The Drug
Effect

Health, crime and society

The Drug Effect: Health, crime and society offers new perspectives on critical debates in the field of alcohol and other drug use. Drawing together work by respected scholars in Australia, the US, the UK and Canada, it explores social and cultural meanings of drug use, and analyses law enforcement and public health frameworks and objectives related to drug policy and service provision. In doing so, it addresses key questions of drug use and addiction through interdisciplinary, predominantly sociological and criminological, perspectives, mapping and building on recent conceptual and empirical advances in the field. These include questions of materiality and agency, the social constitution of disease and neo-liberal subjectivity and responsibility.

Acknowledging the changing national and international drug policy terrain, *The Drug Effect* covers a diverse array of drug types and populations. The book is organised into three sections – drug use as social and cultural practice; health and the medicalisation of addiction; and drugs, crime and the law – which reflect standard divisions in organising research and teaching on drug use. The intention in this volume, however, is to 'trouble' these divisions and the assumptions behind them, offering individual pieces and an overarching critical analysis that can be used both as a research resource and as a teaching tool.

Suzanne Fraser is Associate Professor in the Centre for Women's Studies and Gender Research, School of Political and Social Inquiry, Faculty of Arts, Monash University. She also holds a research appointment with the National Drug Research Institute at Curtin University.

David Moore is Professor in the National Drug Research Institute, Faculty of Health Sciences at Curtin University.

The Drug
Effect

Health, crime and society

Edited by Suzanne Fraser &
David Moore

CAMBRIDGE
UNIVERSITY PRESS

CAMBRIDGE UNIVERSITY PRESS
Cambridge, New York, Melbourne, Madrid, Cape Town,
Singapore, São Paulo, Delhi, Tokyo, Mexico City

Cambridge University Press
477 Williamstown Road, Port Melbourne, VIC 3207, Australia

Published in the United States of America by Cambridge University Press, New York

www.cambridge.org
Information on this title: www.cambridge.org/9780521156059

First published 2011

Cover design by Eggplant Communications
Typeset by Aptara Corp.
Printed in China by Printplus Co. Ltd.

A catalogue record for this publication is available from the British Library

National Library of Australia Cataloguing in Publication data
    Fraser, Suzanne, 1967–
    The drug effect : health, crime and society / Suzanne
    Fraser and David Moore.
    9780521156059 (pbk.)
    Includes bibliographical references and index.
    Drug abuse—Social aspects.
    Drug abuse—Prevention.
    Drug abuse—Treatment.
    Drug addicts—Rehabilitation.
    Drug addicts—Services for.
394.14

ISBN 978-0-521-15605-9 Paperback

Contents

Contributors

Susan Boyd is Professor in the Studies in Policy and Practice Program at the University of Victoria, Canada. She teaches courses on drug law and policy, theory and research methodology. Her research interests include drug law and policy, maternal-state conflicts, film and print media representations, women in conflict with the law, and research methodology. Susan is also a community activist who works with harm reduction and anti-drug war groups.

Nancy D. Campbell is Professor in the Department of Science and Technology Studies at Rensselaer Polytechnic Institute in New York State. Her research and teaching interests include the history of scientific research on drug addiction, the history and sociology of bioethics, global public health, US drug policy, science and technology policy, feminist science and technology studies, and postcolonial science and technology studies. Her major publications include *Using Women: Gender, Drug Policy and Social Justice* (2000), *Discovering Addiction: The Science and Politics of Substance Abuse Research* (2007), *The Narcotic Farm: The Rise and Fall of America's First Prison for Drug Addicts* (2008, with JP Olsen and Luke Walden), and *Gendering Addiction: Drug Treatment in a Neurochemical World* (with Elizabeth Ettorre; forthcoming).

Karen Duke is Principal Lecturer in Criminology at Middlesex University. She has published widely on the development of drugs policy in prisons, the interfaces between drugs and criminal justice policy, and the relationship between research, politics and policy-making. She is the author of *Drugs, Prisons and Policy-making* (2003) and editor of the journal *Drugs: Education, Prevention and Policy*.

Robyn Dwyer is Research Fellow in the National Drug Research Institute at Curtin University. Robyn has extensive experience conducting research among Australian drug-user populations. Her recently completed PhD study was an anthropologically informed ethnographic analysis of the social, cultural and economic processes that constitute street-based drug marketplaces.

Suzanne Fraser is Associate Professor in the Centre for Women's Studies and Gender Research, School of Political and Social Inquiry, Faculty of Arts, Monash University, Melbourne. She also holds a research appointment with the National Drug Research Institute at Curtin University. She is the author of three books on health, the body and society, including *Making Disease, Making Citizens: The Politics of Hepatitis C* (with Kate Seear; 2011).

Helen Keane is Senior Lecturer in the School of Sociology at the Australian National University, Canberra. Author of the widely praised book on contemporary notions of addiction, *What's Wrong with Addiction?* (2002), she has written extensively on illicit drug use, harm reduction and, more recently, pharmaceutical drugs.

Desmond Manderson holds a Canada Research Chair in Law and Discourse at McGill University, Canada. He teaches, supervises and publishes on a wide range of subjects involving interdisciplinary work in law and the humanities, including aesthetics, torts, drug policy and history, ethics and legal education. His major works include *From Mr Sin to Mr Big: A History of Australian Drug Laws* (1993), *Courting Death: The Law of Mortality* (1999), *Songs Without Music: Aesthetic Dimensions of Law and Justice* (2000) and *Proximity, Levinas, and the Soul of Law* (2006).

David Moore is Professor in the National Drug Research Institute at Curtin University, where he leads the Ethnographic Research Program. He has written extensively on the social and cultural contexts of alcohol and illicit drug use, and is currently working on a book provisionally entitled *Habits: Rethinking Addiction* (with Suzanne Fraser; forthcoming).

Kane Race is Senior Lecturer in the Department of Gender and Cultural Studies at the University of Sydney. He works at the intersection of consumption, health, technology and queer studies, and has published numerous articles on technologies of HIV prevention and harm reduction among gay men, as well as the politics and practices of drugs more generally. He is the author of *Pleasure Consuming Medicine: The Queer Politics of Drugs* (2009) and, with Gay Hawkins and Emily Potter, *Plastic Water*, a study of the rise of bottled water (forthcoming).

Craig Reinarman is Professor of Sociology and Legal Studies at the University of California, Santa Cruz. He has been a visiting scholar at the Center for Drug Research at the University of Amsterdam; a member of the board of directors of the College on Problems of Drug Dependence; a consultant to the World Health Organization's Programme on Substance Abuse and a principal investigator on research grants from the National Institute of Drug Abuse and the National Institute of Justice. Reinarman is the author of *American States of Mind* (1987) and co-author of *Cocaine Changes* (1991) and *Crack in America* (1997).

Toby Seddon is Reader in Regulation and Director of the Regulation, Security and Justice Research Centre in the School of Law at the University of Manchester. His research interests include drug-related crime, drug policy, risk and regulatory theory. He has recently completed a major study of drug interventions in the criminal justice system. He is author of *A History of Drugs* (2010).

kylie valentine is Senior Research Fellow in the Social Policy Research Centre at the University of New South Wales. She has a background in cultural and literary theory, feminist criticism, intellectual history and sociology. Her research interests include the politics of (and policies for) families, children and mothers; marginalised communities and individuals; and the translation of research into politics and practice. She is co-author, with Suzanne Fraser, of *Substance and Substitution: Methadone Subjects in Liberal Societies* (2008).

Ian Warren is Senior Lecturer in Criminology at Deakin University, Geelong, where he coordinates the Criminology honours program and has developed several undergraduate units, including Drugs, Crime and Society. His research examines the legal and enforcement dimensions of various criminological problems, including vigilantism, illicit drug supply and the use of emerging surveillance technologies.

Acknowledgements

Many people are involved in turning an idea into a book. We would like to thank Debbie Lee, Susan Hanley and Nina Sharpe at Cambridge University Press for their enthusiastic support for the project. We are also very grateful to the contributing authors, international leaders in their respective research areas, for finding time in their already busy schedules to write their chapters. Robyn Dwyer deserves special thanks for her assistance in researching and collating the proposal on which this book is based. Suzanne Fraser acknowledges the Centre for Women's Studies and Gender Research, School of Political and Social Inquiry, Faculty of Arts, Monash University, and the National Centre in HIV Social Research, University of New South Wales, for their institutional support in undertaking this project, and David Moore acknowledges the core funding received by the National Drug Research Institute from the Australian Government Department of Health and Ageing.

Introduction

Constructing drugs and addiction

Suzanne Fraser and David Moore

The title of this edited collection carries more than a hint of irony. It is clearly multiple. Drugs are often spoken of in terms of their physical or psychological 'effects'. In turn, they are generally treated as the origins or causes of other entities, crime being perhaps one of the most widely assumed. In this respect, beyond the commonplace observation that drugs as substances have 'effects' in the body and on society, we can also say that the *idea of drugs* (their malign powers, their ability to corrupt and so on) itself has effects – at the level of politics and discourse. While the first of these two sets of meanings assumes drugs simply to be self-evidently concrete entities possessed of intrinsic characteristics and producing predictable results, the latter sees drugs and their effects as made in discourse, practice and politics: as constructed. This play on words is our attempt to signal the complexity of the issues canvassed in this collection, and the challenges and rewards that go along with holding these ideas simultaneously. This introduction aims to make this set of challenges and rewards clearer by elaborating key contemporary debates on the constructedness of reality and the nature of material objects, and considering how these ideas can illuminate issues of drug use and addiction.

Knowledge production on drugs, drug use and addiction has long been dominated by the sciences, and many argue that it is on this scientifically defined knowledge that policies and strategies for acting on drug use should be based. An influential trend in recent approaches to drug policy, for example, has been the call for 'evidence-based policy'; that is, policy developed not, it is argued, through moralising approaches to drugs, but through what advocates see as the 'objective', unbiased findings of research. While this approach has several strategic benefits, it also has two weaknesses:

    1 *Its circularity*. Its logic is complicit with neoliberal values of independence and rationality, values usually seen as incommensurate with drug use. This means it tends to promote the very attributes drug users are stigmatised as lacking.

    2 *Its epistemological naiveté*. It tends to take for granted that value-free, objective knowledge about the world *can* be produced.

The latter view – often classified as 'objectivist' or 'positivist' – has come under criticism from many quarters over the last few decades. Among critical social scientists it has been replaced by a range of constructionist perspectives that have been judged better equipped to illuminate drugs, drug use and addiction.

As Goode and Ben-Yehuda explain, the objectivist position assumes that social problems are constituted from concretely real damaging or threatening conditions.[1] In this view, any condition that causes death or disease, shortens life expectancy or significantly reduces quality of life for many people should be defined as a 'social problem'. Another version of the objectivist approach is found in the functionalist paradigm, which sees social problems largely as a product of dysfunction, social disorganisation and violations of social norms; that is, a discrepancy between what is and what ought to be. On the other side of the debate, the constructionist position argues that what makes a given condition a problem is the process of 'collective definition' of that condition as a 'problem', in other words, the level of concern within society about a condition or issue. In this approach, social problems do not exist objectively, as is assumed by the objectivist position, but are constructed by discourse, practice and politics. This can be seen in the fact that the existence of harmful conditions (such as the high rates of injury that go relatively unremarked in certain sports) do not in and of themselves constitute 'social problems'. It is also clear in that a given condition need not even exist for it to be defined as a social problem. Here the persecution of witches in Renaissance Europe and colonial New England is a good example (see Manderson's chapter in this volume). Definitions of social problems emerge out of specific sociocultural conditions and structures, operate within particular historical eras, and are subject to the influence of particular individuals, social classes and so on.

The constructionist approach makes clear that levels of harm or damage do not provide a viable basis for the definition of social problems. As Goode and Ben-Yehuda argue:

It is the discrepancy between concern and the concrete threat posed by or damage caused by a given condition that forces us to raise the question, why the concern over one issue but not another? Or, why concern now but not previously? . . . How do definitions of social problems come about? Why is a social problem 'discovered' in one period rather than another? What steps are taken, and by whom, to remedy a given condition? Why do segments of the society take steps to remedy this condition but not that, even more harmful, one? Who wins, and who loses, if a given condition is recognized as a social problem?[2]

Social constructionism makes visible the social dynamics that help constitute conditions as problems.

Scholars from many fields and disciplines have used the constructionist approach to criticise processes of problem constitution and the often taken-for-granted knowledge that informs or shapes them, raising in the process broader questions about knowledge itself. If we can ask, 'what is a problem?' we can also ask, 'what is knowledge?' This is, of course, an ancient question. If problems and knowledges are socially produced, what do they describe? Do they describe (however imperfectly) a prior, stable 'reality'? Or do they actually produce reality? Could it be that there is no fixed reality beyond that posited, defined and disseminated by discourse, by the production of knowledges? Surely not. For many, reality is, in the last instance, defined by matter (physical objects and so on). And here the debate over the nature of problems and of knowledge itself has been taken up especially intensely by feminists, who have a particularly strong interest in the question of matter and what it represents. This is because the materiality of women's bodies has been used historically to limit their opportunities. Women's bodies, the argument has run, are designed for reproduction, and this imposes an insurmountable obstacle to their participating to the same degree as men in the public sphere, or even to qualifying for equivalent education and rights. Wanting to move beyond biologically deterministic views such as these, feminists have embraced the idea that matter is not in itself a limit to or substrate for social organisation: instead it too can be seen as socially produced in complicated ways through discourse, practice and politics, such as those relating to gender norms and expectations.

Such questions might seem to be a long way from the subject of this book – the relationship between drugs, health, crime and society, but they are crucial to how we think about and respond to drugs as a problem or set of problems. Like feminists, we need to ask whether the things we know about drugs reflect accurately a prior stable reality. If not, do we just need to work harder to produce more objective knowledge, or is unbiased knowledge, knowledge without a perspective, without investments, impossible? Like 'gender', is the reality of drugs socially produced? More specifically, are there irrefutable biological facts with which we can generalise about drugs, or are biological aspects of drugs usefully seen as themselves socially constituted?

These are challenging questions and to help us do justice to them, we can introduce a third set of ideas to deal with the question of matter. Are social constructionist views going too far in emphasising the role of discourse in the production of reality? Do theoretically elegant ideas about reality as socially constituted fail in the face of the biological 'facts'? Who would want to dismiss, for example, a fatal heroin overdose as merely a discursive construction, as if a change in ways of talking and thinking about it would alter it or instantly prevent it from happening?

Retrieving materiality

Karen Barad, a scientist turned feminist scholar, has made the problem of matter a prime topic of her work. Drawing on feminist science studies and science and technology studies, she uses some well-established concepts as well as making some key innovations. In an important 2003 paper, Barad focuses on the understandable tendency among critical scholars seeking to escape biological determinism to understand reality as exclusively shaped by discourse, and to neglect the role of materiality in this process. As she argues:

> Language has been granted too much power. The linguistic turn, the semiotic turn, the interpretive turn, the cultural turn: it seems that at every turn lately every 'thing' – even materiality – is turned into a matter of language or some other form of cultural representation . . . Language matters. Discourse matters. Culture matters. There is an important sense in which the only thing that does not seem to matter anymore is matter.[3]

Barad asks how we can acknowledge the role of materiality in the production of realities without characterising that role as determining, and reality as therefore 'natural' or unchangeable. She explores this dilemma with reference to what physicists call the 'wave-particle duality paradox'; that is, under certain experimental conditions, light exhibits the properties of a wave, and under others it exhibits the properties of a particle. Is light a wave or a particle? Physics has always been certain that phenomena must be one or the other, never both. Carefully explaining and documenting her case, Barad concludes that it is both – physically, in its materiality, in reality – and that what it *is* depends on what instruments are used to measure it. Her case, put simply, is that reality, even in its materiality, does not exist prior to its measurement. In other words, we do not describe reality when we experiment on it; rather, when we measure it, we produce it. But – and this is crucial for our purposes – matter is not passive in this process. The matter of experimental devices, and the matter of light (if, or when, it is measured as a particle), shape each other.

Matter is not merely passive, waiting to be shaped by the 'social' (as has become a common approach, she complains), nor does it determine what the social can be (as has been the traditional view, with dire consequences for women's rights among other things). Instead, she argues, for example, that in an experiment, the observer of the experiment and the object being observed are both constituted by their encounter with each other: that observation changes both the observer and the object of observation. Here, Barad is not suggesting that reality is beyond our comprehension but that it is produced in the process of observation. Each encounter reproduces reality uniquely, based on the specifics of people, objects and concepts encountering each other and being remade by these encounters.

On the basis of her analysis of the wave-particle duality paradox, Barad rejects the commonplace idea that things (such as the observer and the thing being observed) have independent existences, that they possess pre-existing attributes which 'interact' when they encounter each other. Instead, she poses the idea of the 'phenomenon' – that which is made only in its encounters with other phenomena. By moving away from the idea that things possess inherent attributes and properties independent of their encounters with each other, Barad also opens up another issue. She points out that the 'phenomenon' destabilises conventional formulations of causality by troubling conventional causation, which we usually think of in the following way: a pre-formed object (with inherent attributes) enters into subsequent relations with other pre-formed objects, and together they produce predictable, stable effects and meanings. So, for example, her approach would have us question the orthodox causal chain that drug A (e.g. crystalline methamphetamine or 'ice') has B inherent properties (e.g. it is a powerful stimulant), affects people in C specific way (e.g. it induces psychosis and paranoia) and we should respond in D way (e.g. prevent people from consuming it). Some of what most of us consider the most predictable effects of drugs on people turn out to be very heavily dependent upon other factors and how all these factors encounter each other in specific situations. To return to Barad, this process of encounter among things without stable prior attributes she calls 'intra-action', in preference to the more commonly used concept of 'interaction'.

Barad argues that all things, such as physicists, measuring equipment and light – or, we can add, policy-makers, drug treatment services and drugs – are necessarily the product of their encounters with each other and with other phenomena; that they do not exist independently of each other, but are made and remade in their unique encounters. What are the implications of Barad's analysis? What does it mean? Perhaps most importantly, we can observe that where objects do not have inherent attributes separate from the processes of observation or of intra-action with other objects, it makes no sense to see them as acting independently or consistently on other objects, or as 'determining' reality in predictable ways. What they do, what they are, is entirely dependent on their circumstances. What happens when we recognise that material objects – such as those physicists try to measure, or those the police try to control, or those people decide to smoke, swallow or inject – are neither purely the product of discourse, of social practices, or entirely determined by their supposed intrinsic material attributes? What are the effects of treating drugs as phenomena; that is, as continually *remade in their intra-actions with other entities*? Most obviously perhaps, blanket assumptions about the properties of drugs, their actions, their effects (even their physical properties and physiological effects) cannot be made. Furthermore, how we engage with drugs and the problems we assume to unfold from them also needs to be flexible and open to re-evaluation.

Barad also makes clear that the 'human' – what *we* do – needs to be seen as phenomenon too. By this, she means that people, their capacity for action and the ways in which they act are also the product of intra-actions with material objects, concepts and discourse. Thus, agency is not produced by humans in the traditional sense (i.e. it does not emanate from 'within' pre-constituted individuals), but by humans *and* objects, discourse *and* materiality in their intra-action.

To summarise, then, constructionist approaches to knowledge posit that what we know about drugs, and about reality more broadly, even our scientific knowledge of them is the product of social relations, of our values and histories. But this does not mean that we should necessarily seek more 'objective' knowledge about drugs, about reality – to aim for knowledge without the imprint of society. This, as many critics have pointed out, is impossible. Karen Barad's theories introduce ways of understanding matter that move beyond some of the earlier social constructionist scholarship, which tends to assume that our knowledges and practices alone produce reality, and that matter is passive in this process. The materiality of drugs matters but so too do ideas, discourses, practices, histories and politics. All these produce each other and produce drugs, their effects and their circumstances.

Addiction?

If seriously entertained, these observations oblige us to ask a series of critical questions about drugs and drug use. They prompt us to look carefully and sceptically at foundational ideas for the 'problem of drugs', perhaps most obviously, that of 'addiction'. The concept of addiction is a relatively new one. It is treated in public discourse as a more or less established medical fact, and like all medical facts, it is understood as pre-existing its 'discovery' by medical science. By this, we mean that orthodox thinking on addiction understands it as a condition that has always existed in one form or another, but which has only relatively recently been identified and given a name. This 'realist' interpretation of addiction is part of the objectivist approach to medical science and to the world in general critiqued by social constructionism. Realism takes for granted that entities – that is, objects, states and ideas – exist before their entry into discourse, before they are named, analysed, described, experimented upon.

In challenging this assumption, many scholars have argued that the existence of addiction as an idea and a problem is co-extensive with that of Enlightenment notions of reason and rationality.[4] The point here is not that addiction and Enlightenment liberal modernity are merely connected sets of ideas, or that there is a social or cultural 'side' to addiction. What we mean is that addiction and modern society *have made each other, and they continue to rely upon each other for meaning*. In other words, we do not simply argue that our *ideas* about a real, pre-existing thing – 'addiction' – are the product of their times. Instead, the point is that addiction, in *both* its conceptual and material senses, is produced by the times. Thus, the phenomenon of addiction – that is, the idea of addiction as well as the activities and objects associated with addiction, and the state of addiction itself – are produced through social and cultural practices, such as medical procedures, policing practices, media texts and the ways we talk about addiction in everyday life. One of the aims of this book is to offer opportunities for readers to reflect on this constructedness of addiction, and to think about the different political implications of realist and constructionist approaches to addiction.

In keeping with these ideas, for example, Redfield and Brodie argue that 'the addict emerged with the development . . . of a medico-legal discourse capable of reconceiving human identity in the language of pathology'.[5] They give the example of regular and heavy drinking in the USA, which went unlabelled as 'addiction' for centuries before the emergence of the necessary discursive conditions for the generation of the label. Opiate use provides another example in that for centuries it was quite commonplace, considered a minor vice rather than the key evidence of an intrinsically deviant and pathological self. Cocaine use occupied a similar status. While these ideas were developing during the nineteenth century, it was not until the early twentieth century that the notion of the 'drug addict' began to reshape thinking around substance use.

This chronology of labelling is also reflected in the legal history of the term 'addictive substance'. Not until the twentieth century were drugs criminalised in the USA, Great Britain and Australia. In 1901 the Australian Federal Customs Act began regulating the importation of narcotics. In 1906 the US Pure Food and Drug Act removed opiates from patent medicines, and in 1909 the Harrison Act gave the US Government the power to regulate the possession, use and sale of narcotics. In Britain, the 1868 Pharmacy Act began to regulate opium use a little earlier, but it took until the 1916 Defence of the Realm Act and the 1920 Dangerous Drugs Act to seriously criminalise drugs.

Redfield and Brodie argue that this criminalising reflex developed out of two conceptual sources: first, from the powerful typologies of deviance generated by the emerging disciplinary society (and the associated rise of the 'psy' disciplines such as psychoanalysis and psychology), and second, from the emerging ethos of consumption that foregrounded commodity production and consumerism.[6] This confluence of pathologising categories and expanding consumption meant that the twentieth century not only accommodated the idea of addiction: it also nourished and produced it in a multitude of forms.

Redfield and Brodie take their lead partly from Eve Sedgwick's work on addiction.[7] In her view, mainstream definitions of addiction reference a particular relation – a relation to any object, practice or idea that is characterised by a lack of free will. For Sedgwick, Western liberal societies' reliance upon Enlightenment notions of autonomy, rationality and freedom have produced a central dualism: free will and compulsion. She argues that for as long as we have idealised and worshipped the idea of free will, we have also generated its opposite: the denigrated, devalued idea of compulsion. In this model, we must strive for the only good: a pure freedom. Dependence or reliance on, or compulsion to do, anything becomes defined here as a contamination and failure of the will.

Sedgwick argues that the last quarter of the twentieth century had seen the most intense period of 'addiction attribution' to date. But why, she asks, did this intensity emerge when it did? She identifies two features: first, the advent of HIV, which combined two highly stigmatised identities, the homosexual and the drug user, into an archetype of the pathological consumer at a time when, second, consumer culture was itself accelerating. The subsequent anxiety around compulsive behaviour rendered any practice vulnerable to the definition of 'addiction'.

While Sedgwick identifies 'free will' as the key value seen to be compromised or destroyed by addiction, Jacques Derrida identifies this key value as the related concept of 'truth'.[8] According to Derrida, the significance of addiction, the source of its stigmatisation, is our conviction that the drug-using experience, the pleasure or joy that comes from drug use, lacks truth: 'We do not object to the drug user's pleasure *per se*, but to a pleasure taken in an experience without truth.' For Derrida, at the centre of our anxiety about addiction lies the truth of being that society demands from us, rather than any real concern about the thoughts, wishes or indulgences we actually enact. Whatever we do, say or feel, it must be truthful. It must not be fanciful, deluded or the product of chemical intoxication.

Understanding addiction as a broad problem of the truth of being and the freedom of the subject further reveals its role as a key concept in late capitalist modernity. Mark Seltzer argues that the idea of 'addiction' exposes the predicament of the normative subject of late capitalism – the complex tensions at the centre of contemporary existence in that we are expected to desire, pursue and consume to be thought proper modern subjects.[9] We must exhibit drive and a healthily assertive, ambitious attitude. At the same time, we can all too readily be seen as controlled or consumed by these very drives, which themselves can be redefined as 'excessive' and 'pathological'. Sedgwick offers several examples of this dynamic to show that, given the right conditions, there is nothing that cannot be problematised as a form of addiction in contemporary society. She argues that anorexia, bulimia, obesity and even exercise can all be defined as about an excess of control, an inability to manage the desire to control. Even moderation itself, if too rigidly adhered to, if enacted out of habit rather than active thought, can be evidence of compulsion. We might think this apparent multiple bind, this tightrope walk of control, freedom and truth, merely interesting if, as Redfield and Brodie point out,[10] it had not generated a world-wide system of drug prohibition which has vast social, economic and political costs and, many argue, few successes. As such, is worth taking very seriously as an object of study.

In acknowledging that the term 'addiction' has a historical context and political implications, and that the materiality of drugs can neither be dismissed or assumed, we can also question the pharmacology of addiction, the commonly held assumptions about the operations of addiction and the addictiveness of substances. Helen Keane uses the well-known example of research conducted on returned Vietnam veterans to argue that even the most demonised substances can affect people very differently.[11] The research she refers to found that a surprisingly high proportion of US soldiers had used heroin during the Vietnam War, with as many as 20 per cent reporting that they had been 'addicted' to the drug. This research also found, however, that only 10 per cent of this 20 per cent used opiates on their return to the USA. This suggests strongly that the popular representation of heroin as intensely addictive, and associated with unbearable withdrawal symptoms, is quite unreliable. If regular heroin use did not produce painful withdrawal and the usual gamut of social effects such as crime, what is heroin addiction? What, for that matter, is heroin?

In raising these questions, we do not mean to imply that addiction is simply 'made up' and has no effects. Just as the idea of addiction has emerged in a particular time and place, so have experiences of addiction. Where drugs are not prohibited, for instance, they are unlikely to become scarce. Experiences of craving and withdrawal differ under conditions of plenty from those under conditions of scarcity and prohibition. In other words, addiction is partly the product of prohibition in that experiences of craving and compulsion are less likely to materialise where drugs are easy to obtain. This was true of the use of many drugs such as the opiates prior to the late nineteenth century. No doubt some people (some heroin-using US veterans but not others, for example) experience addiction, compulsion, craving and withdrawal in relation to drugs, and these experiences have a serious effect on their lives and the lives of others. But this does not mean that drugs should be seen deterministically as stable objects in possession of fixed characteristics that always produce predictable effects – that is, that their inherent properties *determine* people's experiences, and as such demand particular pre-given responses – for example, that they can and must be 'stamped out'. By the same token, we cannot assume that they have no real effects and are therefore harmless. Sorting out perspectives that offer more than these two extremes, that take proper account of the materiality of drugs as Barad might ask us to do, is one of the key tasks for the field of critical studies of addiction and drugs.

Drugs?

Just as constructionist insights in general and the work of Barad in particular prompt questions about the notion of addiction, they too require a sceptical engagement with the notion of 'drugs' itself. As Derrida points out, in his critique of 'drugs':

> there are no drugs in 'nature' . . . As with addiction, the concept of drugs supposes an instituted and an institutional definition: a history is required, and a culture, conventions, evaluations, norms, an entire network of intertwining discourses, a rhetoric, whether explicit or elliptical . . . The concept of drugs is not a scientific concept, but is rather instituted on the basis of moral or political evaluations: it carries in itself both norm and prohibition, allowing no possibility of description or certification – it is a decree, a buzzword. Usually the decree is of a prohibitive nature.[12]

Here Derrida is pointing to the intrinsically political nature of the category of 'drugs'. He argues that the term does not refer simply or reliably to certain substances with clear-cut attributes or effects. Instead, 'drugs' is a political category that includes some substances and excludes others, depending on the politics of the day. So, for example, until relatively recently, tobacco was not commonly referred to as a drug. What, we are led to ask, will be incorporated into the category of 'drugs' in the future?

This is one sense in which the catch-all category of drugs can be problematised – it refers only to some substances, and in a way that is not systematic. Another critique of the term 'drugs' can be made based on its role in collapsing a range of substances, effects and experiences into a single undifferentiated category. Given the variation in the physical make-up and perceived effects of drugs, can we speak of them as a group at all? As Keane argues, drugs can be seen in terms of Mary Douglas's definition of 'pollution' – as matter out of place.[13] In this sense, too, the category of drugs is an entirely political one; in other words, it contains all substances society disapproves of at a given time, and which society says normal people should avoid, and should want to avoid. This might, perhaps, explain the way that sugar, and even such foods as bread, are coming to be described as drugs in some contexts: the current climate of fear about obesity means that some foods are no longer just foods.[14] They verge on being framed as illicit substances, especially for people classified as 'overweight'.

The terms 'addiction' and 'drugs' need therefore to be seen as social, cultural and political categories. There are, of course, a range of political lines along which drugs and addiction can be analysed. This book aims to illuminate some of these to help resituate our responses to drugs. If addiction is not a straightforward medical condition uncovered by science, and if the category 'drugs' does not include a clearly definable set of dangerous substances that differ from all other substances in measurable, documentable ways, what are they, and what do they do? What does it mean to medicalise addiction under these conditions? What, more specifically, is actually being medicalised: a physical problem, a mental problem or a set of social norms and practices? What does it mean to police drug use and to conduct a 'war on drugs', reduce harm or profess 'zero tolerance'? On what basis can policing of drugs take place? *How* are decisions about which substances are policed made? We hope readers will hold at least some of these questions in mind as they proceed through the chapters of this book.

The chapters

The book is divided into three parts. Part 1 comprises four chapters that offer fresh insights into drug use as social and cultural practice. In the opening chapter, Robyn Dwyer critiques prevailing understandings of illicit drug markets. These, she argues, rely too heavily on mechanisms of supply and demand, ignore the social relations created and reproduced through market participation, and reify the 'market' as an object to be measured rather than a social and cultural process to be understood. On the basis of extensive ethnographic research, she argues that illicit drug markets are animated by the practices of market actors, which are constituted through complex and dynamic social processes, power differentials and cultural understandings. Dwyer also critiques dominant constructions of heroin users and sellers as denigrated, abject 'others' by revealing that, in their daily lives, they negotiate many of the challenges that confront us all. Overall, Dwyer's findings suggest that dominant theoretical conceptions of drug markets and drug market participants are thoroughly inadequate for the task of understanding the circulation of drugs and the role of human and other actors in this circulation.

In chapter 2, Kane Race argues that drugs have been a significant component of the subcultural practices and spaces of pleasure upon which urban gay identity has been built. Although the association between gay social venues and drug use has been the subject of public health research for some time, few studies have explored the productive role of drug practices in the materialisation of gay pleasures, identities and cultures. In order to figure the significance of drug activity within this social and cultural transformation, Race theorises drugs as contingent players within particular sociocultural assemblages. He situates drug use as one practice among the many that produce gay lives and cultures. In doing so, he acknowledges the role of drugs in the formation and transformation of spaces of sexual expressivity without reifying their significance or pharmacological effects.

Susan Boyd (chapter 3) continues the exploration of drug use as social and cultural practice by examining representations of illicit drug use and trafficking in popular cultural forms such as film and music video. Although classed, gendered and racialised depictions of drug use and drug users have been and remain common, alternative representations of pleasure compete with and challenge these conventional discourses. Boyd argues that the diversity, complexity and contradictions in popular cultural representations of drug use, addiction and trafficking highlight the continuing ambivalence about drugs, intoxication, consumption and pleasure. Rather than viewing music, film, and music videos as 'mere entertainment', they can be understood as cultural products that produce and reproduce 'systems of meaning' about drugs, pleasure, drug users, addiction, degradation, crime, treatment, punishment and redemption. These meanings both give impetus to conventional punitive responses to drug use, and create new spaces in which to build alternative responses.

Part 1 on drug use as social and cultural practice closes with chapter 4, which focuses on the production of knowledge about drugs. David Moore explores the politics of multidisciplinary drug research by drawing on his recent involvement in agent-based modelling of drug use. He considers some of the benefits for qualitative researchers of suspending their theoretical and epistemological commitments in order to engage in multidisciplinary research such as agent-based modelling, but also sounds a note of caution. Viewed from the perspective of recent work in science and technology studies that focuses on the role of all research methods in constituting their objects of study, agent-based modelling can be seen to involve a process of simplification that reproduces existing research, policy and practice discourses on individual responsibility and rationality. In this way, Moore observes, it produces specific forms of reality in relation to drugs with specific political effects.

Part 2 of the book features four chapters that explore health and the medicalisation of drug addiction. In chapter 5, Suzanne Fraser formulates a novel approach to disease to argue that poverty, disadvantage and stigma directly shape hepatitis C. Conventional approaches to disease assume: (1) that hepatitis C pre-exists the populations in which it manifests; and (2) that such populations should change their ways to reduce transmission of this pre-existing disease across bodies. Fraser argues, however, that such diseases as hepatitis C are not pre-existing objects waiting to be discovered and understood. Instead they are emergent phenomena, constantly being made and remade in their intra-action with social forces such as stigma. Fraser concludes that, given hepatitis C is made in society and politics, it is necessary to scrutinise carefully legal, policy and social measures and their role in reinforcing or challenging stigma.

Helen Keane's focus in chapter 6 is the use of pharmaceutical remedies to improve workplace performance. She explores the ambivalent meanings attached to two types of medication: 'new generation' sleep medications and stimulant medications used to manage Attention Deficit Hyperactivity Disorder (ADHD). In the first case, Keane argues, medicalised sleep discourse legitimates the use of drugs as a rational response to a debilitating problem that harms not only individuals but also corporations and the national economy. At the same time it produces a counter-discourse of risks and adverse effects, responsibility for which is ultimately borne by the individual. In the second case, Keane finds that stimulant medications are explicitly marketed through the promise of improved productivity and work performance, but that managing the intricate pharmacotherapy of such conditions as ADHD entails processes far more complex than that usually assumed in medicine (restoration of the normal self via medication). Instead, it blurs the boundaries between self, symptom and drug effect. No simple process of performance enhancement, pharmaceutical self-management emerges as an ambiguous practice that highlights both the positive and negative sides of the *Pharmakon*.

In chapter 7, Nancy Campbell investigates five shifts in the 'technologies of addiction' through which struggles over the meaning of 'medicalisation' have played out in US drug policy. In the early twentieth century, the search for a 'magic bullet' to cure drug addiction was inspired by an ethos of pharmacological optimism. This has continued, she argues, through four distinct eras in the development of drug policy in the United States: (1) morphine maintenance; (2) medically assisted detoxification; (3) methadone maintenance; and (4) the development of narcotic antagonists, agonists and partial agonist-antagonists. Each 'technology of addiction therapeutics' co-constitutes subjects – drug users, researchers, clinicians and policy-makers – in different ways that illustrate the inconsistent meanings of 'medical' or 'public health' approaches to addiction therapeutics.

Part 2 on health and the medicalisation of drug addiction closes with chapter 8. Here, kylie valentine notes that most drug use and policy research focuses on drug policy, or a small range of welfare and employment policies, while most social policy research sidelines or ignores drug use and drug policy. Yet social policy, in its broadest terms, would seem to be important to the welfare of illicit drug users. The state and the market, in meeting the needs of drug users, matter enormously. Employment, income support, parenting and family payments, disability policies, carer payments and housing policies have a material impact on the well-being of people who take illicit drugs, many of whom experience vulnerability in the labour market. Her chapter is concerned with how this compartmentalised approach to policy analysis has come about, and how it could be changed. Drawing on feminist welfare regime analysis, and viewing opioid pharmacotherapy as an exemplary intersection of drug policy and social policy, valentine argues that the public provision of services and a broad range of policies are relevant to analysis of national policy frameworks, and could be the basis of comparative study. Other dimensions, often neglected in orthodox welfare regime analysis, are also important, notably privacy, advocacy and difference.

Part 3 of the book focuses on drugs, crime and the law, and consists of five chapters. In chapter 9, Toby Seddon focuses on court-ordered drug treatment, a recent development in the longstanding connection between drugs and criminal justice. After briefly explaining the general rationale and mode of operation of court-ordered treatment, Seddon examines what he calls its 'lexicon of force'. By this he means the family of terms used to describe court-imposed pressure to enter treatment: 'compulsory', 'quasi-compulsory', 'coerced', 'mandated' and so on. Focusing primarily on two British examples – the Restriction on Bail, and the Drug Rehabilitation Requirement – Seddon analyses how these specific interventions (re)produce a distinctive notion of the citizen-subject as a calculating choice-maker.

In chapter 10, Craig Reinarman examines how the growing drug policy reform movement in the USA is challenging cannabis criminalisation and the drug control industry that supports it. Although drug policy reformers tend to understand medicalisation as a useful tool in making their case, he argues that it is multivalent and as such has also been deployed effectively in support of the criminalisation regime. As an example of this, Reinarman critically examines medical research that suggests a link between cannabis and psychosis. The chapter concludes by arguing that medicalisation is unlikely to replace criminalisation or to settle the cannabis policy debate in the US because, ultimately, this debate is not about 'facts' that can be determined by medical science but about the politics of pleasure.

Shifting the focus from the USA to Australia, Ian Warren (chapter 11) argues that the dominant legal discourse of retribution and deterrence ignores the important individual and social factors that help shape drug trafficking offences, authorises the suspension of conventional due process requirements, and legitimises increased law enforcement and harsher punishments associated with the 'war' on drugs. An alternative strategy that aims to reduce drug-related harm appears to be more appropriate, particularly for low-level suppliers who also use illegal drugs. The supervised provision of cannabis or heroin to registered users, recommended by some critics, will not necessarily eliminate all problems associated with illicit drug supply. However, these harm reduction methods can help minimise the destructive effects of questionable legal principles, harsh sentencing and law enforcement corruption under the criminal law and prohibitionist philosophy.

In chapter 12, Karen Duke continues the focus on harm reduction and offers a reconceptualisation of harm reduction in prison settings. Many countries have introduced harm reduction initiatives within their prison systems, yet these are not always as effective as they might be. Employing a 'risk environment' framework, Duke argues that current harm reduction initiatives in prisons (such as health promotion, drug substitution therapy and needle exchange) have focused on individual risk factors, human rights and behaviour change and have consequently ignored the social, political and economic forces that undermine harm reduction. She closes by noting that it is also important to identify and explore the processes and resources that promote health, resilience and well-being and help to create 'enabling environments' for the reduction of drug-related harm in prisons.

Part 3, and the book, concludes with Desmond Manderson's chapter on what he terms the 'unconscious law' of drugs (chapter 13). He opens his chapter by asking why the proponents of 'zero tolerance' approaches to drug use continue to promulgate their position in the face of conclusive evidence of its futility and deleterious impact on individuals, communities and economies. He offers a psychoanalytic reading of drug policies, pointing to the irrational fears and anxieties animating them, and compares this contemporary situation with the Witchcraft Laws of the sixteenth century. Bringing the two stories together, Manderson argues that drug laws are not intended to get rid of drugs any more than the Inquisition wanted to ban the devil.

*

We began this Introduction by noting that objectivist perspectives on drugs and addiction have been the subject of sustained critique by social scientists. These critics, we explained, have sought to replace it with a diverse range of constructionist approaches. The diversity we pointed to is reflected in the chapters gathered together in this volume. Our contributors engage with different strands of contemporary social theory in their analysis of divergent topics and themes. Despite, or perhaps because of, the diversity of its chapters, the book also offers rewards when read as a whole. Not least, we think, it offers readers the opportunity – in some chapters explicitly, in others implicitly – to consider the utility of the post-objectivist insights we outlined. Our sincere hope is that in doing so it emphasises and reinforces the ongoing value of critical, theoretically informed approaches to drugs and addiction.

Notes

1   Goode & Ben-Yehuda, 'Moral panics'.
2   Ibid., p. 152.
3   Barad, 'Posthumanist performativity', p. 801.
4   See, for example, Sedgwick, 'Epidemics of the will'; Derrida, 'The rhetoric of drugs'; Keane, *What's Wrong with Addiction?*; Levine, 'The discovery of addiction'; Redfield & Brodie, Introduction to *High Anxieties*; Room, 'The cultural framing of addiction'.
5   Redfield & Brodie, Introduction to *High Anxieties*, p. 2.
6   Ibid.
7   Sedgwick, 'Epidemics of the will'.
8   Derrida, 'The rhetoric of drugs'.
9   Seltzer, *Bodies and Machines*.
10   Redfield & Brodie, Introduction to *High Anxieties*.
11   Keane, *What's Wrong with Addiction?*
12   Derrida, 'The rhetoric of drugs', p. 2.
13   Keane, *What's Wrong with Addiction?*
14   Fraser, Maher & Wright, 'Between bodies and collectivities'.

References

Barad, K. (2003). Posthumanist performativity: Toward an understanding of how matter comes to matter. *Signs: Journal of Women in Culture and Society*, 28(3): 801–31.

Derrida, J. (1993). The rhetoric of drugs: An interview. *Differences: A Journal of Feminist Cultural Studies*, 5(1): 1–25.

Goode, E., & Ben-Yehuda, N. (1994). Moral panics: Culture, politics, and social construction. *Annual Review of Sociology*, 20: 149–71.

Fraser, S., Maher, J.M., & Wright, J. (2010). Between bodies and collectivities: Articulating the action of emotion in obesity epidemic discourse. *Social Theory and Health*, 8: 192–209.

Keane, H. (2002). *What's Wrong with Addiction?* Carlton South: MUP.

Levine, H. (1978). The discovery of addiction: Changing conceptions of habitual drunkenness in America. *Journal of Studies on Alcohol*, 39(1): 143–74.

Redfield, M., & Brodie, J.F. (2002). Introduction. *High Anxieties: Cultural Studies in Addiction*. Berkeley, Los Angeles, and London: University of California Press, pp. 1–15.

Room, R. (2003). The cultural framing of addiction. *Janus Head*, 6(2): 221–34.

Sedgwick, E.K. (1993). Epidemics of the will. In *Tendencies*. Durham, NC: Duke University Press, pp. 130–42.

Seltzer, M. (1992). *Bodies and Machines*. New York and London: Routledge.

PART 1

Drug use as social and cultural practice

The social life of *smokes*

Processes of exchange in a heroin marketplace

Robyn Dwyer

> Exchange is interesting, because it is the chief means by which useful things move from one person to another; because it is an important way in which people create and maintain social hierarchy; because it is a richly symbolic activity – all exchanges have got social meaning.
>
> Davis, *Exchange*, p. 1

In this chapter, I focus on exchange in order to argue that illicit drug marketplaces are produced and reproduced through complex and dynamic social processes and relations. This understanding contrasts with dominant conceptions of drug (and other) markets that view them as driven by the mechanism of supply and demand, that largely ignore their constituent social relations and that tend to reify the 'market' as an object to be measured rather than a process to be understood.[1] The chapter also challenges dominant and stigmatising constructions of heroin users and sellers (hereafter 'dealers') as denigrated, abject 'others', revealing that, in their everyday lives, they engage in similar practices and struggle with many of the same challenges as do we all.

Using the examples of cigarette exchange between myself and research participants enacted in the course of conducting ethnographic research in a street-based drug marketplace, and of heroin exchange between marketplace participants, I show that drug markets are animated by the behaviour of market actors, with this behaviour being constituted through social relations, power differentials and cultural understandings. Linking the cigarette exchanges between myself and my informants with the heroin exchanges between drug marketplace participants locates the latter exchanges in more generalised processes of social exchange and situates drug market behaviour within wider social and cultural practices.

My analysis draws on two years of participant observation among Vietnamese[2] heroin user–dealers in a street-based heroin marketplace in Footscray, a suburb of Melbourne, Australia's second largest city. I begin with an account of cigarette gift exchange between myself and research participants. These exchanges were a key way through which I was incorporated as an ethnographer into the social field of the drug marketplace.[3] For me as a smoker, cigarette exchange is so taken for granted that I engaged in it unreflexively throughout my fieldwork. It was only later that its enduring and recurring qualities became apparent. My reflections on these processes stimulated my identification and observation of broader processes of exchange around drugs. Thus, cigarette exchanges between myself and drug marketplace participants became an integral source of data and understandings concerning how the drug marketplace operated.

In the remainder of the chapter, I present an account of heroin exchange between participants in the marketplace, drawing out the similarities between these and the cigarette exchanges previously described. In both sections, I show how processes of exchange are used to create and affirm social relationships and, simultaneously, how social relationships shape exchange. This demonstrates how processes and relations of exchange matter, not just to the group under study and the study itself, but also to the method of conducting ethnography.

I conclude that ethnographic methods provide for more nuanced accounts of drug markets and marketplaces by allowing for the apprehension of their constituent social processes and relations. My findings suggest that dominant theoretical conceptions of drug markets and of drug market participants provide inadequate accounts of these sites and of the people who participate in them.

Methods

Fieldwork was conducted between January 2003 and December 2004. I visited the Footscray drug marketplace during daylight hours, on average between four and six days per week for the two-year period. Data consist of approximately 1200 A4 pages of typed fieldnotes made following participant observation. As the social activities that were the focus of my research were illegal, fieldnotes were never recorded while I was in Footscray because of concerns that these might then be accessible to other people. To further protect participants' privacy and ensure anonymity, each person was assigned a pseudonym and personal information was stored only in the file containing their pseudonym. A separate password-protected file contained the key to the pseudonyms. All fieldnotes were recorded using the assigned pseudonyms. On occasions when I recorded details of participants' official encounters with the legal system (e.g. dates of arrests or court cases), I added a further layer of protection by assigning the participant a second pseudonym.

Fieldnotes were coded for themes, concepts and categories expressed in key words and phrases, events and practices. Categories and concepts emerged from the data but were, at the same time, shaped by my initial research interests regarding exchange processes and the social relations and processes constituting the marketplace. Interpretations were discussed with informants. This generated further refinements and, on occasion, provided new data that allowed for the development of more concise definitions of categories and concepts.

In focus

The marketplace

Embedded within Footscray's thriving commercial district – one with a strong Vietnamese presence in the form of restaurants, fresh produce markets and other Vietnamese-owned and -managed businesses – is an equally thriving heroin marketplace. It has operated in its current street-based form since the early 1990s.[a] During the fieldwork period, most drug transactions occurred in and around Footscray's open-air mall, and they were dominated by Vietnamese dealers and their mainly *Aussie*[b] customers. The category *Aussie* includes a mix of people from Anglo-Celtic and second-generation southern or eastern European backgrounds. In this marketplace, the term is used to refer to people who are not 'Asian', Aboriginal or African. The designation *Asian*, or the more specific *Viet*, is employed by the Vietnamese when referring to themselves.

Over the two-year period, I encountered around 300 drug marketplace participants, of whom 123 were Vietnamese dealers. The men and women who appear in this chapter were members of the core group of around 40 Vietnamese dealers who, at some point during my fieldwork, traded almost daily in the marketplace for a period of at least two months. They ranged in age from 19 to 38 years, with seven members of the core group being women. Most had completed four years of secondary school. Although Vietnamese was the dealers' preferred language, drug transactions and conversations with me were conducted mainly in English. Dealers were daily heroin users who met personal drug requirements through the street-based sale of heroin. They were primarily independent entrepreneurs who purchased a larger weight of heroin (usually 1.7g) to divide into smaller portions (known as *caps*) for resale while retaining some heroin for their own use. Most had been involved in this trade for between five and 10 years.

a Byrne, *The Community, the Council and the Police*.
b Emic terms are italicised in text except where they are direct quotations.

Incorporating the ethnographer

Many months after the completion of my fieldwork, two powerful images remain. The first is from an early winter's evening, a few months in. I had been sitting at my regular café table, in the cold, on my own, for hours. It was growing dark and the Vietnamese dealers were, for the first time, not conveniently gathered around the café where I could at least observe them. Instead, they were congregating far away in the centre of the open-air mall, barely discernible in the descending gloom. Just as I was deciding to finish for the day, one of the young men approached. Declaring that I looked lonely and that he felt sorry for me, he announced he had come to talk to me. With much sharing of my offered cigarettes, there ensued an extraordinary conversation about his experiences since arriving in Australia at the age of eight, including his history of using and selling heroin. The intimate connection between this particular young man and me was an engagement that was never repeated.

My second image is of a much later glorious summer's day, towards the end of 12 months of fieldwork. At the same café, on this day, I was in the centre of the gathered Vietnamese dealers. Many were conducting drug trans-actions where we sat. Others approached to show me various documents – bail conditions from the police,[4] letters from Centrelink (the government organisation responsible for the administration of welfare payments) – and to ask me to explain them. People brought Vietnamese food for me to taste, or sought to engage me in conversation, calling, 'Chị hai. Chị hai [Eldest sister]', as they vied for my attention. My fieldwork-acquired sister dozed against me in heroin-induced comfort, and one young man walked up and, wordlessly but with exquisite delicacy, extracted my cigarette packet from my breast pocket in order to help himself to a smoke. How did I travel thus, from stranger to eldest sister? As I argue, cigarette exchanges were one of the vehicles by which I traversed this path.

Processes of exchange were always going to be conceptually significant for my ethnographic research, located as it was in a heroin marketplace where hundreds of drug-related exchanges occur every day. What I had not initially considered was the ways in which I myself would participate in these exchanges, and the ways in which I, and the people among whom I was conducting research, would employ these exchanges to establish and affirm the social relationships that are essential to any fieldwork endeavour.

In preparing myself to commence fieldwork, I familiarised myself with texts on both ethnographic methods[5] and illicit drug scenes.[6] I read that ethnography is both method and text; that ethnography, with its long-term immersion in people's everyday worlds, allows for the apprehension of social processes as these are negotiated and renegotiated through social action; and I read that, with its continuous and intimate engagement, ethnography makes us learn the same procedures that the people we study have themselves learned, thereby allowing for the apprehension of everyday *practical* culture.[7]

The methodological texts and the illicit drug scene ethnographies made similar points in elucidating the ethnographic research process: gain entry; make contact; establish a research presence; develop rapport, acceptance and trust; and lastly, negotiate an identity for oneself. A simple task, perhaps, to reduce such challenging and complex processes of social action to words on a page, but this begged the question of how one actually does these things.

I began by trying to gain entry to the setting and make contact. As my field site was a street-based drug marketplace, gaining entry was relatively easy. I simply needed to go there. The public nature of this marketplace meant that it was entirely possible for me to observe this group of people as they went about their daily lives. In order to participate in these lives, however, it was necessary for me to engage with them and begin to build relationships.

'Would you like a smoke?'

I began by visiting the marketplace on days when drug research colleagues who could introduce me were in the area. They were not there every day, however, so many of my early visits entailed long hours of sitting alone, watching the comings and goings of the locals, nursing a series of *cà phê sữa đá* (Vietnamese-style iced-coffee), smoking cigarette after cigarette, and smiling or saying hello to people whom I might have met previously. If I was lucky I might receive a smile, a nod in greeting or even a 'Hello, how are you?', as someone walked past going about their business. If I was luckier still, I might receive a request for a cigarette or an opportunity to offer one. In these early efforts at engagement, offering cigarettes helped create a space for an encounter. The exchange formed a link that allowed for the possibility of a relationship. Sharing a smoking episode helped establish mutuality. It was an immediate signal of similarity, despite any and all real and perceived differences between us.[8] Further, among smokers, cigarettes are a consensually understood positive gift, with such gifts creating a favourable impression, however fleeting, and helping to foster goodwill.

Participants in the Footscray drug marketplace managed to meet their material needs, and obtain heroin on a reasonably consistent basis, through the employment of a broad repertoire of creative stratagems. Maintaining a supply of tobacco, however, was low on the list of priorities. My repeated offerings of cigarettes disposed people towards me, and it became in their interests to remember me. A person who is regularly present, and apparently willing to provide cigarettes unasked, is someone worth cultivating. This might be achieved by their articulating a relationship between us, for example, employing conversational gambits like: 'I saw you yesterday' or 'You're here a lot' to draw the connection. At first this articulation was for opportunistic reasons alone but over time, with repeated encounters, most of these relationships expanded to offer broader satisfactions or to be based on mutual liking.

'Would you have a smoke, Robyn?'

Gradually, I did begin to establish at least a presence, if not yet a research presence. The process of gaining acceptance was achieved in part through cigarette exchanges, and it was also read by me through temporal changes in the form of these exchanges. My repeated offerings indicated my willingness to provide and, eventually, our developing relatedness enabled people to make requests for cigarettes. The meaning of these requests varied, however, depending on the particular relationship between myself and the demander. It was a mark of acceptance when my friend Thanh, who had always been shy of speaking to me, asked me directly for a cigarette. Before this he had made such requests infrequently, and always through his partner Kelly. Among people I knew less well, a request for a cigarette would be often immediately followed by an apology for asking. With those I was closer to, however, requests for cigarettes could be read as 'demand-sharing', more along the lines of 'give me a cigarette'.

Peterson has argued that demand-sharing signifies the relatedness between the donor and the demander, through the presumption of a right to ask, and the expectation that the demand will be met.[9] Demand-sharing was a common occurrence in this marketplace, with the Vietnamese helping themselves to drinks, cigarettes or food, if these appeared to belong to another Vietnamese person. An encounter involving Linh and her partner Hiêp, two people who at this time I had just begun to speak with more regularly, was expressive of the shift our relationship had recently undergone. Previously, these two would take a cigarette when offered but would rarely ask directly. This day I had pulled my cigarette packet out when Linh came to stand next to me and, looking at me pleadingly, held out her hand to indicate she wanted one. I passed the packet to her and then to Hiêp. Without asking, another young man, Đoan, whom I knew well, also grabbed for the packet to help himself. The shift by Linh and Hiêp to demand-sharing of cigarettes was a signal of my growing incorporation into their social world.

Although I had become a familiar sight and was accepted as a friendly face and provider of cigarettes, the process of negotiating access and trust (in the sense of people accepting my presence and not modifying their behaviour) took more time. In many of my early encounters, people were reluctant to admit their involvement in heroin selling. If they were sitting with me, and were approached by a prospective customer, they might deny they were dealers and send the customer away. Growing acceptance of my presence among them as they went about the business of heroin selling was expressed through practices of inclusion, also achieved and articulated within cigarette exchanges. My new friends were aware of my interest and efforts to learn their language. Their recognition and encouragement of this was signified by requests for cigarettes in Vietnamese and indeed, the question, '*Chị, cho xin em một điếu thuốc?* [Older sister, can I have a cigarette?]' was the second full Vietnamese sentence I understood (the first and most frequently expressed sentence being, '*Anh hai nhiều quá* [Too many police]'). In this marketplace, dealers are well aware of the advantages of communicating in a language that is not understood either by their customers or by the police. It was a marker of my acceptance and inclusion that some were supportive of my efforts to learn their language.

Having begun to establish relationships with at least a few of the core Vietnamese dealers, cigarette exchange was also a means by which we affirmed these relationships. One way of affirming a relationship is through practices of boundary marking. Cigarette exchange was employed in this way when I observed my friend Van approach in the company of a young *Aussie* man whom I had not seen before. Van asked me for a cigarette, and the young *Aussie* man followed his lead. Hearing this, Van screwed up his nose and subtly shook his head to indicate that I should refuse the *Aussie's* request.

Van signified our relatedness – and his consequent right to make, and have met, demands upon me for cigarettes – through his attempt to deny the *Aussie* man this same opportunity. In so doing, Van was marking a boundary in his relationship with me; a boundary that excluded the *Aussie*. Van's act also reproduced the, albeit fuzzy, boundedness of this particular marketplace where *Viets* and *Aussies* were economically, socially and spatially separated. In this location, the Vietnamese and *Aussies* rarely interacted except during drug transactions. They occupied separate areas of the mall and patronised different cafés. As I became more accepted by the *Viet* dealers, I spent more time with them and less time with the *Aussies*, and eventually came to reproduce in my own practice the same socially segregated pattern that had struck me at the outset of fieldwork.

'I buy a packet. I pay you back'

The increasing intimacy of my relationships with *Viet* dealers was articulated through cigarette exchanges. Although initially these exchanges were unbalanced (primarily from me to them), our developing relationships were reflected in a shift to more balanced exchanges, with people making a point of offering to repay me or giving me cigarettes when they had them. In addition to these commensurate returns of cigarettes, reciprocity was also enacted through sharing of food, drinks or services such as information or translation of Vietnamese conversations.[10] On one occasion, for example, two men,

Quàng and Đam, asked me for a 'smoke' and took four from the packet. They did, however, leave me two nectarines in their place.

Reciprocity could also be read as a form of stored credit that allowed people to make claims based on previous giving. One day a young man, called Lam, approached the table where I was sitting and passed me four cigarettes, with the words 'You're always giving them out to me when I ask'. He then departed, but returned to the table an hour or so later. As I was taking a cigarette out of my packet, Lam reached over for one as well, saying he knew it was a good idea to give me some earlier, as his were now all gone.

Over time, with a few people, exchange became generalised such that everyone's tobacco became communal property. During long evenings socialising with my friends Kiều and Lộc, our cigarette packets would be placed out in the open and we would all help ourselves. Kiều and Lộc also shifted to smoking my brand of cigarettes so that our tobacco sharing was indeed commensurate.

This commensurate sharing ultimately entailed other kinds of relational responsibilities. Standing with Kiều outside a local health service, she suddenly asked: 'Have you got ten dollars, chị?' I replied that I did, and she held out a $20 note, telling me to take it and give her $10 in return. 'For smokes,' she stated. I was confused that she seemed to want to give me $10, but Kiều explained she was 'too lazy to buy them'. Still unclear about the point of this arrangement, I did as I usually did with Kiều and complied, taking her $20 and giving her $10. At this point, Kiều then asked for the remainder of my cigarette packet (about a quarter full and therefore worth less than $10). I realised that this had been about buying my remaining cigarettes for the $10, to save her having to go to the shop herself. She added that now she could also ask me for cigarettes another time and feel that she had paid for them: 'You hold for me. An inves-ment.' This episode was both warm and coercive. Our transaction was established as one without a foreseeable end. It was truly reciprocal.

'You always give your cigarettes out to everyone here'

Part of the process of establishing a research presence is the negotiation of a position. While I was always explicit about my role as a researcher, this seemed to be of less salience to the marketplace participants than whether I was a decent person, whether I could be trusted or what I was able to offer in terms of acquaintance or friendship. My gifting of cigarettes emerged as a key characteristic through which people identified and positioned me. Even those people who generally declined my offers of cigarettes still noted and remarked upon my propensity for cigarette distribution. As people came to know and accept me, many took a view of me as 'nice but naïve'. This was articulated through advice to hide my cigarettes so that others would not make demands upon them. This same construction of me was articulated by Thanh's public affirmation of my generosity when he loudly remarked, 'What are you? The Salvation Army or something?' after he witnessed me handing over cigarettes, my mobile phone and a small sum of money in response to a request from Kiều. His comment also served to transmit the respect I had achieved with him, with its implicit warning to me not to allow myself to be exploited and to Kiều not to exploit me.

As Davis argued, exchange is an important way in which people create and maintain social hierarchy.[11] In Vietnamese culture, age-related status, with its conventional representation of respect for elders, is a core feature of this social hierarchy. This is reflected at the most basic level in the age- and kinship-based pronouns for 'I' and 'you'. For example, *em* – meaning younger sibling – is used for, and to, people younger than yourself irrespective of gender, while *chị* and *anh* – meaning older sister and brother respectively – are used for those older than yourself but who are not elderly. Being some ten to fifteen years older than the majority of dealers, I was accorded the status of *chị*. As a consequence, I was due respect.

Cigarette exchange was one of the vehicles by which this ascribed status was expressed and transmitted to other members of the group. One afternoon, a young man, Tư, approached me expectantly and, as I realised he wanted a cigarette, I passed one across to him. Kiều, who was sitting with me, suddenly demanded, 'Did you ask her?' Tư acknowledged my status and the respect I was due by lying and crankily retorting that he had asked.

Returning to the two fieldwork images with which I began this section: from my position as stranger to the local *Viet* dealers in this marketplace, together we used cigarette exchanges (among other things) to incorporate me into their social world, such that, among those I was closest to, although I did not become a heroin user or dealer, I did eventually become *Viet*. As a woman of Anglo-European origins, this identity was admittedly not readily apparent. Indeed, it afforded some bewilderment to a Vietnamese restaurant owner when Kiều, responding to his query regarding whether I could use chopsticks and eat chilli, dismissively asserted that I could because 'She's Viet'.

Cigarette exchanges were one of the ways in which I negotiated the processes of gaining entry, establishing and maintaining a research presence, and establishing a position – processes held to be key in conducting ethnographic research. I both enacted and read these processes through temporal changes in the social meanings of our cigarette exchange. Cigarette exchanges oriented me to the importance of processes and relations of exchange and led me to identify and focus on broader processes of drug exchange that displayed many of the same qualities and purposes. In the next section, I draw out some of the similarities between the cigarette exchanges just described and the everyday drug exchanges occurring in this marketplace. While many useful items and services (e.g. drugs, food, money, mobile telephones, accommodation) were exchanged between participants in the Footscray drug marketplace, I focus on the exchange of heroin.[12]

Heroin exchange within the marketplace

The social science literature has identified two key forms of exchange on the basis of their assumed underlying characteristics. These are market exchange – characterised by trade or barter – and reciprocal or gift exchange – characterised by generalised helping and sharing based on mutual obligations and identity according to kinship and other social relations.[13] In the Footscray drug marketplace, heroin was exchanged through trade (the exchange of heroin for money) and barter (exchanging heroin for other commodities such as clothes, shoes, mobile telephone and other drugs), as well as through employment, service or gifts.

Trade was a central mode of exchange, and it was the exchange form by which the dealers defined their practices ('I sell heroin'; 'I'm a dealer'). Trade is often understood to proceed between people with no social ties,[14] and the ideal market exchange is generally considered a 'spot transaction' where the exchange relationship is concluded immediately.[15] In Footscray, while a substantial proportion of trade transactions were conducted between dealers and customers who were not known to one another, differential opportunities in trade exchanges were available based on different classifications of social relationships. Thus, discounts or credit could be negotiated by *regulars* (customers who purchased frequently from the same dealer) or by other Vietnamese heroin users and dealers who were temporarily without funds. Aware of this, customers worked to develop closer ties with particular dealers through friendly greetings and displays of loyalty. Dealers also benefited by developing regular customers as they could be less concerned about potential thefts and could sell their heroin more quickly. The ways in which social relations shaped opportunites available through heroin exchange reflect the same social processes described in my account of cigarette exchange where the meanings of these exchanges varied depending on the relationship between myself and the other person. Similar processes operate in non-drug marketplaces. For example, research has identified that social relationships between buyers and sellers affect market processes such as price, with goods often being sold at different prices depending on whether customers are family, friends or strangers.[16]

While dealers and customers frequently worked to develop social ties, more intimate social ties were apparent between dealers. These were often based on family or friendship ties and generally underpinned by shared ethnicity. Dealers, particularly younger ones, might 'work' for other dealers, selling heroin on their behalf. Those working for a dealer received shares in the surplus (heroin and cash) generated through the productive activities of purchasing a weight of heroin, breaking it into smaller portions, packaging it into *caps* and then selling these in the marketplace. Shares took the form of heroin, other material goods such as food and cigarettes, accommodation during the period they worked for the dealer and sometimes even small sums of money for minor expenses. Shares were apportioned and distributed according to the decisions of the employing dealer, with some dealers being generous and others less so. Employment exchange relations created and affirmed social hierarchy among Vietnamese dealers in the same manner as cigarette exchanges between the dealers and me expressed and transmitted my social position among this set of people.

More commonly, dealers who were not presently in a position to sell for themselves could provide service to (referred to as *helping out*) another dealer by assisting them secure customers in exchange for a *taste* (an injection of heroin) or a few *caps* with which they could recommence selling for themselves. *Helping out* a Vietnamese dealer was an opportunity largely available only to other Vietnamese as *Aussies* were considered untrustworthy. Although dealers were able to sell without assistance, having a helper offered several advantages. *Caps* could be sold more quickly, thereby reducing the chances of detection by police. With a trusted helper, one person could hold the money while the other held the heroin, thereby minimising potential charges if searched by police. Working in pairs also reduced the risk of violence or robbery. Prestige was also a factor in dealers allowing others to assist, as it suggested that they were generous and in a position to take care of others as well as themselves. At the same time, using helpers could also be risky in that they might steal heroin or *lag* (reveal the dealing activity) to the police if detained or arrested.

Helping out was sometimes constructed as charity (e.g. 'feeling sorry' for the helper, who might be suffering heroin withdrawal) while, at other times, it could be understood in terms of either balanced reciprocity – a counter-gift for past giving or past *helping out* – or generalised reciprocity – informal gift-giving for which no accounts are kept, no immediate or specific return is expected and no source of repayment specified.[17] *Helping out* exchanges were one of the ways in which dealers created and affirmed the social ties that connected them with other Vietnamese heroin users and dealers in Footscray. Through these social processes they produced and maintained the particular social category of Vietnamese identity and acted to reproduce the bounded nature of the marketplace. Similar boundary marking practices were a feature of the cigarette exchanges described previously, for example, when Van requested a cigarette while simultaneously suggesting I should refuse an *Aussie's* request.

In addition to employment and *helping out*, heroin was also exchanged through gifts. Gift exchange is understood to create, extend and maintain

social relations.[18] In contrast to market exchanges, where the 'exchange relation of a commodity is a relationship between things', the 'exchange relation
of gifts [...] is one between persons'.[19] Furthermore, gift exchanges are forward transactions (they have a temporal dimension in contrast to the spot
transactions of market exchange) and they carry the implication that the
exchange remains open. Mauss, one of the earliest theorists of gift exchange,
argued that gifts constitute social relations by creating obligation and indebtedness. Mauss was concerned with gift relations in societies seen as operating
through gift systems, and argued that these systems were based on three obligations: 'giving, receiving, repaying'.[20] By creating obligations, gifts tie people
together in a temporal, lasting cycle of giving, receiving and repaying. Mauss
further recognised the power inherent in exchange whereby 'the donor gains
prestige and power by transforming the recipient into a debtor'.[21] Thus gift
exchange, while producing social solidarity, was also coercive, with its cycle
of indebtedness and obligation.

Based on their social purposes, I distinguished three key forms of gift
exchange: gifts to maintain, gifts to substantiate and gifts to (re)incorporate.
Maintaining gifts could be read as charity. These were generally provided
when the recipient was *hanging out* (in heroin withdrawal) and the donor
'felt sorry' for the person. Such gifts were, for the most part, offered only
to other Vietnamese. Gifts to maintain were shaped by notions of social
obligation – either directly, as repayment for past gifts (the recipient had
directly helped out the donor on previous occasions), or indirectly, through
perceived obligations based on friendship or shared experience (e.g. the discomfort of heroin withdrawal). These gifts served to maintain the recipient
within the local network of Vietnamese heroin dealers. Individuals sometimes withdrew from the network if they were unable to maintain their
heroin habit, as it was through their use of heroin that people came to be
members of this local heroin dealer scene. These gifts were also maintaining
in that they contributed to the donor's prestige and reputation.

Gifts to substantiate took the form of sharing (or *shouting*) of heroin
and other goods, whether the recipient needed these things or not. Sharing
exchanges usually occurred between kin, fictive kin or close friends, and were
used to express and substantiate these social relations. Substantiating gift
exchanges usually implied people using the heroin together and, in this,
sharing heroin also expressed sociality. My account of reciprocal sharing
of cigarettes during evenings socialising with Kiều and Lộc may also be
understood as sharing to substantiate our intimate social ties.

The third form of gift exchange was that of gifts to (re)incorporate
someone into the donor's social network. In contrast to maintaining gifts,
(re)incorporating gifts were unsolicited and the recipient was not defined
as being in need. (Re)incorporating gifts also differed from substantiating
(sharing) gifts because consumption of the gift was not communal and the

relationship between donor and recipient was more socially distant. A key occasion that elicited such gift-giving was when people were released from prison. They would return to the marketplace and be given a *cap* or a *taste*. Such gifts served as a way of reaffirming relationships between people, of reincorporating them into the network of social relations.

(Re)incorporating gifts could be used by the recipients, or they could be re-exchanged through trade. Thi had spent an afternoon sitting with me, albeit with much to-ing and fro-ing to speak with other people. Returning after one of these trips away, she announced, 'That was good', explaining that earlier someone had given her three *caps*. She did not want to use them all herself and, as she was returning to the table, someone had asked her if she had heroin so she was able to sell two of them. Thi's interpretation of this gift was that the donor sought to incorporate her in a new form of relationship to him: 'to make me an *em*'. In this context, '*em*' refers to bringing her into a girlfriend relation. It also carries implications of subordination. Regardless of their respective ages, Vietnamese male–female intimate relations (boyfriend–girlfriend or husband–wife) are nearly always expressed as '*anh–em*' (older male–younger female) relations, structuring the man in a higher social position than the woman.

Employment, service and gift exchanges more explicitly rely on, and produce, more intimate social relations than do trade exchanges. However, all the modes of exchange described in this section were constituted through the networks of social relations within which they were embedded, and these particular networks of social relations were, simultaneously, made and remade through these processes of exchange. Furthermore, as the discussion has highlighted, exchange was used both instrumentally (to pass useful things between each other) and symbolically (to produce and maintain social hierarchy, to create and affirm social relationships or to establish prestige).

Conclusion

Ethnographic research knowledge is practical knowledge. It is only by doing it that one can come to fully understand *how* to do it. Exchange of cigarettes was, simultaneously, one of the ways I *did* ethnography, and one of the ways I came to a practical understanding of both the method of ethnography and of the social and cultural processes that I sought to investigate through my ethnographic research. Reflecting on our cigarette exchanges contributed to a realisation that *all* the exchanges and transactions in this marketplace were both a means of passing useful things between people and richly symbolic, creating and recreating the social order of this particular world. As the marketplace participants and I did with cigarettes so, too, they did with all the drug-related exchanges they transacted each day, strategically employing these exchanges to establish and affirm their social relationships and, through their social actions, to produce and reproduce this particular local drug marketplace. If we are to understand drug markets and market-places, we must recognise that such sites are embedded in particular social, cultural and economic contexts, that drug marketplace participants engage in similar practices for similar purposes as do we all and that, finally, the term 'market' (or 'marketplace') is always only an abstraction from the practices and relations of a set of people.

Acknowledgements

This research was supported by a National Drug Research Institute (NDRI) Postgraduate Scholarship. I am indebted to Monica Minnegal and Peter Dwyer for stimulating the reflections that led to the development of this chapter. I thank them, David Moore, Suzanne Fraser and the anonymous reviewer for thoughtful comments throughout the writing process. I am grateful also to the people who participate in this drug marketplace.

Notes

1 For further elaboration of this critique, see Dwyer & Moore, 'Understanding illicit drug markets in Australia'.
2 While Vietnamese people have been in Australia for several decades, by 1996 only 24 per cent of the total Vietnamese-background population were Australian-born (Khoo, McDonald, Giorgas et al., *Second Generation Australians*). Among the Vietnamese drug marketplace participants I came to know, with some being as young as 18 years of age, all had been born in Viet Nam. They will be referred to as 'Vietnamese'.
3 It is important to note that cigarette exchange was not a strategic or instrumental element of my research methods. Rather, it is part of my culturally embodied practice as a smoker. Being asked for cigarettes or offering them to other smokers is a regular occurrence across all areas of my everyday life.
4 When people are arrested they may either be remanded in custody to await their court appearance or released on bail to later appear at court under their own recognisance.
5 See, for example, Hammersley & Atkinson, *Ethnography*, and Agar, *The Professional Stranger*.
6 See, for example, Maher, *Sexed Work*, and Bourgois, *In Search of Respect*.
7 Bloch, *How We Think They Think*.
8 See also Dennis, 'Four milligrams of phenomenology', on the capacity of smoke and smoking to dissolve 'social and conversational boundaries' between people.
9 Peterson, 'Demand sharing'.
10 Reciprocity, in addition to being part of what creates and affirms social relationships, should also be considered an essential component of ethical research practice. Similarly concerned with reflections on the initiation and maintenance of relationships with research participants, Higgs, Moore & Aitken, reporting on research conducted in the same drug marketplace some years earlier (in 'Engagement, reciprocity and advocacy'), noted the importance of reciprocity, particularly among marginalised ethnic Vietnamese

participants, in contributing to ethical harm reduction research practice. Likewise Maher, in 'Don't leave us this way', discussed how her involvement in the illegal distribution of sterile injecting equipment in the United States provided a 'measure of reciprocity' that brought her closer to the women she studied and helped her move beyond cultural explanations towards an understanding of the structures that helped sustain vulnerability to HIV/AIDS.

11 Davis, *Exchange*.
12 For more detail, see Dwyer & Moore, 'Beyond neo-classical economics', and 'Interrogating conceptions of drug dealers'.
13 Wilk, *Economies and Cultures*.
14 Slater & Tonkiss, *Market Society*.
15 Danby, 'The curse of the modern'.
16 Kaneff, 'The shame and pride of market activity'.
17 Sahlins, *Stone Age Economics*.
18 See, for example, Gregory, *Gifts and Commodities*; Osteen, 'Introduction: Questions of the gift'; Sykes, *Arguing with Anthropology*; Thomas, *Entangled Objects*.
19 Thomas, *Entangled Objects*, p. 14.
20 Mauss, *The Gift*, p. 37.
21 Yan, 'Unbalanced reciprocity', p. 68.

References

Agar, M. (1996). *The Professional Stranger: An Informal Introduction to Ethnography*. San Diego: Academic Press.

Bloch, M. (1998). *How We Think They Think: Anthropological Approaches to Cognition, Memory and Literacy*. Boulder, CO: Westview Press.

Bourgois, P. (1995). *In Search of Respect: Selling Crack in El Barrio*. Cambridge: Cambridge University Press.

Byrne, F. (1992). *The Community, the Council and the Police: A Combination to Reduce Crime in Footscray*. Australian Institute of Criminology. Retrieved 13 May 2004. www.aic.gov.au/conferences/natovcp/index.html.

Cellarius, B.A. (2000). 'You can buy almost anything with potatoes': An examination of barter during economic crisis in Bulgaria. *Ethnology*, 39(1): 73–92.

Danby, C. (2002). The curse of the modern: A post-Keynesian critique of the gift/exchange dichotomy. *Research in Economic Anthropology*, 21: 3–42.

Davis, J. (1992). *Exchange*. Buckingham: Open University Press.

Dennis, S. (2006). Four milligrams of phenomenology: An anthro-phenomenological exploration of smoking cigarettes. *Popular Culture Review*, 17(1): 41–57.

Dwyer, R. & Moore, D. (2010a). Understanding illicit drug markets in Australia: Notes toward a critical reconceptualisation. *British Journal of Criminology*, 50(1): 82–101.

—— (2010b). Beyond neo-classical economics: Social process, agency and the maintenance of order in an Australian illicit drug marketplace. *International Journal of Drug Policy*, 21(5): 390–8.

—— (forthcoming). Interrogating conceptions of drug dealers: Community exchange of heroin in an Australian drug marketplace. *Ethnography*.

Gregory, C.A. (1982). *Gifts and Commodities*. London: Academic Press.

Gudeman, S. (2001). *The Anthropology of Economy: Community, Market and Culture.* Malden, MA: Blackwell Publishing.

Hammersley, M., & Atkinson, P. (1995). *Ethnography: Principles in Practice.* London & New York: Routledge.

Higgs, P., Moore, D., & Aitken, C. (2006). Engagement, reciprocity and advocacy: Ethical harm reduction practice in research with injecting drug users. *Drug and Alcohol Review,* 25(5): 419–23.

Kaneff, D. (2002). The shame and pride of market activity: Morality, identity and trading in postsocialist rural Bulgaria. In R. Mandel & C. Humphrey (eds), *Markets and Moralities: Ethnographies of Postsocialism* (pp. 33–52). Oxford & New York: Berg.

Khoo, S., McDonald, P., Giorgas, D. & Birrell, B. (2002). *Second Generation Australians: Report for the Department of Immigration and Multicultural and Indigenous Affairs.* Canberra: DIMIA.

Maher, L. (1997). *Sexed Work: Gender, Race and Resistance in a Brooklyn Drug Market.* Oxford: Clarendon Press.

—— (2002). Don't leave us this way: Ethnography and injecting drug use in the age of AIDS. *International Journal of Drug Policy,* 13(4): 311–25.

Mauss, M. (1974). *The Gift: Forms and Functions of Exchange in Archaic Societies.* Trans. I. Cunnison; intr. E.E. Evans-Pritchard. London: Routledge & Kegan Paul.

Osteen, M. (2002). Introduction: Questions of the gift. In M. Osteen (ed.), *The Question of the Gift: Essays Across Disciplines* (pp. 1–41). London & New York: Routledge.

Peterson, N. (1993). Demand sharing: Reciprocity and the pressure for generosity among foragers. *American Anthropologist,* 95(4): 860–74.

Sahlins, M. (1972). *Stone Age Economics.* London: Tavistock Publications.

Slater, D., & Tonkiss, F. (2001). *Market Society: Markets and Modern Social Theory.* Cambridge: Polity.

Sykes, K. (2005). *Arguing with Anthropology: An Introduction to Critical Theories of the Gift.* London & New York: Routledge.

Thomas, N. (1991). *Entangled Objects: Exchange, Material Culture and Colonialism in the Pacific.* Cambridge, MA, & London: Harvard University Press.

Wilk, R.R. (1996). *Economies and Cultures: Foundations of Economic Anthropology.* Boulder, CO: Westview Press.

Yan, Y. (2002). Unbalanced reciprocity: Asymmetrical gift giving and social hierarchy in rural China. In M. Osteen (ed.), *The Question of the Gift: Essays Across Disciplines* (pp. 67–84). London & New York: Routledge.

Party animals

The significance of drug practices in the materialisation of urban gay identity

Kane Race

> Respectable gays like to think that they owe nothing to the sexual
> subculture they think of as sleazy. But their success, their way of living,
> their political rights and their very identities would not have been possible
> but for the existence of the public sexual culture they now despise.
>
> Berlant & Warner, 'Sex in public'

Understanding the emergence of contemporary gay identity is impossible without considering the history of parties. A party is an event: a provisional and temporary coming together of diverse elements, people and things. A festive mode of social participation. Neither temporally permanent nor spatially fixed, parties nevertheless leave their imprint on cultural memory, urban geography – even political identity. And although party practices are immensely variable and historically diverse, patterns can be traced that reveal much about the shifting relations between sexual minorities, social authorities and cultural economies. In *Pleasure Consuming Medicine*, I argued that greater attentiveness to pleasure and its varieties and social dynamics might enable new ways of reflecting on policies and practices of care.[1] Here I supplement that analysis with a more historically and geographically specific investigation of parties as they have featured in the formation and imagination of urban gay identity, with a particular focus on Sydney and some of the metropolitan histories on which its gay community draws, such as that of New York.[2]

Drugs have been a significant component of the practices of gay sociability from which gay political identity has emerged. This is not to say that all gay men do drugs, or that illicit drug use is a feature of homosexuality in general, but that drugs have been a significant component in the subcultural practices and spaces of pleasure upon which urban gay identity has been built. Of course, gays and lesbians have made use of many spaces to find each other in the heteronormative context. But bars, parties and nightclubs have played a special role as agents of gay socialisation.[3] In turn, the materialisation of gay political identity would not have been possible without reference to the urban gay subcultures that constituted it as a recognisable source of collective identity. While many studies have noted the association between gay social venues and drug use – usually as a problem for public health[4] – few have explored the part played by drug practices in the pleasures, identities and cultures that have emerged.[5] My claim in this chapter is that psychostimulant drugs played a productive part in the materialisation of gay political identity in the twentieth century. But how does one figure the significance of drug activity within such social and cultural transformations? Grasping chemistry as a meaningful cultural force requires us to situate drugs as contingent players within particular sociocultural assemblages.[6] Hence my focus on party practices. Situating drug use as one practice among the many that make up lives and cultures may allow an acknowledgement of their activity in the formation and transformation of spaces of sexual expressivity without reifying drugs as fixed, in terms of their significance or effects.

Pleasure, escape and gay sociability

'The city' is by now well recognised as a significant component in the emergence of modern gay identities and communities.[7] The journey to urban centres on the part of sexual outsiders can be understood in (at least) two ways: as an escape from oppressive heteronormative contexts, and as part of a search for sexual partners and sexual community. From the beginning of the twentieth century, such cities as New York, Berlin, Paris and London have featured as an 'elsewhere' in the homosexual imagination – safe havens where fellow sexual outsiders might be found. In the context of stigmatised identity, the mix of anonymity and critical mass to be found in cities has afforded many queer individuals a greater sense both of individual freedom and of community. Where some scholars have considered the forms of stranger sociability and erotic attraction that characterise the city as 'precisely the obverse of community',[8] it is possible to appreciate in this context how erotic pleasure has featured as the very *basis* of community. But this is assembled community – not the taken-for-granted community of transparent recognition that is thought to precede heterosexual self-formation. And the forms of

pleasure that animate this community are themselves textured by the structures of the city. Thus for Henning Bech, 'the city is not merely a stage on
which a pre-existing, preconstructed sexuality is displayed and acted out; it
is also a space where sexuality is generated'.[9]

A similar ambiguity around escape versus pleasure could be thought to
characterise explanations of drug use within gay and lesbian populations.
Just as movement to the city could be understood in terms of escape from an
oppressive normative order, drugs may be used to escape cognitive awareness
of oppressive norms around sexual identity and sexual practice. In *The Boys
in the Band*, the theatrical depiction of a birthday party among gay friends in
a New York loft, one of the main characters coins the 'Christ, was I drunk
last night syndrome' to discuss the ways in which alcohol can be used to
mediate the stigma and shame around homosexuality: 'You know, when
you made it with some guy in school, and the next day when you had to
face each other there was always a lot of shit-kicking crap about, "Man, was
I drunk last night! Christ, I don't remember a thing!"' Although initially
this is discussed among the gay friends at the party as a ploy that closeted
youth use to justify homosexual activities after the event, in the discussion
that ensues it is quickly acknowledged to comprise a more deliberate and
widespread strategy. So when Michael expands: 'You see, in the Christ-was-
I-drunk-last-night syndrome, you really *are* drunk. That part of it is true. It's
just that you also *do remember everything*. [General laughter.] Oh God, I used
to have to get loaded to go in a gay bar!' One guest responds, 'A lot of guys
have to get loaded to have sex', depicting intoxication less as a loss of control
than as a deliberate, if less than ideal, strategy.[10]

This use of alcohol to mediate intensities of guilt, stigma and shame in
relation to homosexual practice and identity might be read as a product of the
times (and indeed a reviewer of a revival of the film in 1999 complained of the
characters' 'self-lacerating vision of themselves [which] belongs to another
time'.[11] It finds support in much of the sociological literature that attributes
homosexual drug use to depression, alienation, and the stigmatised status
of homosexuality.[12] But the involvement of alcohol in the course of the
drama itself suggests that intoxication played a part also in the processes
of banter, rivalry, play, confrontation, disclosure and affective exchange that
characterised the elaboration of (some) gay friendship networks in this context. A focus on the pleasures afforded by intoxicants, however temporary
and ambiguous these may seem, may give some insight into the experiential
shape and texture of particular social worlds and the conditions through
which participants attempt certain transformations or escapes.

The sometimes maudlin depiction of gay intoxication offered by *The Boys in
the Band* could be set alongside Andrew Holleran's 1978 novel *The Dancer from
the Dance*, which lyrically depicts New York's gay club scene of the 1970s.[13]
Here, drugs appear to be indispensably involved in the shaping of an entire

subculture and set of practices: the drug-saturated disco culture with its distinctive and exuberant practices of dance, glamour, friendship, music and sex. Drugs are everywhere in this text – poppers, angel dust, amphetamines, cocaine, Quaaludes, valium, alcohol – but they are generally subordinated to the pleasures of context:

> Some of the dancers are on drugs and enter the discotheque with the radiant faces of the Magi coming to the Christ Child; others, who are not, enter with a bored expression, as if this is the last thing they want to do tonight. In half an hour they are indistinguishable, sweat-stained, ecstatic, lost. For the fact was drugs were not necessary to most of us, because the music, youth, sweaty bodies were enough. And if it was too hot, too humid to sleep the next day, and we awoke bathed in sweat, it did not matter: We remained in a state of animated suspension the whole hot day. We lived for music, we lived for Beauty and we were poor.[14]

While the disco culture depicted in *Dancer from the Dance* is unimaginable without drugs, drugs are dispersed as an ancillary component to the primary activities of dancing and sexual sociability. Meanwhile, dancing itself features as a means of elaborating social bonds that suspend the couple form, perhaps indefinitely: 'Now of all the bonds between homosexual friends, none was greater than that between friends who danced together. The friend you danced with, when you had no lover, was the most important person in your life; and for people who went without lovers for years, that was all they had. It was a continuing bond.'[15] No longer simply a mechanism to assuage guilt or enable sexual coupling, intoxication emerges as one aspect of a culture of playful participation and socio-sexual interaction that has a particularity of its own.

The depiction of drugs in *Dancer from the Dance* suggests that it is important to consider the social organisation of urban gay life when accounting for homosexual drug use. It is inadequate to rely on explanations of social stigma alone.[16] Yet it would be too simplistic to separate the theme of escape from a more positive consideration of the contexts of pleasure altogether. Rather, what is needed is an appreciation of how the different sides of this polarity fold into one another at different moments in different lives, and how agencies of pleasure respond specifically and substantially to broader contexts of judgement and everyday pressure. Indeed, in both these texts the use of intoxicating substances has an acknowledged complexity, featuring as an escape from overbearing normative standards, an opportunity for self-expression and self-justification, and a means of producing new contexts of social and sexual interaction that might otherwise be difficult to achieve.

With these considerations in mind, what follows is a discussion of some of the forms of public sociability that have been important in the formation of urban gay culture. Drugs and alcohol have been a significant part of these practices, sometimes incidentally (simply because they have gone with the territory) and sometimes in terms of their perceived capacity to conjure new materialities – the contexts of action and interaction I have discussed above. The practices of sexual sociability in which drugs and alcohol are bound up have attracted intense surveillance and intervention on the part of social authorities. These scenes of illicit sexuality and consumption have comprised key targets in disciplinary attempts to privatise and normalise sexuality. But they have also been incorporated into regimes of economic value – for example, in official efforts to promote tourism and consumption in the 'post-liberation' context. These contradictory investments in the scene of gay partying give drugs an ambiguous but volatile status within the regimes of consumer society, as I will go on to illustrate with reference to contemporary disputes around drug policing in Sydney.

Disorderly premises

Although sometimes depicted as a phenomenon of post-Stonewall consumer culture, parties and partying have been significant forces in the formation of urban gay culture in a sense that precedes and exceeds the relatively short history of gay liberation. Historically excluded from some of the key institutions of private life, such as marriage and the family, homoerotically inclined men have long made use of public and semi-public venues – such as bars, coffee shops, parties, parks, public restrooms, bookshops and bathhouses – to meet other men and pursue social and sexual ties. George Chauncey depicts a thriving urban gay culture spread out across a host of commercial establishments, social events, dances and public spaces, even before the 1920s in New York.[17] More locally, the attraction of many single men to the city led to the concentration of identifiably homosexual clientele in some city pubs and bars as early as the 1920s and 1930s in Sydney, while the influx of servicemen during World War II boosted the clientele of these venues and led to the emergence of Kings Cross as a key nightlife district with a growing homosexual presence.[18]

Not surprisingly, the legal prohibition of homosexuality at this time meant that public gathering spots and venues frequented by gay men were subject to frequent police raids. In his history of the gay subculture in Sydney, Gary Wotherspoon provides an account from a patron of Black Ada's, a popular underground nightclub based in an old dance studio in the city in the 1930s:

> The place was packed to the hilt, dim lights, a bottle of 'plonk', lots of 'knowall' girls as a front and in the half light everyone looked beautiful. The dancing was real, body to body, pre-war stuff and you haven't lived unless you've really danced – asking some beaut guy for a dance, clasping him in your arms and

cheek to cheek – sex on the dancefloor! About 1am the Vice Squad used to make its routine call and when Black Ada opened the door and saw them she would press a bell and we'd all scatter for our seats leaving only the blokes dancing with the girls. So by the time the Vice Boys got to the top of the stairs it looked like a Sunday School hop and Ada used to call out in time to the music, 'One, two, turn – one, two. Will the couple on the right keep in step!' We all pissed ourselves at the tables trying to look as if we were studying the waltz.[19]

Black Ada's became increasingly popular during World War II, but was soon closed by the Vice Squad, who considered it too 'corrupting' an influence to leave open.

Parties and balls were one of the main forms of more conspicuous socialising among Sydney's homoerotically inclined men.[20] Parties relied on extended friendship networks and were often hastily arranged before city pubs closed at 6pm. Balls were more elaborate affairs, some even being held annually in public halls. Some of the bigger parties, such as the Drag and Drain parties of the 1930s and '40s and Artists and Models Balls of the 1950s and '60s, catered to a wider bohemian set, and drag and cross-dressing were regular features of these events. These were exuberant affairs, by all accounts: Wotherspoon writes of drag queens arriving in removalist vans, since their gowns and wigs were so elaborate that there was no other way to get there.[21] When police harassment and surveillance of homosexual activity reached a peak in the post-war period, especially in the context of the Cold War, these private and semi-public parties took on a new significance in sustaining Sydney's homosexual subcultures. Organisers now had to go to extreme lengths to avoid police attention, including selling tickets only very close to the event, refusing to sell tickets to unknown guests, meeting at suburban railway stations and organising travel to the dancehall from there. While larger events such as the Artists Ball continued to attract police attention (the constant harassment eventually forcing them to be abandoned), these larger-scale events were in many ways the precursors of the RAT parties in the 1980s (discussed below),[22] which started a craze for giant dance parties in Sydney and popularised dance music and the drug ecstasy in Australia.

In his stunning history of New York, George Chauncey shows how the alcoholic beverage control laws developed in the 1930s after Prohibition expanded the state's ability to regulate public sociability, which had a profound impact on urban gay sociality.[23] Where Prohibition had transformed the boundaries of acceptable public sociability by allowing an unanticipated intermingling of the classes and sexes in the underground demimonde of the speakeasy (precisely the opposite of what was intended), the establishment of the State Liquor Authority as the exclusive authority for licensing the sale of alcohol in the post-Prohibition context led to a sanitisation of the night-time

environment, which effectively suppressed public expressions of homosexual sociability. In particular, the mechanism of the licence made proprietors
responsible, under threat of revocation of licence, for ensuring that premises
did not become 'disorderly'. This gave authorities a new way to reinforce the
boundaries of respectable public sociability by regulating the public spaces
where people met to drink. While the legislature did not specifically prohibit
bars from serving homosexuals, the State Liquor Authority made it clear in
practice and numerous legal instances that the mere presence of gay men,
lesbians, prostitutes, gamblers or other 'deviant' figures was enough to condemn an establishment as 'disorderly' and lead to a revocation of licence. 'In
the two and a half decades that followed, it closed literally hundreds of bars
that welcomed, tolerated, or even failed to notice the patronage of gay men
or lesbians.'[24]

While there is less evidence of liquor licensing provisions being used in
this way in Sydney, the constant police harassment of public and semi-public
parties makes it possible to see how forms of public sociability involving
the consumption of intoxicating substances have formed a key target in disciplinary attempts to privatise and normalise sexuality more broadly. The
convergence of various regulatory operations around illicit sexuality, intoxication and public sociability reveal this site to be an important nexus for
understanding configurations of regulatory power, social experimentation
and queer resistance.[25] But these proscriptive arrangements also suited certain entrepreneurial interests. The demand for gay social spaces in the context
of illegality turned gay bars into very attractive propositions for organised
crime. In Australia, the illegal status of homosexuality enabled the development of close links between organised crime, corrupt police and the owners of
gay commercial establishments in Sydney, some of whom allegedly paid huge
sums of money in order to operate.[26] In her 'true crime' account of relations
between organised crime and gay commercial establishments in Sydney in
the early 1980s, Sandra Harvey describes how Patch's – one of the first of the
popular disco-style nightclubs designed to cater to a gay clientele on Oxford
Street – contained a large wooden tea chest stuffed with cash used to pay off
the police.[27] The criminalisation of homosexuality created conditions that
were well suited to exploitation by corrupt organisations.

A similar concentration of police surveillance, illicit gender and sexual
expression, organised crime and underground consumption subtended the
events that precipitated the Stonewall Riots in 1969 in New York (commonly
referred to as the birth of the modern gay and lesbian rights movement).
Like many venues frequented by sexual minorities at this time, the Stonewall
Inn did not have a liquor licence but was owned and controlled by a mafia
family, who were in the habit of paying off police to prevent raids.[28] Police
harassment and entrapment of homosexuals for solicitation was so intense
in New York over this period that bars had become one of the few places

where gays, lesbians and transgender individuals could openly congregate without being arrested.

When police raided the Stonewall Inn one busy summer night, many patrons refused to produce their identification. Police responded with mass arrests. The crowd that gathered in Greenwich Village that night to witness these arrests soon broke out into a series of demonstrations and violent confrontations with police. The ensuing events are generally regarded as a catalyst for the more outspoken forms of gay activism that gained shape in this period and have been discussed more extensively elsewhere.[29] Among the sporadic protests and actions undertaken by insurgents over the next few days was the distribution of a leaflet that read 'Get the Mafia and the Cops out of Gay Bars' – an indication of widespread frustration with the existing regimes of underground consumption and surveillance.[30]

A magical and volatile formula

The emergence of a lucrative market for heterosexual prostitution during the Vietnam War prompted a change in the spatial configuration of gay sub-cultural venues in Sydney. In Kings Cross, where a nascent camp culture had gradually emerged, 'even the streets themselves, with their pimps, working women, and drunken, often abusive clients, were increasingly hostile to camp men', and many businesses catering to a gay clientele turned their attention to nearby Oxford Street.[31] Oxford Street became the site of a new, American-influenced, much more visible enactment of gay identity over the 1970s, complete with nightclubs, bars, American-themed cafes, and sex venues. For gay men, a much more studied, masculinised, 'clone' look replaced the effeminacy that for so long had defined homosexual male subculture, while the popularity of such groups as the Village People was matched by the adoption of many of the accoutrements of disco, including amyl-nitrate poppers: 'the drug that defined an era, fuelling both the ecstatic twirl of the dancers at nightclubs and . . . sexual hedonism'.[32]

Perhaps the event that most firmly established Oxford Street as a place of political significance for gay culture was Mardi Gras, which began in 1978 as a procession commemorating the Stonewall Riots, but culminated in a violent clash with police leading to the arrest of 53 people. Mardi Gras grew into an annual street parade and massive party and one of Australia's most popular and distinctive public events. The history of Mardi Gras is complex and has been discussed extensively elsewhere.[33] Here I merely identify a number of features that might help to contextualise the significance of drugs in the materialisation of public gay identity in Australia.

The first of these is the way Mardi Gras successfully fused political activism with the forms of cultural recreation and subcultural pleasure that characterised the emerging commercial gay scene. In the 1970s there was a perceived disjuncture between recreational participants in the bar and club scene and the more politically minded activists intent on social and legal reform, and some degree of mutual suspicion existed between these groups.[34] The first parade was designed as a form of 'political outreach', and the mix of fancy dress, dancing, marching and chanting distinguished it from more conventional genres of protest march. Such chants as 'Out of the bars and onto the streets!' successfully attracted participants from among the Saturday night patrons on Oxford Street, significantly boosting the scale of the event. This formula was retained and expanded upon in later years, with the addition of huge, irreverent, satirical floats designed by Sydney's queer artistic talent. The event was rescheduled to a night in summer to capitalise on the warmer, more festive atmosphere. As a later president of the organisation, Richard Cobden, emphasised more than a decade later, 'In 1978 our community in Sydney happened across a magical and volatile formula – a political protest blended with in-your-face extravagance and creativity. The magic and volatility worked. We created a lesbian and gay protest quite unlike anything else in the world – a celebration.'[35] Whatever sentimentality might be evident in this analysis, it is clear that Mardi Gras provided a powerful source of collective identification for differently motivated gay, lesbian and transgender individuals. By bringing an innovative form of public and political expression to the city's streets that emphasised play and parodic performance, the history of the event belies conventional distinctions between political activism and pleasure.[36]

Second, Mardi Gras contributed to a culture of public partying that was participatory, spectacular and widely accessed. In this respect, the dance parties associated with the event drew on many of the conventions of the drag balls of previous eras while taking them to a new degree of intensity and scale.[37] Dance parties are often overlooked in political histories of Mardi Gras beyond their function as principal fundraisers for the organisation. But these events became key sources of collective identification and popular involvement, uniquely implicated in elaborations of queer belonging. The Mardi Gras dance party was held in the enormous pavillions of the Royal Agricultural Showgrounds directly after the parade and soon came to attract crowds of more than 15 000 people. While drug use was more obviously associated with the dance party rather than the parade, the event as a whole can best be characterised in terms of a culture of public partying in which drug use featured as a widely acknowledged, if variably accessed, component. With multiple relays and intersections between the parade, the dance parties, and the commercial and street-based recovery parties that invariably followed over the next few days, the Mardi Gras party was characterised by wider and more diverse forms of participation than perhaps is typical of the North American 'circuit party'. Actively referencing as well as influencing the many other gay-friendly public parties that emerged in Sydney at this time (such as the RAT parties and Sleaze Ball), Mardi Gras parties featured creative design concepts, individual themes, dance music, party drugs such as ecstasy and LSD, extravagant live performances, guest celebrities and audio-visual effects, and attracted thousands of gays, lesbians and drag queens as well many heterosexual bohemians.[38] With recorded electronic dance music spun by DJs, flamboyant display on the part of participants, the stimulation afforded by party drugs, and gender experimentation, these parties contrasted sharply with the heteromasculine pub rock scene of the 1980s mainstream and its drinking culture. Party drugs were a staple component of these events and were valued for their ability to construct new contexts of intimacy, eroticism, affection, play, expressivity, sensation and perception. The Mardi Gras parties and RAT parties started a craze for giant dance parties in Sydney that did much to transform the city's nightlife and general character by popularising gay-friendly dance music and associated practices.

The third aspect of Mardi Gras that deserves comment in this context is its unanticipated impact on concepts and practices of public health. In particular, Mardi Gras made it possible to imagine new styles of public health that thematised community education and pleasure.[39] At the beginning of the AIDS crisis in 1983–84 there were calls to ban the parade, with one of the government's principal advisers on AIDS describing the post-parade party as a 'Bacchanalian orgy'.[40] What was at issue at this juncture was the strategy for responding to AIDS: a punitive legal and medical regime or community education, partnership and participation. A legal framework for the protection of civil rights had been enacted during the early 1980s, including anti-discrimination measures and the decriminalisation of homosexuality. The sense of a coherent, organised, identifiable community that Mardi Gras appeared to embody made it possible to imagine a 'community response to AIDS', a phrase that soon worked its way into policy discourse and became an effective basis for further mobilisation. The transformation in consciousness was so complete that the same medical adviser reversed his position in 1985 and suggested that 'Mardi Gras would provide a perfect forum for large-scale education about AIDS'.[41]

Elsewhere I have written about the significance of the construct of 'community' in gay responses to HIV/AIDS.[42] The sense of community that was enacted at dance parties 'helped sustain a collective sense of predicament, power, care and commitment – a shared ethos enabling wide-ranging cooperation and transformative activity'.[43] This transformative activity included the invention and promotion of a safe-sex ethic, and the creation and sustenance of friendship networks outside the family form, which became important in the context of social exclusion, death and dying. What is less frequently acknowledged is the participation of drugs such as ecstasy in the materialisation of this community response.[44] The feelings of peace, empathy, openness and caring stimulated by ecstasy contributed to relational intensities, embodied dispositions and wider structures of feeling, which, for many, gave further force, coherence and meaning to a whole range of caring and bonding practices. Indeed, the recent clinical proposals to test such drugs as ecstasy and ketamine for their efficacy in treating post-traumatic stress disorder and depression respectively may simply represent a more formalised version of some forms of collective experimentation that were taking place on gay dance floors during the 1980s and 1990s in response, at least in part, to HIV/AIDS.

Of course, the running of dance parties presented needs of its own, and it was in this context that further innovations in care practice developed. The participation of people with AIDS in the Mardi Gras dance parties at the start of the crisis required the services of a medical tent, and organisers pulled together front-line volunteer teams of nurses, doctors, paramedics and first aiders to service these large-scale events.[45] The needs of HIV-positive patrons ranged from emotional support to feelings of illness, fatigue and other mishaps requiring medical attention or rest. But the team was soon called upon to service a much more diverse range of presentations and needs, ranging from physical injuries to costume mishaps and, more topically, drug-related emergencies and accidents. The latter category of situations demanded a particular approach to care that was non-judgemental, responsive to circumstances, and avoided moralism. Certain strategies were adopted, such as the exclusion of any authority figures from the medical tent (security officers, licensees or police) in order to maintain confidentiality and ensure effective communication and safe treatment of patrons. With only a tiny percentage of patrons presenting for care requiring emergency transfer to local hospitals, the Mardi Gras medical tent pioneered a pragmatic and effective first-line health service that served as a model for drug harm reduction at dance parties.

The final aspect of Mardi Gras that is relevant to this discussion is its contribution to Sydney's international reputation, such that in 2000 it could be described in a mainstream international academic publication as a 'principal signifier of Sydney' whereby 'images of Sydney as exuberant (homo)sexuality become mainstream, as gay men and lesbians, alongside heterosexual couples, families, tourists and households, turn out to celebrate the city in its public spaces'.[46] The transformation in the public image of Sydney's sexual subcultures from a stigmatised and despised minority to a position of symbolic centrality in the city's international imaginary was nothing short of extraordinary. Indeed, local spectators watching the closing ceremony of Sydney's Olympic Games in 2000 – with its giant floats, inclusion of drag queens, pink-suited dancing boys, and pop singer and well-known gay icon Kylie Minogue – could not but be struck by the constant reference to the spectacular conventions of Sydney's urban queer subcultures and open appropriation of their codes[47] – albeit without reference to the drug practices with which many of these cultural artefacts were associated.

There has been some discussion in the critical literature of how state and municipal authorities appropriate counterpublic spaces to gear their urban landscapes to a consumer environment and reposition the city as a tourist magnet in the global economy.[48] The discussion of the effects of this sort of economic success is very useful for understanding subsequent transformations in Sydney's urban spaces, as I will discuss further below. But it is noteworthy that the growth of Mardi Gras over this period occurred despite, rather than because of, the entrepreneurial activities of official bodies. Notwithstanding contemporaneous efforts on the part of authorities to refashion Australian cities as key players in the global economy through the promotion of hallmark events (mainly sports), Mardi Gras was tolerated at best and largely ignored by state authorities for almost two decades. Indeed, as late as 1990 the Minister for Tourism ordered the NSW Tourism Commission to remove material relating to Mardi Gras from its premises and databases on 'moral grounds'.[49]

It was only in its third decade, after the commissioning of several economic impact statements by the organisation itself, that Mardi Gras came to be explicitly embraced and promoted on the basis of its contribution to the regional economy (which was assessed to be greater than that of any other national hallmark event).[50] Nevertheless, with its capacity to draw crowds of up to 750 000 people to the city streets to watch the parade, the event had successfully positioned itself as a lucrative commodity and tourist drawcard by the late 1990s, attracting significant commercial sponsorship, broadcast live on television across the country and internationally, advertised in tourist promotions, its cultural artefacts featuring in galleries, books and museums.

Perhaps one of the most remarkable cultural transformations associated with Mardi Gras is the changing relation between sexual minorities and the police – a relation that could in many ways be taken as a barometer of citizenship status. While traditionally relations between police and sexual minorities were extremely hostile, the organisers of the 1984 Mardi Gras became involved in efforts to establish direct liaison between police and the emerging gay and lesbian organisations (as recommended in state anti-discrimination reports a few years earlier).[51] Mardi Gras provided a key opportunity for brokering relationships between gay and lesbian organisers and the police: indeed cooperation and interaction with police was crucial in maintaining such a large-scale public event. Despite some initial tensions, over the next few years there was a general improvement in relations and an increased acknowledgement on the part of the police of their role in supporting the event. When the Sisters of Perpetual Indulgence, a satirical order of gay male nuns, decided to exorcise the Darlinghurst police station of 'the demon of homophobia' on the occasion of its closure in 1987, the contingent of New South Wales police who gathered to watch the event did little but stand 'bemusedly looking on'.[52] In 1990 police gave Mardi Gras a community award for 'ongoing cooperation and crowd and safety control measures'.[53] In 1991 they started advertising in the Mardi Gras Guide. By 1998 they were marching in the parade. This was an extraordinary transformation in relations. During the 1990s community-based anti-violence initiatives tackling homophobia built on these improved relations, successfully interpellating police in lesbian, gay, bisexual and transvestite (LGBT) concerns and constituting LGBT populations as legitimate recipients of state care, rather than targets of state intervention and violence.[54] While police were aware of the drug use associated with gay party culture in this period,[55] drug consumption did not comprise an explicit priority of public operations in the context of the discourses of harm minimisation that were prevalent at the time.

Step back in time

A couple of weeks after Mardi Gras 2009 an opinion piece appeared in one of Sydney's gay and lesbian newspapers entitled 'Step back in time'. Written by lesbian barrister Kathy Sant, the piece argued that NSW Police should be banned from marching in the Mardi Gras parade until hostile and oppressive police actions at gay and lesbian events ceased. In particular, Sant criticised the large police presence at the Mardi Gras party and the use of sniffer dogs to instigate searches of partygoers inside and outside the party. 'Lots of things are better in 2009 but for some reason the NSW Police Force has chosen to take a step back in time,' Sant wrote. She went on to compare recent police operations to the violent confrontations of the first Mardi Gras:

> Just like in 1978, there was police hostility, harassment and unjustified violence (in the form of invasive searches) against innocent people in 2009. There was roughly the same number of arrests as at the first Mardi Gras. Once again people were frightened about losing their jobs or damage to their reputations. Perhaps the magnitude of the abuse is less but the police again seem willing to disregard the law and their own policies. We are again targets for policing from a police force even when we are not hurting anyone, rather than being accepted as members of the public who deserve protection from our police service.[56]

Sant's article elicited a wave of support in the letters pages, with many writers agreeing with her comments and criticising police. This prompted a written response from the Assistant Commissioner, Catherine Burn, who defended police actions on the night and constructed drug searches as a reasonable response to 'anti-social behaviour'. Pointing to the use of sniffer dogs at a number of recent music festivals and non-gay specific dance parties, Burn rejected the idea that police operations were homophobically motivated or that they unfairly singled out gay and lesbian spaces. 'Drug possession is not just an offence, but drug use is dangerous and harmful to one's health and wellbeing,' Burn wrote. 'There should be a focus on educating the community rather than condemnation of police for doing their job.'[57]

The community outcry revealed much about the significance of party practices in the constitution and recreation of gay and lesbian identity in Sydney. While police had conducted similar operations at non-gay raves and music festivals as Burn indicated, rarely had they received such sustained and extensively voiced public criticism of these operations on the part of participants in the event. Notable here was the tacit community acknowledgement of the significance of drug practices in the viability of this cultural form. While Mardi Gras itself disowned the drug use of participants, a former president of the organisation speculated in the gay press that 'Mardi Gras has faced serious crises during its 30 years, but this one [police use of sniffer dogs] has the potential to take down the organization once and for all'.[58] The exchange between police and their critics reveals how powerfully the drug raid reverberates with historical narratives and cultural memories of state intervention in gay social practices. By invoking the legacy of disciplinary attempts to suppress gay practices of public sociability under the guise of regulating consumption, critics construct an affective basis for resisting this instance of social government. But is this just another instance of homophobic state action, continuous with the past? Does identity politics provide a sufficient means of resisting and contesting these policing practices?

The threat to gay space embodied in current practices of drug policing represents a new chapter in the government of liminal consumption. To understand its dynamics, we must consider the effects of the forms of economic investment in gay spaces that have taken place in the contemporary consumer context – in particular, the emergence of the night-time economy as a particular sort of problem for, and object of, government.[59] Whereas previous interventions in the scene of gay partying targeted deviant expressions of sexuality and gender through direct police intervention and the mechanism of the licence, it would appear in this instance that gay and lesbian social spaces have been caught up in the broader social government of 'anti-social behaviour' and night-time violence in a way that nonetheless threatens the continuation of some expressions of gay-friendly urban culture. Given the historical use of dance drugs to elaborate its particular modes of urban belonging, it is not surprising that the gay community has become the locus of some of the most vocal objections to this policing strategy. But behind this drama is not simply homophobic policy but also an inadequate analysis of the cultural activity of drugs.

The conflations of 'anti-social behaviour'

The extraordinary popularity of Mardi Gras by the end of the 1990s brought a greater volume of mainstream consumers to the recreational precincts of Oxford Street on weekend nights. Within the marketing discourses and cultural narratives associated with night-time consumption, gay space offers various degrees of liminal experience: intrigue, excitement, transgression, novelty and adventure, a zone where day-time identities and norms may be momentarily suspended.[60] For sexual minorities, the marketing of this space to non-gay consumers and the increasing heterosexual presence within these zones can represent a loss of control over crucial spaces of communal elaboration and some degree of disenfranchisement.[61] Indeed, the desexualisation of gay space within discourses of cultural economy, and the loss of symbolic meanings associated with these spaces as sites of resistance to heteronormative society, is perfectly illustrated in the discourse on city branding cited above, which sees 'images of Sydney as exuberant (homo)sexuality become mainstream, as gay men and lesbians, alongside heterosexual couples, families, tourists and households, turn out to celebrate the city in its public spaces'.[62]

The expansion of Oxford Street's night-time economy, and the attraction of increased numbers of recreational consumers to the area on weekend nights, brought with it many of the problems associated with the expansion of night-time leisure in urban centres more generally around the world: violence and disorder, accident and injury, congestion, public drunkenness and so-called anti-social behaviour.[63] Tensions surfaced over police inaction after a spate of attacks on gay men in the late-night precinct. While many within the gay community interpreted these attacks as homophobic, a broader discourse on public drunkenness, drug and alcohol-associated violence and antisocial behaviour had developed in association with the expansion of night-time leisure over the previous decade, and the problems on Oxford Street were largely interpreted through this lens.[64]

Investigation of the sexual dynamics of this violence was subsumed to the more predominant police discourse of drug and alcohol-associated violence. Perhaps the best illustration of the paradoxical impact of this discourse on gay venues came in 2007 when the Lord Mayor and the Minister for Police answered the call of a local drag identity, Maxi Shield, to walk down Oxford Street on Saturday night to 'witness first-hand the nightly antisocial behaviour' associated with a change in venues and patrons. Police responded a couple of weekends later with Operation Gilligan's, a high-profile operation in which police took drug dogs through a number of venues on Oxford Street (gay and straight), leading to the arrest of several people for possessing drugs and the closure of the Manacle, one of the few remaining queer-friendly venues on the strip, for breaching its licensing conditions! Paradoxically, the equation of 'anti-social behaviour' with illicit intoxication produced further assaults on, and elimination of, gay-friendly space in this precinct.

The use of drug dogs in such operations has been justified by police in terms of confronting drug- and alcohol-associated violence and the illegality of drugs. But the conflation of drugs and alcohol in this discourse fails to think through the assemblages within which specific substances participate and their variable effects: the narratives, relations, spaces, meanings, affects and gendered performances with which they are enacted. The gay dance culture differentiates itself, both substantially and practically – in terms of consumption practices – from the heteromasculine drinking culture with which much night-time violence in associated.[65] Gay events are rarely places of in-group violence: the Mardi Gras party attracts 20 000 people to public pavilions in inner Sydney in what could be described as a scene of liminal consumption *par excellence* – yet few incidents of violence are ever recorded within party grounds. The coherence of police discourse on drug and alcohol-associated violence is dubious at best, given the not so distant cultural memory of NSW Police praising New Year's Eve crowds for their behaviour and attributing the lack of violent incidents to the widespread use of ecstasy![66] If peaceful night-time sociability is the aim of state operations, it would appear that police are happy to ignore their own corporate memory and intelligence.

While sniffer dogs have now become a staple feature of police responses to 'anti-social behaviour', their use was originally substantiated in relation to drug enforcement quite specifically. Drug dogs appeared in Sydney shortly after the Sydney 2000 Olympics, and their use was formalised in the *Police Powers (Drug Detection Dogs) Act* of 2001 after a court ruling challenged their legality. This form of policing can be interpreted as a form of 'show-policing': one of the first operations involved 300 police officers and the media units of all the major newspapers raiding a straight nightclub on Oxford Street, leading to the arrest of only two people.[67] The effectiveness of the strategy has been thoroughly debunked in a review of the legislation conducted by the NSW Ombudsman.[68] The practice appears to be driven more by the state's desire to be *seen to be doing something* than any serious attempt to address any problem associated with drugs. As a policing strategy, it stages an intense but ultimately superficial battle between the amoral market and the 'moral' state in an exercise of power I have described elsewhere as 'exemplary power'.[69] Almost certainly, the strategy is disproportionately affecting those forms of urban culture that have been elaborated around the use of illicit drugs. As one letter-writer to the Sydney *Star Observer* put it recently: 'Understandably things change, but for a gay scene to have been almost obliterated is puzzling.'[70] Just as distressingly, it has led to a significant deterioration of relations between sexual minorities and the police, relations that had been built up carefully over many years. Hence, when in 2010 a poster appeared around inner Sydney featuring a large image of the commander of the Local Area Police alongside the text *'Homophobic violence is NOT acceptable. Report all violence to the police'*, many gay and lesbian participants in Sydney's nightlife precincts found it difficult to figure out whether this communication should be taken as an act of reassurance or a threat. For drug policing had itself produced a series of performative effects, materialising as aggressive and homophobic – if not in intention, then certainly in effect.

Conclusion

Drug practices have played a significant role in the materialisation of urban gay identity. Obviously, they are not the only practices through which gay identity has been elaborated. Gay social practices have developed in parks, coffee shops, churches, sporting organisations, political groups and online media as well. It remains to be seen whether drug practices will continue to play such a significant role in the constitutive practices of urban gay culture given its public diversification in recent years. But it would be difficult to understand the materialisation of urban gay identity – including political identity – without accounting for their cultural and historical activity. Over the last century, forms of public sociability involving the consumption of intoxicating substances have also formed a key target in disciplinary attempts to privatise and normalise sexuality. But where previously police intervention targeted deviant expressions of sexuality and gender explicitly, in the post-liberation context it would appear that gay and lesbian social spaces have been ineptly caught up in the government of night-time violence and the night-time economy in a way that nonetheless threatens these forms of public sociability. The public panic over night-time violence and the 'antisocial behaviour' associated with night-time economies has generated a desire on the part of the state to be *seen to be doing something* in the highly mediatised environment of contemporary law and order, and this has led to the adoption of strategies of surveillance and intimidation that are not only ill-suited to the problem at hand but also disproportionately affect the forms of culture that have relied on party practices for their elaboration and reproduction.

These interventions can be situated as part of ongoing disciplinary efforts to eradicate forms of public sociability that do not organise themselves around the family or the market. Given the historical use of dance drugs to elaborate its particular modes of urban belonging, it is not surprising that gay community has become the locus of some of the most vocal objections to this policing strategy. But while this strategy disproportionately affects gay space, and is prone to homophobic abuse, a successful counter-response need not rest on the argument that these interventions unfairly target a minority identity exclusively. Rather, it should be grounded in the innovative and effective practices of social care and government associated with queer responses to HIV/AIDS and drug harm, which emphasise pleasure, care and cooperation rather than fear, demonisation and intimidation. On this basis, the care practices that make up good party practices might well achieve an exemplary power of their own.

Notes

1 Race, *Pleasure Consuming Medicine*.
2 The author wishes to thank Gary Wotherspoon and Robin Room for their guidance in relation to some of the historical material consulted for this piece, and Melissa Gregg and Rebecca Brown for conversations about the night-time economy.
3 Southgate & Hopwood, 'Mardi Gras says "be drug free"'; Green, '"Chem-friendly"'.
4 Stall & Wiley, 'A comparison of alcohol and drug use patterns of homosexual and heterosexual men'; Lewis & Ross, *A Select Body*; Halkitis, Parsons & Stirratt, 'A double epidemic'.
5 Southgate & Hopwood, 'Mardi Gras says "be drug free"'; Green, '"Chem-friendly"'.
6 Gomart & Hennion, 'A sociology of attachment'; Race, 'The death of the dance party'; Malins, 'Machinic assemblages'.
7 D'Emilio, *Sexual Politics, Sexual Communities*; Chauncey, *Gay New York*; Bell & Binnie, *The Sexual Citizen*; Eribon, *Insult and the Making of the Gay Self*.
8 Young, *Justice and the Politics of Difference*, p. 239.
9 Bech, *When Men Meet*, p. 118.
10 Crowley, *The Boys in the Band*, pp. 41–3.
11 Guthmann, '70s gay film has low self-esteem'.
12 Stall & Wiley, 'A comparison of alcohol and drug use patterns of homosexual and heterosexual men'; McKirnan & Peterson, 'Alcohol and drug use among homosexual men and women'; Lewis & Ross, *A Select Body*; Halkitis, Parsons & Stirratt, 'A double epidemic'.
13 Holleran, *Dancer from the Dance*.
14 Ibid., p. 115.
15 Ibid., pp. 111–12.
16 Green, '"Chem-friendly"'.
17 Chauncey, *Gay New York*.
18 Wotherspoon, *City of the Plain*.
19 Ibid., p. 61.
20 Ibid.
21 Ibid., p. 135.
22 RAT parties were dance parties hosted by the Recreational Arts Team, a group of artists and friends who used creative design concepts to throw extravagant and wildly popular dance parties throughout the 1980s in Sydney. The parties attracted an inner-city crowd of heterosexual bohemians as well as gay men, lesbians and drag queens, and are often credited with popularising dance culture and the drug ecstasy in Australia.
23 Chauncey, *Gay New York*.
24 Ibid., p. 339.
25 Race, *Pleasure Consuming Medicine*.
26 Faro, *Street Seen*; Hurley, 'Sydney'.
27 Harvey, *The Ghost of Ludwig Gertsch*, p. 124.
28 Duberman, *Stonewall*.
29 Adam, *The Rise of a Gay and Lesbian Movement*; Duberman, *Stonewall*; Carter, *Stonewall*.

30　Duberman, *Stonewall*, p. 205.
31　Faro, *Street Seen*, p. 223.
32　Ibid., p. 245.
33　Marsh & Galbraith, 'The political impact of the Sydney Gay and Lesbian Mardi Gras'; Carbery, *A History of the Gay and Lesbian Mardi Gras*; Haire, 'Mardi Gras'.
34　Faro, *Street Seen*.
35　Ibid., p. 236.
36　Marsh & Galbraith, 'The political impact of the Sydney Gay and Lesbian Mardi Gras'; Hurley, 'Sydney'; Race, *Pleasure Consuming Medicine*.
37　Wotherspoon, *City of the Plain*; Faro, *Street Seen*.
38　Faro, *Street Seen*.
39　Ballard, 'Australia'; Marsh & Galbraith, 'The political impact of the Sydney Gay and Lesbian Mardi Gras'; Sendziuk, *Learning to Trust*; Race, *Pleasure Consuming Medicine*.
40　Haire, 'Mardi Gras', p. 101.
41　Marsh & Galbraith, 'The political impact of the Sydney Gay and Lesbian Mardi Gras', p. 308.
42　Race, 'The death of the dance party', and *Pleasure Consuming Medicine*.
43　Race, *Pleasure Consuming Medicine*, p. 22.
44　Bardella, 'Pilgrimages of the plagued'.
45　Masters, 'We promised never to tell!'
46　Gibson & Connell, 'Artistic dreamings', p. 308.
47　Markwell, 'Mardi Gras tourism'.
48　Quilley, 'Constructing Manchester's "new urban village"'; Hurley, 'Sydney'; Haire, 'Mardi Gras'; Hobbs et al., *Bouncers*; Waitt & Markwell, *Gay Tourism*; Bell & Binnie, *The Sexual Citizen*.
49　Marsh & Galbraith, 'The political impact of the Sydney Gay and Lesbian Mardi Gras', p. 313.
50　Haire, 'Mardi Gras'.
51　Marsh & Galbraith, 'The political impact of the Sydney Gay and Lesbian Mardi Gras'.
52　Faro, *Street Seen*, p. 237.
53　Marsh & Galbraith, 'The political impact of the Sydney Gay and Lesbian Mardi Gras', p. 317.
54　Tomsen, 'Queer and safe'.
55　Southgate & Hopwood, 'Mardi Gras says "be drug free"'.
56　Sant, 'Step back in time'.
57　Burn, 'Time to work together'.
58　McLachlan, 'Serious threat'.
59　Hobbs et al., *Bouncers*.
60　Waitt & Markwell, *Gay Tourism*.
61　Quilley, 'Constructing Manchester's "new urban village"'; Waitt & Markwell, *Gay Tourism*.
62　Gibson & Connell, 'Artistic dreamings', p. 308.
63　Hobbs et al., *Bouncers*.
64　A number of high-profile police operations targeting 'drug and alcohol associated violence and anti-social behaviour' were conducted throughout Sydney over the summer of 2007 and 2008, while licensing restrictions were imposed on a number of late-night venues in 2008. Even when the possibility of homophobic violence was raised, this generally translated into a call for 'more police'.
65　Lewis & Ross, *A Select Body*.
66　Bearup, 'Love's in the air, alcohol nowhere'.
67　Police Powers (Drug Detection Dogs) Bill, Second Reading, Legislative Assembly, NSW Parliament, 6 December 2001. Hansard & Papers.
68　The review found that the strategy yielded traffickable quantities of drugs in only the tiniest percentage of indicated searches while three out of four searches failed to yield

any illicit substances at all. Meanwhile, the strategy was found to generate even riskier practices of consumption as users attempt to avoid detection. NSW Ombudsman 2006, *Review of the Police Powers (Drug Detection Dogs) Act 2001.*

69 Race, *Pleasure Consuming Medicine.*
70 Marcus, 'Memorial plaque'.

References

Adam, B. (1987). *The Rise of a Gay and Lesbian Movement*. Boston: Twayne Publishers.

Ballard, J. (1992). Australia: Participation and innovation in a federal system. In D.L. Kirp & R. Bayer (eds), *AIDS in Industrialized Democracies: Passions, Politics and Policies*. Piscataway, NJ: Rutgers University Press.

Bardella, C. (2002). Pilgrimages of the plagued: AIDS, body and society. *Body and Society*, 8(2): 79–105.

Bearup, G. (2000, 4 January). Love's in the air, alcohol nowhere. *Sydney Morning Herald*, p. 4.

Bech, H. (1997). *When Men Meet: Homosexuality and Modernity*. Cambridge: Polity Press.

Bell, D., & Binnie, J. (2000). *The Sexual Citizen: Queer Politics and Beyond*. Cambridge: Polity Press.

——— (2004). Authenticating queer space: Citizenship, urbanism and governance. *Urban Studies*, 41(9): 1807–20.

Berlant, L., & Warner, M. (1998). Sex in public. *Critical Inquiry*, 24(2): 547–66.

Burn, C. (2009, 1 April). Time to work together. *SX News*. Retrieved 20 April 2011. http://sxnews.gaynewsnetwork.com.au/feature/we-are-not-the-enemy-005219.html.

Carbery, G. (1995). *A History of the Gay and Lesbian Mardi Gras*. Parkville, Vic: Australian Gay and Lesbian Archives.

Carter, D. (2004). *Stonewall: The Riots That Sparked the Gay Revolution*. New York: St Martin's Press.

Chauncey, G. (1994). *Gay New York: Gender, Urban Culture, and the Making of the Gay Male World 1890–1940*. New York: Basic Books.

Crowley, M. (1969). *The Boys in the Band*. London: Secker & Warburg.

D'Emilio, J. (1983). *Sexual Politics, Sexual Communities: The Making of a Homosexual Minority in the United States 1940–1970*. Chicago: University of Chicago Press.

Duberman, M. (1993). *Stonewall*. London: Penguin Books.

Eribon, D. (2004). *Insult and the Making of the Gay Self*. Durham, NC: Duke University Press.

Faro, C. (2000). *Street Seen: A History of Oxford Street*. Carlton, Vic.: Melbourne University Press.

Gibson, C., & Connell, J. (2000). Artistic dreamings: Tinseltown, Sin City and suburban wasteland. In J. Connell (ed.), *Sydney: The Emergence of a World City*. Oxford: Oxford University Press.

Gomart, E., & Hennion, A. (1998). A sociology of attachment: Music amateurs, drug users. *Sociological Review*, 46(S): 220–47.

Green, A.I. (2006). 'Chem-friendly': The institutional basis of club drug use in a sample of urban gay men. In B. Sanders (ed.), *Drugs, Clubs and Young People: Sociological and Public Health Perspectives*. Aldershot, UK: Ashgate.

Guthmann, E. (1999, 15 January). 70s gay film has low self-esteem. *San Francisco Chronicle*.

Haire, B. (2001). Mardi Gras. In C. Johnston & P. Van Reyk (eds), *Queer City: Gay and Lesbian Politics in Sydney*. Sydney: Pluto Press.

Halkitis, P., Parsons, J., & Stirratt, M. (2001). A double epidemic: Crystal methamphetamine drug use in relation to HIV transmission among gay men. *Journal of Homosexuality*, 41(2): 17–35.

Harvey, S.D. (2000). *The Ghost of Ludwig Gertsch*. Sydney: Pan Macmillan.

Hobbs, D., Hadfield, P., Lister, S., & Winlow, S. (2003). *Bouncers: Violence and Governance in the Night-time Economy*. Oxford: Oxford University Press.

Holleran, A. (1978). *Dancer from the Dance: Nights in the City in Gay New York*. London: Penguin.

Hurley, M. (2001). Sydney. In C. Johnston & P. Van Reyk (eds), *Queer City: Gay and Lesbian Politics in Sydney*. Sydney: Pluto Press.

Lewis, L.A., & Ross, A. (1995). *A Select Body: The Gay Dance Party Culture and the HIV/AIDS Pandemic*. New York: Cassell.

McKirnan, D.J., & Peterson, P.L. (1989). Alcohol and drug use among homosexual men and women. *Addictive Behaviors*, 14: 545–53.

McLachlan, M. (2009, 13 October). Serious threat. *Sydney Star Observer*. Retrieved 23 March 2011. www.starobserver.com.au/news/2009/10/13/letters-to-the-editor-56/17098.

Malins, P. (2004). Machinic assemblages: Deleuze, Guattari, and an ethico-aesthetics of drug use. *Janus Head*, 7(1): 84–104.

Marcus (2009, 20 October). 'Memorial plaque'. *Sydney Star Observer*. Retrieved from www.starobserver.com.au/news/2009/10/20/letters-6/17412.

Markwell, K. (2002). Mardi Gras tourism and the construction of Sydney as an international gay and lesbian city. *GLQ*, 8(1–2): 81–99.

Marsh, I., & Galbraith, L. (1995). The political impact of the Sydney Gay and Lesbian Mardi Gras. *Australian Journal of Political Science*, 30(2): 300–20.

Masters, J. (2007). We promised never to tell!! Confusions from the medical tent. Paper presented at *Queer Space: Centres and Peripheries*, University of Technology Sydney, Sydney, 20–21 February.

NSW Ombudsman (2006). *Review of the Police Powers (Drug Detection Dogs) Act 2001*. Sydney: NSW Government.

Quilley, S. (1997). Constructing Manchester's 'New Urban Village': Gay space in the entrepeneurial city. In G.B. Ingram, A.M. Bouthillette & Y. Retter (eds), *Queers in Space: Communities, Public Places, Sites of Resistance*. Seattle, WA: Bay Press.

Police Powers (Drug Detection Dogs) Bill, Second Reading, Legislative Assembly, NSW Parliament, 6 December 2001. Hansard Papers. Retrieved 16 April 2011. www.parliament.nsw.gov.au/Prod/parlment/hansart.nsf/V3Key/LA20011206063.

Race, K. (2003). The death of the dance party. *Australian Humanities Review*, 30 (October). Retrieved 23 March 2011. www.australianhumanitiesreview.org/archive/Issue-October-2003/race.html.

—— (2009). *Pleasure Consuming Medicine: The Queer Politics of Drugs*. Durham, NC: Duke University Press.

Sant, K. (2009, 18 March). Step back in time. *SX News*. Retrieved 20 April 2011. http://sxnews.gaynewsnetwork.com.au/feature/step-back-in-time-005133.html.

Sendziuk, P. (2003). *Learning to Trust: Australian Responses to HIV/AIDS*. Sydney: UNSW Press.

Southgate, E., & Hopwood, M. (1999). Mardi Gras says 'be drug free': Accounting for resistance, pleasure and the demand for illicit drugs. *Health*, 3(3): 303–16.

Stall, R.S., & Wiley, J. (1988). A comparison of alcohol and drug use patterns of homosexual and heterosexual men: The San Francisco Men's Health Study. *Drug and Alcohol Dependence*, 22: 63–73.

Tomsen, S. (2001). Queer and safe: Combating violence with gentrified sexual identities. In C. Johnston & P. Van Reyk (eds), *Queer City: Gay and Lesbian Politics in Sydney*. Sydney: Pluto Press.

Waitt, G., & Markwell, K. (2006). *Gay Tourism: Culture and Context*. Binghamton, NY: Haworth Press.

Wotherspoon, G. (1991). *City of the Plain: History of a Gay Subculture*. Sydney: Hale & Iremonger.

Young, I.M. (1990). *Justice and the Politics of Difference*. Princeton, NJ: Princeton University Press.

Pleasure and pain

Representations of illegal drug consumption, addiction and trafficking in music, film and video

Susan Boyd

Since the criminalisation of a number of drugs in Western nations, popular culture has become saturated with drug references, iconic imagery and symbolism. In fact, drug prohibition appears to have spurred a proliferation of racialised, gendered and class-biased drug imagery in film and musical lyrics about forbidden, outlawed and officially condemned practices. Through visual imagery, narrative and music, films communicate meaning about drugs and the people who take them. These both reflect and produce understandings of illicit drugs, playing a part in public perceptions of drug use and in policy and other responses to perceived drug crises. Drawing on critical and feminist criminology, sociology and cultural studies, this chapter analyses the representation of illicit drug use in popular culture, focusing on music in drug films and music videos. These texts illuminate the diversity and complexity of representations of drug consumption, addiction and trafficking, in popular culture. They point to our ambivalence about drugs, intoxication, consumption and pleasure. Using qualitative research methods I explore the narrative themes of drug trafficking, drug consumption and addiction that emerge in a sample of texts produced between 1960 and 2010. Rather than viewing music, film and music video as 'mere entertainment', I understand them to be cultural agents that produce and reproduce 'systems of meaning' about drugs, pleasure, drug users, addiction, degradation, crime, treatment, punishment and redemption.[1] In turn, I argue, these meanings both give impetus to conventional punitive responses to drug use and create new spaces in which to build alternative responses.

Background

Drug use has appeared in popular film and other entertainment from its earliest days. A number of films made in the 1920s and 1930s represent drugs such as marijuana, cocaine and opiates as pleasurable, mainstream and compatible with non-criminal lifestyles. Similarly, a number of positive drug songs such as 'Reefer Man', depicted in the 1930s Hollywood comedy, *International House* (1933), and Ella Fitzgerald's 1938 song about cocaine, 'Wacky Dust', were popular. Following drug prohibition, positive film representations of criminalised drugs were eventually banned in the USA and elsewhere. In contrast, prohibitionist films such as *Narcotic* (1923) and *Reefer Madness* (1935) entertained and educated moviegoers about the horrors of drugs and addiction. These propagandist anti-drug narratives depict the supposed degradation associated with opium/heroin and marijuana addiction and jazz music, portray violent dealers threatening white moral society, and call for more policing and laws.

The 1960s marked a significant rupture in drug war discourse, and oppositional films and music proliferated. As early rock 'n' roll merged into the mainstream, its association with youth culture, illegal drug taking and resistance was represented in many songs and films. Representations of an array of legal prescription drugs also emerged.[2] In many of these films, music is central to the narrative of the story. Ruptures in and challenges to drug war discourse continue to appear in film and other forms of popular culture today, and numerous contemporary films and songs about illegal drugs emphasise not only risk and danger but also pleasure and play.

It can be argued, however, that the pleasure associated with drug consumption is still treated with much suspicion and hostility both on and off the screen. Individuals who 'seek bodily pleasure through practices regarded as harmful' and criminal often become 'objects of fear and revulsion'.[3] Historically, drug consumption among poor and marginalised peoples is more likely to be seen as deviant, pathological and linked to crime, addiction, compulsion and social misery, rather than pleasure.[4] White women's drug use and pleasure are also historically and cinematically linked to the breakdown of moral society. Women are seen as failing in their gender-specific roles, refusing to act like women, and abandoning the home and family,[5] and racialised women and men are constructed as more deviant and criminal than their white counterparts.[6] Our most hateful condemnation is reserved for the drug trafficker,[7] and film representations of them are fairly consistently negative over time.[8] However, as will be discussed in this chapter, alternative representations compete with and challenge conventional discourse. A century of drug prohibition has done little to appease our appetite for illegal drugs, especially marijuana. Pleasure is central to many references in popular culture to marijuana and other drugs. Indeed, the hundreds of films and songs about illegal drug use and selling produced over the last century suggest that our consumption of these film images and musical lyrics can also be understood as a form of vicarious pleasure.

Representation of illegal drugs

Although representations of illegal drugs in popular culture are diverse, the criminalisation of specific drugs is justified by their perceived danger. It is also argued that drug prohibition is fuelled by fear of the Other. Scholars such as Frantz Fanon, Edward Said and, later, Michael Foucault make clear how the Other came to be identified and disciplined. The identification and regulation of racialised, drugged, addicted and criminal bodies emerged in the nineteenth century accompanied by the rise of the penitentiary and such professions as criminal justice, medicine, psychiatry and social work, which 'encourage individuals to behave in ways commensurate with the interests of a liberal, well-tempered, regulated society'.[9] Sobriety and self-control became the template of white middle-class respectability. These shifts in the moral regulation of drug users were accompanied by increased surveillance and discipline of individuals and groups, and drug war imagery and representation, especially through film, throughout the twentieth and twenty-first centuries.

Drug prohibition and film emerged during the same era, and since the late 1800s and early 1900s stories about drugs, drug users, traffickers, addiction and punishment have been popular in Western societies. Each visual image, drug film or song carries its own, specific meaning. However, film images, narratives and music also 'accumulate meanings' by making references to earlier images and cultural references.[10] Through the deployment of visual and narrative stereotypes, including the reduction of people who use and sell criminalised drugs to a narrow set of simple, racialised, essential characteristics, the construction of 'otherness', fantasy and the fetishism of drug associated imagery and paraphernalia (such as 'shooting-up' scenes), we come to make sense of or understand the films we watch and the music lyrics we hear by drawing from earlier and contemporary references.[11] Stuart Hall argues that stereotyping occurs when there are extreme 'inequalities of power'. He makes clear how representational practices and stereotyping are key elements 'in this exercise of symbolic violence'.[12] Thus, the war on drugs and its associated harm is accompanied by symbolic violence; commonly expressed in cultural products such as movies. Films reproduce stereotypical references that work to reiterate social hierarchies.

Although illegal drug use in Western nations has been officially understood primarily through the lens of criminal justice, crime and punishment – and, to a lesser degree, health – popular culture also contributes to our knowledge and perceptions about both illegal and legal drug use. Fraser, valentine and Roberts observe that Western culture is a 'scientific and biomedical one, saturated with drugs and drug-taking: legal and illegal'.[13] 'Non-criminal' drug consumers, such as marijuana and ecstasy users, are also commonplace in popular cultures.[14] Pleasure is represented as central to drug use.[15] Thus, there is no single message about illegal drugs in popular culture.[16] Popular culture contributes to and reinforces stereotypes and myths, transmitting ideas about the scope of illegal drug use and trafficking, notions about pleasure and harm, and addiction and sobriety. It also offers a critique of the war on drugs and provides alternative narratives. Film narratives and images racialise and Other their subjects at the same time as they produce a multitude of pleasures and horrors associated with drug use and drug selling. In other words, these film representations are potentially unstable in the meanings they convey about drugs.

In focus

Analysing popular culture on drugs

Cultural studies and cultural criminology perspectives provide a lens to understand drug films, music and videos. These perspectives offer a mode of analysis sensitive to images, meaning and representation in popular culture. Although illegal drug use is associated with harm, pleasure is central to many popular cultural representations. Stuart Hall highlights the politics of representation and the ideological significance of visual images and the interdependency of narrative and image in popular culture.[a] Ien Ang makes clear how pleasure derived from popular culture 'eludes our rational consciousness'. She illuminates the multiplicity of meaning in popular culture and notes that the pleasure audiences experience is 'uncertain and precarious'.[b] Through cultural criminology, we gain a critique of the uncritical acceptance of the expansion of Western criminal justice practice and policy and the proliferation of media representations of crime and deviance linked to the use and production of illegal drugs.[c]

a Evans & Hall, 'What is visual culture?'; Hall, 'The determination of news photographs', and *Representations*.
b Ang, *Watching Dallas*, p. 85.
c Ferrell & Websdale, 'Materials for making trouble'; Hayward & Young, 'Cultural criminology', p. 259.

Rock 'n' roll and drug films

A number of films produced in the 1960s and '70s, such as *Chappaqua* (1966), *Easy Rider* (1969), *Alice's Restaurant* (1969), *Performance* (1970) and *Pure Shit* (1975), are in sharp contrast to earlier morality anti-drug films. These films normalise illegal drug use, and drug dealers are sometimes portrayed as sympathetic characters. The music in these films is central to the narrative of the story. The film *Easy Rider* is a good example; although the soundtrack is not original, current songs of the era were used 'as part of the narrative'.[17] Many of these songs accompany references to drugs in the film, such as the sharing of marijuana by Fraternity of Man: 'Don't bogart that joint my friend/Pass it over to me/roll another up/Just like the other one.'

The film depicts two white, counterculture motorcycle-riding men, crossing the United States after completing a cocaine deal that will provide them with enough cash to be free. Acts of challenging conventional society and illegal drug use are portrayed as positive in the film. The film prophetically opens with Steppenwolf's 1968 song, 'The Pusher':

> I smoked a lot of grass
> Oh lord, I popped a lot of pills
> But I never touched nothin'
> That my spirit could kill
> . . . But the pusher don't care if you live or if you die
> I say God damn the pusher.

Other songs on the soundtrack suggest psychedelic ambience. Nevertheless, in *Easy Rider*, the main characters are punished for their transgressions and murdered at the end of the film. The film director notes that the main characters blew their chances for freedom. In their pursuit of the American Dream, to get rich through one drug deal in order to drop out of society, they lose sight of their freedom.[18] The film does not necessarily condemn drug use and dealing; rather, 'get rich quick' schemes associated with the pursuit of the American Dream and conventional society are under scrutiny. In *Easy Rider*, it is not the drug that produces harm (a dominant theme in earlier films); rather it is conventional society that is represented as dangerous, embodied in the form of working-class Southern white men. In addition, the lyrics about the 'pusher' at the beginning of the film signal ambivalence about drug dealers.

Funk, soul, blues

Societal and political changes, including anti-colonial efforts and the civil rights and Black Panther movements in the USA, led to the emergence of a number of black filmmakers and actors in the early 1970s. The film

Superfly (1972), directed by Gordon Parks, Jr, represents this new genre. *Superfly* is about the plight of poor black men and women in the ghettos of New York City. The soundtrack is central to the story. *Superfly*'s main character, Priest, is depicted as a sensitive and thoughtful cocaine dealer (who uses the drug recreationally) engaged in the only job in town available for a black man in racist, class-biased urban America. The film opens with the song 'Ghetto Child' by legendary musician Curtis Mayfield: 'Little child, runnin' wild/watch awhile/You see he never smiles.' In the film, the white police, who control the higher level of the drug trade, are depicted as corrupt and violent. Black power and agency are depicted as desirable for long-subjected communities. Curtis Mayfield is shown singing 'Pusherman' in the film: 'I'm your pusherman... Solid life of crime/a man of odd circumstances/a victim of ghetto demands.' Mayfield's songs accompany the film narrative, and the soundtrack can be considered as a character in itself. The song lyrics function as a 'Greek chorus', both commenting upon and criticising the onscreen action.[19] The lyrics evoke themes about the appeal of the drug economy and economic necessity, coupled with the threat of violence and self-destruction and the quest for the 'American Dream'.

In both *Easy Rider* and *Superfly*, recreational drug use is normalised and cocaine dealers are not vilified but rather they are humanised. In both films, conventional society rather than the lone dealer is depicted as a threat to freedom. The music strengthens the narrative, providing another layer of meaning to the story.

Pop, new wave/punk and hip-hop

Cocaine consumption and dealing are also depicted in a number of films of the 1980s such as *Scarface* (1983), *Bright Lights, Big City* (1988) and *Clean and Sober* (1988). These films differ significantly from *Easy Rider* and *Superfly*; no longer is recreational cocaine consumption normalised or dealers represented sympathetically. Rather, in *Scarface*, racialised, foreign drug dealers and cocaine consumers are depicted as violent and a threat to the nation. In *Bright Lights, Big City* and *Clean and Sober*, upper-class characters are represented as quickly becoming addicted to powder cocaine, which leads to their moral downfall. Jimmy Reed's blues lyrics, 'Bright lights, big city/Gone to my baby's head', alludes both to the allure of the immoral city and to a seemingly naturalised relationship with cocaine. In *Clean and Sober* abstinence, Twelve-Step ideology, addict identity and the disease model of addiction are represented as the only route to salvation. In the film, the Fleetwoods' pop song of love and obsession provides another layer of understanding to the images of destructive cocaine addiction depicted on the screen: 'Come softly darling, come to me stay/you're my obsession, forever and a day.'

Whereas older narratives of redemption and sobriety are realised on the screen for the white upper-class lead characters in *Bright Lights, Big City* and *Clean and Sober*, death and destruction is the fate of Tony, the lead character, who sells and uses cocaine in *Scarface*. Although the music in *Scarface* is not as powerful as the soundtrack of *Easy Rider* or *Superfly*, the song 'Rush Rush' by new wave/punk musician Debbie Harry provides context to the shift in the history of representations of cocaine users and the people who sell the drug. She sings: 'He's a real speed demon . . . /The son of a devil, he wants more and more/Oh, he's a high, high climber.' The lyrics and chorus 'rush rush' and 'give me yeyo' (i.e., cocaine) provide context to the images in *Scarface* that potentially link violence, cocaine, drug dealing, wealth and ultimately the destruction of the self and others.

Shifts in drug taking and responses to it are also reflected in films and music produced in the 1990s. *New Jack City* (1991) is about inner-city life, crack cocaine and the drug trade in New York City during the conservative 1980s Reagan era and the 'crack scare'. This film draws on older narratives of death and destruction and potent tropes of drug use produced throughout the 1980s. The negative impact of violence related to the drug trade on black urban communities is depicted in the movie. Film representations of drug trafficking and addiction are often shown to be relational. In order to make clear the impact of drug trafficking, depictions of harrowing addiction are included in the film's storyline.

The hip-hop soundtrack features several prominent rappers such as Queen Latifah who sings about the drug trade: 'Don't let money change you . . . money, money, money.' Ice T is depicted as a 'righteous, good cop' in the film. Flavor Flav, of Public Enemy, also appears in the film as a DJ at the nightclub Spotlight. However, in this film, black power is turned on its head and constructed within a drug war discourse that pits 'bad' black users and dealers against the emergence of a 'good' black cop. This construction is in sharp contrast to the political discourse in *Superfly*, produced 20 years earlier. In *New Jack City*, drug war ideology is reaffirmed. Local black dealers are represented as greedy and evil, a violent threat to communities. The 'undisciplined pleasure' of crack use is swiftly punished by severe and inescapable addiction. Crack use is equated with degradation, poverty, disorder and the threat of violence. In the film, women's drug use is sexualised – they are represented as willing to do anything for another hit of the drug – and masculinity is expressed through violence. Theorist James Nadell questions how culpability and responsibility are problematically formulated in racist ways in representations of 'drug-crazed or drug-dealing Black' people, noting, 'African Americans do not control the means of narcotics production, refinement, or international transshipment, and only marginally control the retail, low-end domestic distribution network.'[20]

Esan explores the connection between hip-hop, drugs and the struggle for identity, and discusses how both music and drugs are 'features of a vibrant youthful scene'.[21] The hip-hop songs featured in *New Jack City* and other films and music videos are varied, revealing the pleasures and dangers associated with drugs, the negative impact of the war on drugs, the reality of the drug trade, and the marginalisation and criminalisation of poor black and Hispanic people in and outside the USA. Critical researchers argue that the creation of 'lyrics and poetry' by youth 'is a political act' since hip-hop provides a social space for marginalised youth to tell their story.[22] The ambiguity of the narrative in *New Jack City* is revealed through music. The music in the film stands in partial opposition to the overall dominant message of the film's narrative. The subversive potential of the music is contained and also acts to undermine the negative representations of drugs and dealing in the film. Thus, multiple readings of the film are possible.

Stoner films and reggae

Not all drug films are dramas, nor are they all set in the inner city; comedic stoner flicks emerged in the late 1970s, and they continue to be produced today. The comedy team Cheech and Chong developed record albums and films that celebrate and exaggerate their love for cannabis. Comedy, pleasure, play and anti-authoritarianism are central to stoner flicks, as is the male-buddy theme. Cheech and Chong's breakout film, *Up in Smoke* (1978), highlights their antics, and the theme song of the same name makes clear the duo's ethos: 'I take a toke/And all my cares/Go up in smoke.' A number of contemporary comedies, such as *Harold and Kumar Go to White Castle* (2004) and *Trailer Park Boys: The Movie* (2006) (and their sequels), also represent marijuana users, growers and sellers outside the inner city. In these films, representations of normalised and exaggerated marijuana consumption and drug selling prevail. Although *Harold and Kumar Go to White Castle* is a subversive film when it comes to race, it is conventional in its representation of gender (as are Cheech and Chong productions). Thus the performances of gender often undermine the anti-hegemonic potential of some drug films, while they support a particular view of masculinity. In these films, similar to Cheech and Chong productions, whiteness, racial stereotypes, and criminal justice and the drug war are problematised, and pleasure is central to the narrative. Yet, in illegal drug policy debates, the experience of pleasure remains fairly unacknowledged in both research and policy initiatives; instead, discourses of harm and risk dominate.[23]

The films above include positive representations of recreational marijuana consumption, growing, drug selling and importing. The classic Jamaican film, still popular today, *The Harder They Come* (1972), illuminates both recreational and *spiritual* use of the plant and the drug trade. Foremost, Henzell, the film's director, wanted to make a movie about reggae. He also wanted to show the interlock between the music and ganja business and the police. Reggae musician Jimmy Cliff plays the main character in the film. In addition, the director wanted to comment on Rastafarians, who believe that marijuana, or ganja as it is referred to, is not evil or illegal; rather it is a sacrament and a blessed substance.[24] Esan notes that songs about marijuana by reggae musicians Peter Tosh and Bob Marley also reflect their consideration of the plant in Rastafarian culture.[25] The film *The Harder They Come* is a critical commentary on reggae, poverty, the drug trade, criminal justice and Rastafarian culture. The director of the film asserts that the reggae music in the film by Jimmy Cliff, such as 'The Harder They Come', 'You Can Get it if You Really Want' and 'Many Rivers to Cross', strengthens the pictures in each scene.[26]

Music videos

The film *Get Him to the Greek* (2010) is a good example of how the film, music and video industries come together to package and sell a product. The emergence of music videos and MTV in the 1980s, followed by YouTube and other internet sites, provided a more global reach for communicating popular culture. In *Get Him to the Greek*, all these industries capitalise on the bad boy reputation of British comedian and actor Russell Brand, who plays rock star Aldous Snow in both the film and the music video. Brand's past drug and sex addiction are vividly captured in two memoirs, comedy acts and media depictions.

Get Him to the Greek is a male-buddy narrative that centres on getting Aldous from London to LA within 72 hours to give a comeback performance. Comedy and copious drug use, both alcohol and illegal substances, accompany his travels. Brand also directs, sings and performs in the music video that accompanies the film, titled *Just Say Yes*. The official MuchMusic video shows Aldous bringing his future bride home to meet his eccentric drug-consuming family. The chorus, 'Just say yes, just say yes', is repeated throughout the video as images of exaggerated drug use and drug paraphernalia are depicted. In both the music video and the film, excessive and pleasurable drug use is normalised.

Multiple meanings associated with drug use are purposely represented in the video. This is most evident in the video's coupling of drug consumption, pleasure and harm with racialised and sexualised representations of women. In the music video, racialised women's bodies serve to articulate century-old myths about the connections between the socially constructed Other and her insatiable desire for drugs and sex. As Bhabha suggests, this 'Other' operates as both 'an object of desire and derision'.[27] bell hooks argues that popular culture perpetuates the links between some ethnicities and the sexualised Other as a forbidden delight to 'liven up mainstream white culture'.[28] The video's performances of gender thus serve to undermine its potentially subversive narrative by reinvoking familiar stereotypes of drug use by using women's bodies as the vehicle for containment.

As Stuart Hall suggests, meanings are intertextual in that they are shaped by other texts. In the case of Amy Winehouse, media commentary and cultural references, including her own body of work, help shape the meaning we attach to her music videos. The music video of Amy Winehouse's popular Motown-infused 2006 song, 'Rehab', for example, may be understood by viewers and listeners against the backdrop of sensationalised media depictions of her colourful public life and drug use as portrayed in popular magazines such as *Hello!* and *Rolling Stone*. In the music video, Winehouse is filmed in an old tenement-style apartment surrounded by her band mates. She sings, 'They tried to make me go to rehab I won't go go go/I'd rather be at home with Ray, I ain't got 70 days.' The following verse, 'I ain't got the time and if my daddy thinks I'm fine', confirms her position on the matter. Here Winehouse writes back to her critics and attempts to reframe how her subjectivity is shaped and understood by popular media depictions of her drug use.

Winehouse's defiance and her rejection of self-improvement and rehab are slightly diminished in the video by her sexualised attire (in comparison to her band mates) and stereotypical gender concerns, such as losing her man. Similarly, at the end of the video Winehouse and her band mates are depicted in a room that is reminiscent of a stark rehab room. 'Rehab' depicts drug and alcohol consumption and addiction in relation to weariness and 'depression'. Winehouse refuses 'therapeutic' intervention, professional expertise, addict identity and the superficiality of 'being on the mend'. Twelve-Step models and rehab practice often expound neoliberal notions of the sober, rational citizen taking personal responsibility for his or her behaviour; yet, contradictorily, addiction is understood as a disease and as a 'lifelong social identity'.[29] Winehouse's video contests professional treatment and conventional conceptions of addict identity.

In sharp contrast, Rap musician Eminem's 2010 song titled 'Not afraid' is described as a 'therapeutic new single' on his CD titled *Recovery*. Rather than rejecting rehab, the song is said to be part 're-hab session group' accompanied by lyrics about addiction and getting off drugs.[30] He raps:

> I'm not afraid to take a stand
> Everybody come take my hand
> We'll walk this road together, through the storm . . .
> It was my decision to get clean, I did it for me
> Admittedly I probably did it sublimely for you
> So I could come back a brand-new me.

The music video shows Eminem trapped inside a room, crashing through the walls of it and emerging into the light on the other side, soaring up like a superhero over the city. The video ends with Eminem rapping: 'You're not alone'.

In contrast to Winehouse, Eminem publicly embraces dominant fellow-ship concepts of recovery and identity in his latest song. In an interview with *Rolling Stone*, Eminem describes his problematic addiction to an array of drugs such as Vicodin, Valium and Ambium.[31] Despite Eminem's humble roots, he is now a privileged multimillionaire with many resources and sources of support available to him. In the video, he is represented as a 'decontexualised' individual taking personal responsibility for regulating his behaviour and remaking himself.[32] Abstinence is represented as a personal choice. His well-meaning and fantastical message to his fans ignores such political and social structures as the war on drugs and such factors as race, class and gender that shape people's lives, choices and drug use, including their access to support and publicly funded voluntary drug treatment and private care.

Similar to the narrative of Eminem's 'Not afraid', recovery and Twelve-Step ideology and practices inform contemporary drug policy and treatment, and for many, these programs are invaluable, as is maintaining abstinence. However, Twelve-Step programs and ideology, including AA, NA and drug courts, often render invisible other support that individuals receive. Such support includes services not covered by publically funded health-care plans, legal drugs that people consume in order to achieve or maintain sobriety, including prescribed drugs and tobacco and caffeine,[33] recreational and spiritual forms of substance use, and alternative models of drug use and addiction. Twelve-Step models also coexist and collude with criminal justice institutions, harsh drug laws, punishment and imprisonment of 'offending addicts' who 'do not comply with treatment' goals.[34] Poor and racialised people are over-represented in mandatory treatment programs and prisons in the USA (and elsewhere). The emergence of drug courts in the USA, Canada and the UK speaks to the expansion of treatment through criminal justice, rather than voluntary access. Historically, representations of harmful drug use and addiction, fuelled by greedy drug pushers, have served to bolster the war on drugs and criminal justice expansion.

Rather than understanding addiction through the lens of Twelve-Step or disease models, Keane and Valverde argue that addiction does not need to be 'understood' as a centralised or fixed pathological identity; rather it could be understood as a matter of 'habit and conduct'.[35] Keane reveals how contemporary understanding of drug consumption and addiction focuses on feelings, underlying pathology and an inability to self-regulate emotional states, on 'one's sense of self'. She explores 'addiction' in terms of the search for intimacy, whereby humans make 'connections with substance, things, and other humans', and she illuminates how 'the production and solicitation of repetitive, serial desire is a central goal of consumer societies'. Thus, addiction can be understood as a form of intimate and emotional attachment, rather than 'compensation for its absence'.[36] Bruce Alexander notes that addiction is neither good nor bad; he argues that problematic drug use is one social response (among many) to 'prolonged dislocation' that emerges in free-market economies, where traditional culture and social relationships are destroyed.[37] Angela Garcia also illuminates how addiction is shaped by historical dispossession, longing, chronicity and melancholy ('mourning without end').[38]

As we can see from the discussion above and the films, music and videos included in this chapter, people's experience of drug use and addiction are diverse. The music videos highlight how celebrity musicians such as Eminem, Brand and Winehouse express their private and public lives and their experiences with drugs in their creative output. Unlike official drug discourse, the videos are diverse (e.g. exaggerated consumption, rejection of rehab and celebration of rehab fellowship); yet, inadvertently, all three illuminate class and white privilege (with little concern about criminal justice intervention). Nevertheless, the diversity of music videos, in contrast to official discourse, provides more nuanced understandings of addiction and pleasurable recreational illegal drug use. It can be argued that 'one-dimensional' perspectives of drugs, addiction and selling hinder our understanding of them and produce simplistic and ineffective national and international drug policy and practice.[39]

Conclusion

Film, music and music videos are 'social spaces' within which constructs of the war on drugs and addiction are articulated.[40] Binaries of outlaws/citizens, addicts/criminals, order/disorder, moral/immoral and pleasure/risk continue to inform both music and films. While these binary pairs are familiar territory for most popular culture consumers, their deployment is by no means consistent or predictable across time or genre. Images and narratives related to Otherness, racialisation, gender, sexuality and class both disrupt and confirm conventional discourses. Hegemonic depictions of gender, for example, often help to limit the potentially subversive narratives in some drug films. Drug war stereotypes and century-old notions of excess, desire, addiction, fear, pleasure, disorder and violence are continually played out through narrative, music and visual representations, but not always along the condemnatory, moralising lines we might expect. The films, songs and music videos discussed in this chapter reveal that popular culture provides competing narratives about drugs, drug dealing/trafficking, criminal justice, addiction, recovery, spirituality, pleasure and pain. Most significant is the diversity of the lyrics and visual representations in film and music videos. These contribute significantly to representational practices and discourse about illegal drugs, yet much remains to be learnt about these practices and their effects. Unlike conventional prohibitionist discourse, popular culture provides a 'multiplicity of meanings',[41] and a relatively nuanced account of people's diverse experience. In this way, I would argue, it helps create social spaces in which alternative understandings and drug policy can emerge.

Acknowledgements

I would like to thank David Moore, Suzanne Fraser, Connie Carter and Jade Boyd for instructive editorial comments.

Notes

1   See Doyle, 'How not to think about crime in the media'.
2   Since the 1950s, an ever-expanding selection of legal drugs has become available to consumers (e.g. Valium, Prozac) (Healy, *The Antidepressant Era*).
3   MacLean, 'Volatile bodies', p. 376.
4   Ibid., p. 377; valentine & Fraser, 'Trauma, damage and pleasure', p. 410.
5   Campbell, *Using Women*.
6   Boyd, *From Witches to Crack Moms*.
7   Coomber, *Pusher Myths*.
8   Boyd, *Hooked*.
9   Hyatt, 'From citizen to volunteer', p. 205.
10 Hall, *Representations*, p. 232.
11 See ibid.
12 Ibid., pp. 258, 259.
13 Fraser, valentine & Roberts, 'Living drugs', p. 123.
14 Manning, 'An introduction to the theoretical approaches and research traditions'.
15 Duff, 'The pleasure in context'; Moore, 'Erasing pleasure from public discourse on illicit drugs'.
16 Boyd, *Hooked*; Esan, 'Echoes of drug culture in urban music'; Fraser, valentine & Roberts, 'Living drugs'; Manning, 'An introduction to the theoretical approaches and research traditions'; Shapiro, *Shooting Stars*; Starks, *Cocaine Fiends and Reefer Madness*; Stevenson, *Addicted*.
17 Dennis Hopper, director, commentary, *Easy Rider*, 1969.
18 Ibid.
19 Commentary, Chapter 1, *Superfly*, 1972.
20 Nadell, 'Boyz N The Hood', p. 452.
21 Esan, 'Echoes of drug culture in urban music', pp. 196, 198.
22 Hanley, 'Close to the edge', p. 146.
23 Duff, 'The pleasure in context'; Moore, 'Erasing pleasure from public discourse on illicit drugs'; O'Malley & Valverde, 'Pleasure, freedom and drugs'.
24 Commentary notes, *The Harder They Come*, 1972.
25 Esan, 'Echoes of drug culture in urban music'.
26 Commentary notes, *The Harder They Come*, 1972.
27 Bhabha, 'The Other question', p. 19.
28 hooks, *Black Looks*, p. 21.
29 Valverde, *Diseases of the Will*, p. 122.
30 Dolan, 'Shady comes clean', p. 72.
31 Eells, 'Eminem', p. 52.

32   Wagner, *The New Temperance*, p. 69.
33   See Martin, 'The drunk's club'.
34   Garcia, 'The elegiac addict', p. 727.
35   Keane, *What's Wrong with Addiction?* and Valverde, *Diseases of the Will*.
36   Keane, 'Disorders of desire', pp. 193, 191, 201, 203.
37   Alexander, 'The roots of addiction in free market society', p. 29.
38   Garcia, 'The elegiac addict', p. 721.
39   Coomber & South, *Drug Use and Cultural Contexts 'Beyond the West'*.
40   See Holloway, *Cultures of the War on Terror*, and Thobani, 'Slumdogs and superstars', on the war on terror.
41   Ang, *Watching Dallas*, p. 88.

References

Alexander, B. (2001). The roots of addiction in free market society. *Canadian Centre for Policy Alternatives*, 1–31. Retrieved 29 March 2011. www.policyalternatives.ca

Ang, I. (1996 edn). *Watching Dallas: Soap Opera and the Melodramatic Imagination*. London: Routledge.

Bhabha, H. (1983). The Other question: The stereotype and colonial discourse. *Screen*, 24(6): 18–36.

Boyd, S. (2004). *From Witches to Crack Moms: Women, Drug Law, and Policy*. Durham, NC: Carolina Academic Press.

—— (2008). *Hooked: Drug War Films in Britain, Canada and the United States*. Toronto: University of Toronto Press.

Campbell, N. (2000). *Using Women: Gender, Drug Policy, and Social Justice*. New York: Routledge.

Coomber, R. (2006). *Pusher Myths: Re-situating the Drug Dealer*. London: Free Association Books.

Coomber, R., & South, N. (eds) (2004). *Drug Use and Cultural Contexts 'Beyond the West': Tradition, Change and Post-Colonialism*. London: Free Association Press.

Dolan, J. (2010, 27 May). Shady comes clean: Eminem's 12-Step rap. *Rolling Stone*, 1105, 72.

Doyle, A. (2006). How not to think about crime in the media. *Canadian Journal of Criminology and Criminal Justice*, 48(6): 868–85.

Duff, C. (2008). The pleasure in context. *International Journal of Drug Policy*, 19: 384–92.

Eells, J. (2010, 25 November). Eminem: The road back from hell. *Rolling Stone*, 1118: 48–54.

Esan, O. (2007). Echoes of drug culture in urban music. In P. Manning (ed.), *Drugs and Popular Culture: Drugs, Media and Identity in Contemporary Society* (pp. 196–210). Cullompton, Devon: Willan Publishing.

Evans, J., & Hall, S. (1999). What is visual culture? In J. Evan & S. Hall (eds), *Visual Culture: The Reader*. London: Sage.

Ferrell, J., & Websdale, N. (1999). Materials for making trouble. In J. Ferrell & N. Websdale (eds), *Making Trouble: Cultural Constructions of Crime, Deviance, and Control* (pp. 3–21). New York: Aldine de Gruyter.

Fraser, S., valentine, k., & Roberts, C. (2009). Living drugs. *Science as Culture*, 18(2): 123–31.

Garcia, A. (2008). The elegiac addict: History, chronicity, and the melancholic subject. *Cultural Anthropology*, 23(4): 718–46.

Hall, S. (1981). The determination of news photographs. In S. Cohen & J. Young (eds), *The Manufacture of News: Social Problems, Deviance and the Mass Media* (rev. edn, pp. 226–43). London: Constable.

—— (1997). *Representations: Cultural Representations and Signifying Practices*. London: Sage.

Hanley, M. (2008). Close to the edge: The poetry of hip-hop. In D. Silberman-Keller, Z. Bekerman, H. Giroux & N. Burbules (eds), *Mirror Images: Popular Culture and Education* (pp. 145–58). New York: Peter Lang.

Hayward, K., & Young, J. (2004). Cultural criminology: Some notes on the script. *Theoretical Criminology*, 8(3): 259–73.

Healy, D. (1997). *The Antidepressant Era*. Cambridge, MA: Harvard University Press.

Holloway, D. (2008). *Cultures of the War on Terror: Empire, Ideology, and the Remaking of 9/11*. Montreal: McGill-Queen's University Press.

hooks, bell (1992). *Black Looks: Race and Representation*. Boston: South End Press.

Hyatt, S. (2001). From citizen to volunteer. In J. Goode & J. Maskovsky (eds), *The New Poverty Studies: The Ethnography of Power, Politics, and Impoverished People in the United States* (pp. 201–35). New York: New York University Press.

Keane, H. (2002). *What's Wrong with Addiction?* New York: New York University Press.

—— (2004). Disorders of desire: Addiction and problems of intimacy. *Journal of Medical Humanities*, 25(3): 189–204.

MacLean, S. (2008). Volatile bodies: Stories of corporeal pleasure and damage in marginalised young people's drug use. *International Journal of Drug Policy*, 19: 375–83.

Manning, P. (2007). An introduction to the theoretical approaches and research traditions. In P. Manning (ed.), *Drugs and Popular Culture: Drugs, Media and Identity in Contemporary Society* (pp. 7–28). Cullompton, Devon: Willan Publishing.

Martin, C. (2011). The drunk's club: A.A., the cult that cures. *Harper's Magazine*, 332(1928): 28–38.

Moore, D. (2008). Erasing pleasure from public discourse on illicit drugs: On the creation and reproduction of an absence. *International Journal of Drug Policy*, 19: 353–8.

Nadell, J. (1995). Boyz N The Hood: A colonial analysis. *Journal of Black Studies*, 25(4): 447–64.

O'Malley, P., & Valverde, M. (2004). Pleasure, freedom and drugs: The uses of 'pleasure' in liberal governance of drug and alcohol consumption. *Sociology*, 38(1): 25–42.

Reinarman, C. (2005). Addiction as accomplishment: The discursive construction of disease. *Addiction Research and Theory*, 13(4): 307–20.

Shapiro, H. (2003). *Shooting Stars: Drugs, Hollywood, and the Movies*. London: Serpent's Tail.

Starks, M. (1982). *Cocaine Fiends and Reefer Madness: An Illustrated History of Drugs in the Movies*. New York: Cornwall Books.

Stevenson, J. (ed.) (2000). *Addicted: The Myth and Menace of Drugs in Film*. New York: Creation Books.

Thobani, S. (2009). Slumdogs and superstars: Negotiating culture and terror. *Studies in South Asian Film and Media*, 1(2): 227–48.

valentine, K., & Fraser, S. (2008). Trauma, damage and pleasure: Rethinking problematic drug use. *International Journal of Drug Policy*, 19: 410–16.

Valverde, M. (1998). *Diseases of the Will: Alcohol and Dilemmas of Freedom*. Cambridge: Cambridge University Press.

Wagner, D. (1997). *The New Temperance: The American Obsession with Sin and Vice*. Boulder, CO: Westview Press.

Film

Alice's Restaurant (1969). Dir. A. Penn. USA.

Bright Lights, Big City (1988). Dir. J. Bridges. USA/Japan.

Chappaqua (1966). Dir. C. Rooks. USA/France.

Clean and Sober (1988). Dir. G.G. Caron, USA.

Easy Rider (1969). Dir. D. Hopper. USA.

Get Him to the Greek (2010). Dir. N. Stoller. USA.

Harold and Kumar Go to White Castle (2004). Dir. D. Leiner. Canada/USA/Germany.

Narcotic (1934). Dir. D. Esper & V. Dodar't. USA.

New Jack City (1991). Dir. M. Van Peebles. USA.

Pure Shit (1975). Dir. B. Deling. Australia.

Reefer Madness (Tell Your Children) (1936). Dir. L.J. Gasnier. USA.

Scarface. (1983). Dir. B.D. Parlma. USA.

Superfly (1972). Dir. G.J. Parks. USA.

The Harder They Come (1972). Criterion Collection, 2000. Dir. P. Henzell. Jamaica.

Trailer Park Boys: The Movie (2006). Dir. M. Clattenburg. Canada.

Up in Smoke (1978). Dir. L. Adler. USA.

Music videos

Just say Yes. (2010). Dir. R. Brand. USA.

Not Afraid. (2010). Dir. R. Lee. USA.

Rehab. (2006). Dir. P. Griffen. UK.

Discography

Allen, Lilly (2009). *Everyone's at It*. EMI/Parlophone.

Cheech & Chong (1979). *Up in Smoke*. Warner Bros. Records.

Fleetwoods (1959). *Come Softly to Me*. Dolphin.

Fraternity of Man (1968). *Don't Bogart Me*. ABC Records.

Harry, Debbie (1983). *Rush Rush*. Chrysalis Records.

Mayfield, Curtis (1972), *Ghetto Child*. Curtom Records.

Mayfield, Curtis (1972), *Pusherman*. Curtom Records.

Reed, Jimmy (1969). *Bright Lights, Big City*. Vee Jay Records.

Steppenwolf (1968), *The Pusher*. American Recording.

The ontological politics of knowledge production

Qualitative research in the multidisciplinary drug field

David Moore

In recent decades, numerous calls for the development of multidisciplinary understandings of drug use and related harm have led to several methodological innovations. These have included the development of mixed-method research approaches such as drug ethno-epidemiology (i.e. combining ethnographic fieldwork and epidemiological surveys)[1] and complex systems approaches such as agent-based modelling (see 'Agent-based modelling' below).[2]

In focus

Agent-based modelling

Agent-based modelling uses qualitative and quantitative data to develop virtual environments that represent simplified versions of 'real-world' processes. These virtual environments are then used to model the consequences of manipulating key 'input variables' on 'attitudinal and behavioral outputs'.[a] The advocates of such modelling argue that it enables the development and testing of theories in a way that might not be possible using other analytical and experimental methods, and allows for the exploration of policy scenarios by developing explicit hypotheses about the ability of 'agents' (i.e. individuals) to cope with or adapt to changes in their environment.

a Gorman, Mezic & Gruenewald, 'Agent-based modeling of drinking behavior', p. 2055.

In the various commentaries and debates calling for and reflecting on these methodological developments, some have argued that qualitative researchers should suspend their theoretical and epistemological commitments in order to engage in multidisciplinary research.[3] Drawing on my recent involvement in agent-based modelling of amphetamine-type stimulant (ATS) use and related harm in Australia and on recent work in science and technology studies that focuses on the role of all research methods in constituting their objects of study, the chapter considers what might be won and lost when qualitative researchers adopt this 'suspension' mode of multidisciplinary engagement. It does not aim to resolve the question of the most appropriate mode of multidisciplinary engagement for qualitative researchers, but to begin sketching an alternative way of thinking about the processes and politics of multidisciplinary drug research, as a stimulus to further discussion and debate.

The multidisciplinary turn

During the 1980s and 1990s, there was increasing recognition within drug research of the explanatory limitations of quantitative approaches.[4] One consequence was the development of various forms of mixed-methods research on drugs in which qualitative research was given increased prominence. These approaches emphasised 'cross-methodological and analytical dialogue' across multidisciplinary research teams.[5] In this way, some of the limitations of the two forms of data collection could be minimised (e.g. the limited generalisability of qualitative research and the limited depth of quantitative research) and some of their advantages could be reinforced (e.g. the richness of qualitative research and the use of large samples in quantitative research).

In the commentaries and debates concerning multi-method and multidisciplinary research, a primary focus has been on ways of improving the integration of qualitative and quantitative methods so as to provide better understandings of the complex combination of factors influencing drug use and to inform the development of multilevel interventions.[6] Less attention has been paid to the politics of multidisciplinary drug research (see 'The politics of multidisciplinary drug research' below) and, in particular, to the question of how theoretical and epistemological differences between the disciplines involved in multidisciplinary projects might be managed and possibly reconciled.

In focus

The politics of multidisciplinary drug research

As a 'social field',[a] the production of knowledge about drugs is constituted through a network of positions occupied by individuals (e.g. researchers, policy-makers, practitioners, community members) and institutions (e.g. research centres; federal, state and local government; drug services). These positions are related through relations of domination, subordination or equivalence, and through struggles over a distribution of power that enables and reproduces access to scarce resources (e.g. research funding, 'impact' on policy and practice). Subjugated knowledges, such as qualitative accounts of drug use, struggle for equal legitimacy with the dominant discourses of biomedicine and epidemiology. The need to produce knowledge that is 'policy relevant' and 'accessible' also tends to stifle innovation and critical research.

a Wacquant, 'Towards a reflexive sociology'.

One response to the politics of multidisciplinary knowledge production in the drug field has been offered by Philippe Bourgois, a US anthropologist who has conducted extensive ethnographic research on drug use:

> I agree with the postmodern position that realities are fragmented and multiplicitous. [. . .] For the sake of engendering a good faith dialogue with outsiders, however, it is necessary for ethnographers to shed postmodern anthropology's somewhat rigid cultural and intellectual value judgments and accept (conditionally and inconsistently) in a culturally relative way the public health researcher's belief in scientifically documentable realities. [. . .] This is necessary [. . .] if we are to enter the popular [f]ray and translate participant-observation into terms understandable to epidemiologists and public health practitioners and researchers.[7]

Encapsulated within the position advocated by Bourgois (and in some of his other published work) is the tension between qualitative research *in*, or *for*, the drug field and qualitative research *on* the drug field.[8] The former aims to apply qualitative research findings to improve understandings of drug use and to inform policy development. In order to participate in this work, qualitative researchers produce knowledge about phenomena already established by 'science' and must often suspend their bedrock theoretical and epistemological commitments: for example, that researchers have no direct, unmediated access to the 'objective' world, that qualitative data are created intersubjectively (i.e. between researchers and subjects) rather than 'collected' and that there are multiple interpretations of qualitative data.[9]

In qualitative research *on* the drug field, drug research and policy, and their underlying theories, methods, assumptions and ideological bases, become the object of critical inquiry. Those engaged in such critical analyses sometimes portray those engaged in applied research as colluding in expert-driven forms of social control. The improvements made to drug research and policy are seen as little more than new forms of neoliberal governmentality. Those engaged in applied research sometimes characterise critical qualitative research as being theoretically elegant but of little practical value. In urging drug ethnographers (and by extension other qualitative researchers) to 'shed' their theoretical and epistemological commitments and accept (albeit 'conditionally and inconsistently') those of public health, Bourgois calls for what I term a 'suspension' mode of engagement.[10]

Theoretical approach

In considering what might be won and lost in adopting a suspension mode of multidisciplinary engagement and in canvassing other potential forms of engagement, I draw on three insights from recent work in science and technology studies and feminist science studies.[11] These are the kinds of insights that would presumably be set aside if qualitative researchers followed injunctions to suspend their theoretical and epistemological commitments. First, this work argues that scientific processes – of observation, measurement and diagnosis – produce their objects rather than describe a pre-existing 'reality'; that is, the tools and practices of knowledge production help to constitute the very phenomena under observation. Karen Barad, a feminist science studies theorist, provides a particularly compelling example when she considers how different observational techniques in physics produce light as either a particle or wave: '... this is contrary both to the ontology assumed by classical physics, wherein each entity (e.g. the electron) is either a wave or a particle, independent of experimental circumstances, and to the epistemological assumption that experiments reveal the preexisting determinate nature of the entity being measured.'[12]

A second insight from recent work in science and technology studies and feminist science studies, which builds on the argument that scientific processes produce their objects rather than describe a pre-existing 'reality', is found in the work of Annemarie Mol. She introduces the term 'ontological politics'. According to Mol, this is 'a composite term':

> It talks of *ontology* – which in standard philosophical parlance defines what belongs to the real, the conditions of possibility we live with. If the term 'ontology' is combined with that of 'politics' then this suggests that the conditions of possibility are not given. The reality does not precede the mundane practices in which we interact with it, but is rather shaped within these practices [i.e. the first insight described above]. So the term *politics* works to underline this active mode, this process of shaping, and the fact that its character is both open and contested.[13]

Third, recent work in science and technology studies and feminist science studies has focused on the related issues of simplification and complexity. Mol and Law pose the following question, which is highly relevant to thinking through the implications of agent-based modelling: 'How might complexity be handled in knowledge practices, nonreductively, but without at the same time generating ever more complexities until we submerge in chaos?'[14] They suggest that one way of thinking about complexities in knowledge practices involves the notion of 'multiplicities'. In standard forms of scientific inquiry (e.g. epidemiology), a single order organises the simplification of complex phenomena and reveals aspects of a pre-existing 'reality'. However, according to Mol and Law, when multiple orders are gathered together, the dichotomy between 'simple' and 'complex' begins to dissolve. This is because the various 'orderings' of a specific object or topic render 'reality' in different ways and do not always produce and reinforce the same kinds of simplification. In situations of 'multiplicity', the various modes of ordering 'include, exclude, depend on, and combat one another' and may also overlap and interfere with one another.[15] This means that we need a way of conceptualising how multiplicities hold together – that is, how they become 'more than one but less than many'.

For Mol and Law, if reality hangs together, it is not because the world precedes knowledge of it but because the various 'coordination strategies' involved in situations of multiplicity succeed in reassembling multiple versions of reality:

> If there are different modes of ordering that coexist, what is reduced or effaced in one may be crucial in another so that the question no longer is, Do we simplify or do we accept complexity? It becomes instead a matter of determining *which* simplification or simplifications we will attend to and create and, as we do this, of attending to what they foreground and draw our attention to, as well as what they relegate to the background.[16]

Adopting this view of knowledge production, we can see that research methods inevitably shape phenomena as they observe and measure them. Because different research methods produce different realities, the process by which particular versions come to be taken as legitimate is contested and therefore open to change. And that forms of simplification are an inevitable (and necessary) part of any knowledge enterprise. This framework allows us to ask some important questions about the politics of multidisciplinary drug research such as agent-based modelling. What kinds of coordination strategies does agent-based modelling deploy to reassemble multiple versions of reality? Which simplifications are created and what do they foreground and relegate? How, for example, does agent-based modelling produce 'drug users'? What kinds of capacities are they taken to possess? What effects result from these framings? Are there alternative ways of producing drug users, and alternative forms of simplification, that might result in different framings and effects?

In order to explore such questions and to consider what might be won and lost in adopting different modes of multidisciplinary engagement, I discuss my recent involvement in agent-based modelling of ATS use and related harm among young Australians. I begin with an account of the research methods involved in this project that would befit a conventional positivist epistemology before beginning to sketch an alternative way of thinking about the processes and politics of multidisciplinary drug research.

Agent-based modelling of ATS use and related harm

The agent-based modelling in which I was involved focused on ATS use and related harm among young Australians (18–30 years old) and employed an ethno-epidemiological design: ethnographic fieldwork, in-depth interviews and two epidemiological surveys with young people using ATS in Melbourne and Perth. The research team included agent-based modelling alongside the ethnographic and epidemiological research for two reasons: (1) to overcome a key barrier to the development of mixed methods research – the genuine integration of data;[17] and (2) to model the outcomes of various policy scenarios on the prevalence of ATS-related harm.[18]

Building SimAmph: An agent-based model

Drawing on our ethno-epidemiological data, secondary data sources and previous research, we built a model of ATS use called 'SimAmph'. This process was guided by two principles. First, collective design involved the input of data and concepts produced by the ethnographers and epidemiologists.[19] Summaries of ethnographic data were sent to the modellers approximately every three months, while the epidemiological data supplied the patterns and prevalence of ATS use and related harm. Iterative questioning by the modellers of these data and concepts allowed the research team to create a common ontology over time (i.e. a specific set of terms and assumptions for describing the reality created by the model). Second, incremental design led to the development of an initial agent-based model which was then modified through the collective design process, thus allowing for partial verification at each stage of the process.[20] Because the research team was physically located in four cities (Perth, Melbourne, Canberra and Sydney), with data collection occurring simultaneously in three research sites, adhering to these design principles required regular teleconferences, email discussions and face-to-face meetings between team members. As noted by one team member, the modelling process evolved as a 'tool for managing the conversation', an ongoing forum for structuring dialogue between the ethnographic and epidemiological components.

In SimAmph, each *agent* represents a young person whose ATS use fluctuates with time and according to circumstances. *Agents* have individual attributes, are able to access different types of drugs and move through different social settings for drug use, each with their own characteristics. The *agents* in SimAmph move through five *stages of social engagement* in weekend partying:

- *novices*: drug use is limited mainly to alcohol and cannabis
- *occasional users*: use ATS monthly or less
- *regular users*: use ATS weekly
- *hardcore users*: engage in 'binges' over 1–3 days involving ATS, alcohol and cannabis
- *marginal users*: use ATS daily, plus alcohol and cannabis.

For the purposes of the model, we also added a *pool* stage, which consists of young people who have yet to engage in weekend partying and ATS use.

Drawing on our ethnographic data,[21] two variables describe the movement of *agents* between these stages. First, young people increase their involvement in ATS use through a 'peer influence' variable, which is a function of the drug-using patterns of friends in a particular stage and the drug-related norms of the venues they typically visit. Second, young people decrease their involvement in ATS use through a 'health experience' variable, which is a function of their experience and assessment of their own mental and physical health and that of their friends.

In SimAmph, *agents* visit different *venues* (e.g. clubs, dance parties and private homes), which are characterised by different levels of drug *accessibility* and *tolerance*. *Accessibility* refers to the availability and use of drugs in a *venue*. *Tolerance* refers to the cultural acceptability of drug use in that *venue*.

While engaging in ATS use with their friends, *agents* experience different forms of harm. A probabilistic model links the behavioural patterns of *agents* to their chances of developing one or more of these forms of harm that, in turn, result in short or long-term consequences for their mental or physical health. We used our epidemiological data to calculate the probability of experiencing specific forms of harm and their likely impact over the short term and long term.

We used a computing platform called Cormas[©] to run a series of simulations.[22] The simulations run on weekly time-steps, reflecting our interest in weekend patterns of partying and drug use. Each simulation includes a set number of *agents*, initially located in the *pool*. To validate the model, we ran a base scenario to compare the results generated by the model with findings from existing research. This is sometimes called the 'proof of concept' – that is, using the model to tell us something that we already know. The base scenario simulated the behavioural patterns of *agents* over a period of four years. It aimed to create a benchmark against which the outcomes of simulations of drug policy scenarios could be evaluated. We compared the outcomes of the simulation for the proportions of drug users in each stage with the results from the 2004 National Drug Strategy Household Survey

(NDSHS, n = 29 445). The percentage of *agents* in each of the stages derived from the NDSHS displayed a reasonable match with those produced by the base-scenario simulation.

Modelling policy scenarios

Building SimAmph allowed us to test some 'what-if' situations. We ran further simulations to model the potential impact of various interventions on ATS-related harm by making empirically based assumptions about how changes in the environment would affect the behaviour of *agents*. We modelled the likely impact of three types of intervention on levels of ATS-related harm (see 'The use of ecstasy pill-testing', 'The use of passive-alert detection dogs by police at public venues' and 'The introduction of a mass-media drug prevention campaign' below). We chose these interventions because they are all options in the Australian drug policy landscape and their possible outcomes cannot be answered easily by an empirical study.

In focus

The use of ecstasy pill-testing

The question we asked was: if adulterated pills enter the ecstasy market and the market share of these pills varies between 10 and 50 per cent, what percentage of young ATS users would need access to pill testing in order to ensure that the prevalence of a major medical condition (defined as an overdose or other situation requiring medical intervention) remained at 'usual' levels (i.e. < 5 per cent according to our epidemiological data)?

The results show that as the market penetration of the adulterated ecstasy pills increases from 10 to 50 per cent, the percentage of young ATS users who need access to pill testing in order to ensure that the prevalence of major medical conditions remained at less than 5 per cent increases from 30 to 85 per cent. This simulation suggests that in situations where adulterated ecstasy pills become widely available in a drug market, pill testing needs to be readily accessible in order to reduce acute drug-related harm.

In focus

The use of passive-alert detection dogs by police at public venues

The aims of passive-alert detection (PAD) dog programs are to detect drugs in public places and to deter drug use; however, their effectiveness is largely unknown. In the absence of such data, we used SimAmph to test a range of detection rates and user reactions in order to explore issues around the impact of PAD dogs on the behaviour of our modelled *agents*. First, what is the likely impact of the use of PAD dogs on the prevalence of young drug users consuming all of their drugs in a single dose, rather than, as planned, over a period of time? Second, when drug users experience or witness major adverse health consequences resulting from drug consumption, what is the impact on their own drug use?

The findings from this simulation suggest that only very high rates of detection will reduce the drug use of *agents* and, even with detection rates of 60 to 80 per cent, these effects are driven mainly by a four-fold increase in negative health consequences as detection rates rise. In other words, the law enforcement 'benefit' of reduced drug use comes at the 'cost' of greater rates of harm.

In focus

The introduction of a mass-media drug prevention campaign

The problem we addressed in this simulation related to the appropriate targets and levels of persuasion required of mass-media campaigns. What levels of persuasion would need to be achieved by the campaign in order to reduce the prevalence of physical and mental health problems, and the proportion of young people using ATS on a regular basis? Would the required persuasion levels differ when the campaign targets different groups of drug users?

In this simulation, our agent-based modelling showed that the mass-media prevention campaign had little effect on the behaviour and experience of heavier drug users. However, it led to small reductions in the prevalence of health-related conditions among moderate ATS users as long as the rate of persuasion is at least 30–40 per cent. It also prevented moderate drug users from becoming heavier users, as long as the rate of persuasion is at least 25 per cent.

SimAmph and the suspension mode of multidisciplinary engagement

For its proponents, and viewed from within the suspension mode of multidisciplinary engagement, participating in agent-based modelling delivers several clear benefits for qualitative research *in* or *for* the drug field. At a pragmatic level, linking ethnographic research with 'legitimate' sciences such as epidemiology and with innovative approaches such as agent-based modelling may improve its chances of winning research funding and achieving greater prominence in the field more generally. Given that qualitative research traditionally struggles for financial support, as well as to get published in drug journals,[23] this is no small matter. For qualitative researchers committed to 'making a difference',[24] participating in agent-based modelling of policy scenarios may also mean that qualitative research is more 'transferable' in terms of policy and practice. The qualitative focus on cultural logics created and reproduced by drug users, and the ethnographic focus on drug-using practices, can also improve the quality of methods adopted in other disciplines – for example, by improving the design of epidemiological instruments and of agent-based models. Conversely, agent-based modelling can improve the process of multidisciplinary integration by identifying some of the limitations of ethnographic data.

Such models as SimAmph also provide a way of integrating ethnographic data on the individual perceptions, peer influences and social settings that shape drug use and related harm with those derived from epidemiological surveys. They can be used to explore the complex reciprocal relationships between environments and individuals, where *agents*, interacting in non-linear ways, continually evolve within their environments. This integrated approach – combining original ethno-epidemiological data, existing datasets and expert knowledge – goes some way towards overcoming the compartmentalisation that characterises existing data, as well as helping to identify what other data might be needed to build better models. SimAmph has the capacity to link behavioural patterns with health-related risks and harm, and its structure, variables and values – for example, the probabilities of risk and harm, and *agent* characteristics and relationships – can be modified as new data and understandings emerge. Agent-based models like SimAmph can be potentially valuable tools for assisting policy-makers and practitioners to think through the likely impacts of various policy options and interventions. They can be used to inform policy directions by providing reasonable estimates of what might happen under specified conditions and assumptions.

Multiplicity and the ontological politics of agent-based modelling

Viewed from the perspective provided by recent work in science and technology studies and feminist science studies (that scientific processes produce their objects, that the conditions of possibility are both open and contested, and that various modes of ordering reality 'include, exclude, depend on, and combat one another'), a different set of questions about SimAmph emerges, questions that derive from an interest in qualitative research *on* the drug field. What kinds of coordination strategies does SimAmph deploy to reassemble multiple versions of reality? Which simplifications are created, and what do they foreground and relegate? How does SimAmph produce 'ATS users'? What kinds of capacities are they taken to possess? What effects result from these framings? And are there alternative ways of producing ATS users, and alternative forms of simplification, that might result in different framings and effects?

Agent-based modelling draws on ethnographic and epidemiological data, and in this sense can be seen as 'more than one but less than many'. It draws together ethnography and epidemiology around pre-constituted aspects of 'reality' – drug-using subjects ('young ATS users'), forms of drug use ('ATS use'), drug-using consequences ('health-related harm') and social practice ('peer influence') – rather seeing ethnography and epidemiology as producing different realities. How does agent-based modelling hold these different versions of ATS users and ATS use together? On the one hand, both the ethnographic and epidemiological research components proceed independently and according to appropriate epistemological and conceptual perspectives. On the other, they come to be defined in relation to one another, to be co-produced: each becomes the mirror of the other (even if, as I note below, the modelling ultimately relies heavily on quantitative data). The ethnographic findings refer to small samples and provide in-depth understandings of the social relations and cultural meanings of ATS use in particular places at particular times. The epidemiological research tests the insights of the ethnographic research amongst larger samples of ATS users and informs future ethnographic research. The agent-based modelling, in turn, shapes and draws on both ethnographic and epidemiological versions of ATS use and users but then turns them into a third version – so that they are contained within the agent-based modelling version but not contained by it.

SimAmph aims to develop the 'simplest' version of the 'complex' reality of ATS use. Two conditions of modelling shape this process. First, although the structure of SimAmph is based on the ethnographic research findings, the values of the various parameters within this structure are drawn (mainly) from the epidemiological findings. Because SimAmph uses behavioural algorithms, any aspect that cannot be quantified is left out. This means that some aspects of the 'social' or 'cultural' introduce too much complexity to be comfortably managed. Second, resource limitations also shape decisions about what counts as 'too complex'. As the model becomes more complex, greater computing resources (i.e. time, money) are required.

What outcomes emerge from this process of simplification? SimAmph produces 'ATS users' in particular kinds of ways, and I focus on two such aspects here. First, although it takes into account the social relationships between its *agents* and the social settings in which they use drugs, it focuses primarily on the actions of monadic individuals. Individual *agents* decide whether to increase or decrease their drug use; individual *agents* choose to make use of pill-testing to check on the purity of drugs; individual *agents* decide to consume (or not consume) all of their drugs on seeing PAD dogs; and individual *agents* are persuaded (or not persuaded) by drug education campaigns. Second, these monadic individuals are taken to possess particular capacities. SimAmph is based on a behavioural algorithm that emphasises a rational, prudentially minded drug-using subject – young ATS users weigh up the benefits and risks of drug use and increase or decrease their involvement accordingly.

What effects result from these framings? In its rendering of ATS users as monadic individuals, with particular kinds of capacities, SimAmph reproduces and reinforces the long-standing emphasis on individual decision-making and practice in public health conceptualisations of drug use. As other researchers have argued,[25] this framing has contributed to the increased responsibilisation of drug users in policy and practice and has diverted attention from structural inequalities and the material constraints on human agency. The emphasis on a rational, prudential subject also has political implications. While ascribing to drug users neoliberal capacities such as rationality and responsibility may confer benefits upon them, this framing of drug users may not allow for the multiple ways in which bodily pleasure, emotion and desire figure in drug use and may therefore limit the conception of effective strategies for harm reduction.[26] These effects make clear that the process of simplification, which produces the focus on individual *agents* and their capacities, is far from neutral.

What are some of the alternatives? Answering this question properly would require a separate chapter, but here I indicate one possibility. In relation to SimAmph's framing of ATS users as monadic individuals, freely making decisions about their drug use and responses to public health interventions, the model might place greater emphasis on the fluid social relations amongst drug users.[27] As currently formulated, the *agents* in SimAmph increase and decrease their engagement in different stages of drug use relatively easily when compared with the findings of social research on drug scenes. For example, recent research on the influence of network topology on patterns of drug use suggests that SimAmph's friendship networks need to be more flexible to allow *agents* to select new acquaintances as they move through their drug careers.[28] Such a move might prompt us to ask different questions about appropriate responses to ATS use.

Conclusion

In this chapter, I have begun to sketch an alternative to what I have called the 'suspension' mode of multidisciplinary engagement. This mode of engagement prevents us from asking a series of important questions about the relationships between research methods, the realities they produce and the political implications of these realities. Seen in conventional research terms, agent-based modelling is one way of developing more complex understandings of drug use and related harm, through the integration of data produced by qualitative and quantitative methods. Modelling the likely impact of various policy scenarios can also provide a potentially valuable tool for promoting dialogue about policy options. Viewed from the perspective of recent work in science and technology studies, however, agent-based models such as SimAmph involve a series of coordination strategies and simplifications that foreground and relegate specific aspects of the phenomenon under investigation. For example, they reproduce existing research, policy and practice discourses on individual responsibility and rationality. In this way, they produce certain forms of reality with specific political effects. Identifying and acknowledging the political consequences of research methods and the realities they produce should be a central element in future debates on multidisciplinary drug research.

Acknowledgements

The SimAmph project was funded by a National Health and Medical Research Council Project Grant (#323212). I am indebted to research colleagues involved in the project: in alphabetical order, Gabriele Bammer, Paul Dietze, Anne Dray, Rachael Green, Susan L. Hudson, Rebecca Jenkinson, Lisa Maher, Pascal Perez and Christine Siokou. The description of agent-based modelling presented here draws on material that appears in Moore et al., Perez et al. and Perez et al.[29] The National Drug Research Institute receives core funding from the Australian Government Department of Health and Ageing. I thank Suzanne Fraser, Helen Keane and an anonymous reviewer for Cambridge University Press for their insightful comments on an earlier version.

Notes

1   For example Agar, 'Recasting the "ethno" in "epidemiology"'; Bourgois, Martinez, Kral et al., 'Reinterpreting ethnic patterns among white and African American men who inject heroin'; Clatts, Welle, Goldsamt et al., 'An ethno-epidemiological model for the study of trends in illicit drug use'; Pach & Gorman, 'An ethno-epidemiological approach for the multi-site study of emerging drug abuse trends'.
2   For example Agar, 'Another complex step'; Agar & Wilson, 'Drugmart'; Hoffer, Bobashev & Morris, 'Researching a local heroin market as a complex adaptive system'; Gorman, Mezic & Gruenewald, 'Agent-based modeling of drinking behavior'; Dray, Mazerolle, Perez et al., 'Policing Australia's "heroin drought" using an agent-based model to simulate alternative outcomes'; Galea, Hall & Kaplan, 'Social epidemiology and complex system dynamic modelling as applied to health behaviour and drug use research'.
3   For example Bourgois, 'Theory, method and power in drug and HIV-prevention research', and McKeganey, 'Quantitative and qualitative research in the addictions'.
4   Rhodes & Moore, 'On the qualitative in drugs research: Part one'.
5   Bourgois, Martinez, Kral et al., 'Reinterpreting ethnic patterns among white and African American men who inject heroin'.
6   Sussman, Stacy, Johnson et al., 'Transdisciplinary focus on drug abuse prevention'.
7   Bourgois, 'Theory, method, and power in drug and HIV-prevention research', p. 2167. Although Bourgois writes about his own discipline, anthropology, his observation is also relevant to qualitative drug researchers working within other theoretical and/or disciplinary traditions (e.g. feminist theory, post-structuralism and, more recently, science and technology studies).
8   See also Nettleton & Bunton, 'Sociological critiques of health promotion'.
9   Moore, 'Vacating the committee chair'.
10   Although beyond the scope of this chapter, I am indebted to Helen Keane for making the general observation that it might not be possible for scholars to suspend their theoretical

and epistemological commitments because these are not external to subjectivity but form part of their scholarly habitus.

11 For example Mol & Law, 'Complexities: An introduction'; Law, *After Method*; Mol, *The Body Multiple*; Latour, *Reassembling the Social*.

12 Barad, *Meeting the Universe Halfway*, p. 106.

13 Mol, 'Ontological politics', pp. 74–5.

14 Mol & Law, 'Complexities: An introduction', p. 1.

15 Mol & Law, 'Complexities: An introduction', pp. 9–10.

16 Ibid., p. 11.

17 Bryman, 'Barriers to integrating quantitative and qualitative research'.

18 For further detail on the methods used in this project and the outcomes of the modelled scenarios, see Moore, Dray, Green et al., 'Using agent-based modelling to improve understanding of drug use and related harms'; Perez, Dray, Moore et al., 'SimAmph'; and Dray, Pascal, Moore et al., 'Are drug detection dogs and mass-media campaigns likely to be effective policy responses to psychostimulant use and related harm?'.

19 Perez, Dray, Ritter et al., 'SimDrug'.

20 Townsley & Johnson, 'The need for systematic replication and tests of validity in simulation'.

21 Siokou & Moore, 'This is not a rave!'; Green & Moore, '"Kiddie drugs" and controlled pleasure'; Siokou, Moore & Lee, '"Muzzas" and "Old Skool Ravers"'.

22 Bousquet, Bakam, Proton et al., 'CORMAS'.

23 Moore, 'Ethnography and the Australian drug field'; Rhodes, Stimson, Moore et al., 'Qualitative social research in addictions publishing'.

24 Maher, 'Don't leave us this way'.

25 For example Fraser, 'It's Your Life!'

26 Measham, 'Drug and alcohol research'; Moore & Fraser, 'Putting at risk what we know'.

27 Moore, 'Beyond Zinberg's "social setting"'.

28 Galea, Hall & Kaplan, 'Social epidemiology and complex system dynamic modelling as applied to health behaviour and drug use research'.

29 Moore, Dray, Green et al., 'Using agent-based modelling to improve understanding of drug use and related harms'; Perez, Dray, Moore et al., 'SimAmph'; and Dray, Pascal, Moore et al., 'Are drug detection dogs and mass-media campaigns likely to be effective policy responses to psychostimulant use and related harm?'.

References

Agar, M. (1996). Recasting the 'ethno' in 'epidemiology'. *Medical Anthropology*, 16: 391–403.

——— (2001). Another complex step: A model of heroin experimentation. *Field Methods*, 13(4): 353–69.

——— (2005). Agents in living color: Towards emic agent-based models. *Journal of Artificial Societies and Social Simulation*, 8-1. Retrieved 28 March 2011. http://jasss.soc.surrey.ac.uk/8/1/4.html.

Agar, M., & Wilson, D. (2002). Drugmart: Heroin epidemics as complex adaptive systems. *Complexity*, 7: 44–52.

Barad, K. (2007). *Meeting the Universe Halfway: Quantum Physics and the Entanglement of Matter and Meaning*. Durham, NC, & London: Duke University Press.

Bourgois, P. (1999). Theory, method, and power in drug and HIV-prevention research: A participant observer's critique. *Substance Use and Misuse*, 34(14): 2155–72.

Bourgois, P., Martinez, A., Kral, A., et al. (2006). Reinterpreting ethnic patterns among white and African American men who inject heroin: A social science of medicine approach, *PLoS Med*, 3. Retrieved 28 March 2011. www.plosmedicine.org/article/info per cent3Adoi per cent2F10.1371 per cent2Fjournal.pmed.0030452.

Bousquet, F., Bakam, I., Proton, H., & Le Page, C. (1998). CORMAS: Common-Pool Resources and Multi-Agent Systems. *Lecture Notes in Artificial Intelligence*, 1416: 826–37.

Bryman, A. (2007). Barriers to integrating quantitative and qualitative research. *Journal of Mixed Methods Research*, 1: 1–18.

Clatts, M.C., Welle, D.L., Goldsamt, L.A., et al. (2002). An ethno-epidemiological model for the study of trends in illicit drug use: Reflections on the 'emergence' of crack injection. *International Journal of Drug Policy*, 13: 285–96.

Dray, A., Mazerolle, L., Perez, P., et al. (2008). Policing Australia's 'heroin drought' using an agent-based model to simulate alternative outcomes. *Journal of Experimental Criminology*, 4(3): 267–87.

Dray, A., Pascal, P., Moore, D., et al. (in press). Are drug detection dogs and mass-media campaigns likely to be effective policy responses to psychostimulant use and related harm? Results from an agent-based simulation model. *International Journal of Drug Policy*.

Fraser, S. (2004). 'It's Your Life!': Injecting drug users, individual responsibility and hepatitis C prevention. *Health*, 8(2): 199–221.

Galea, S., Hall, C., & Kaplan, G.A. (2009). Social epidemiology and complex system dynamic modelling as applied to health behaviour and drug use research. *International Journal of Drug Policy*, 20: 209–16.

Gorman, D., Mezic, J., & Gruenewald, P.J. (2006). Agent-based modeling of drinking behavior: A preliminary model and potential applications to theory and practice. *American Journal of Public Health*, 96(11): 2055–60.

Green, R., & Moore, D. (2009). 'Kiddie drugs' and controlled pleasure: Recreational use of dexamphetamine in a social network of young Australians. *International Journal of Drug Policy*, 20(5): 402–8.

Hoffer, L.D., Bobashev, G., & Morris, R.J. (2009). Researching a local heroin market as a complex adaptive system. *American Journal of Community Psychology*, 44: 273–86.

Latour, B. (2005). *Reassembling the Social: An Introduction to Actor-Network-Theory*. Oxford: Oxford University Press.

Law, J. (2004). *After Method: Mess in Social Science Research*. London & New York: Routledge.

McKeganey, N. (1995). Quantitative and qualitative research in the addictions: An unhelpful divide. *Addiction*, 90: 749–51.

Maher, L. (2002). Don't leave us this way: Ethnography and injecting drug use in the age of AIDS. *International Journal of Drug Policy*, 13(4): 311–25.

Measham, F. (2004). Drug and alcohol research: The case for cultural criminology. In J. Ferrell, K. Hayward, W. Morrison, & M. Presdee (eds), *Cultural Criminology Unleashed* (pp. 219–30). London: Glasshouse Press.

Mol, A. (1999). Ontological politics: A word and some questions. In J. Law & J. Hassard (eds). *Actor Network Theory and After* (pp. 74–89). Oxford & Keele: Blackwell & the Sociological Review.

—— (2002). *The Body Multiple: Ontology in Medical Practice*. Durham, NC, & London: Duke University Press.

Mol, A., & Law, J. (2002). Complexities: An introduction. In J. Law & A. Mol (eds). *Complexities: Social Studies of Knowledge Practices* (pp. 1–22). Durham, NC, & London: Duke University Press.

Moore, D. (1993). Beyond Zinberg's 'social setting': A processual view of illicit drug use. *Drug and Alcohol Review*, 12(4): 413–21.

—— (1994). Vacating the committee chair: Paving the way for synthesis in the addictions. *Addiction*, 89(1): 16–18.

—— (2002). Ethnography and the Australian drug field: Emaciation, appropriation and multidisciplinary myopia. *International Journal of Drug Policy*, 13: 271–284.

Moore, D., Dray, A., Green, R., et al. (2009). Using agent-based modelling to improve understanding of drug use and related harms. *Addiction*, 104(12): 1991–7.

Moore, D., & Fraser, S. (2006). Putting at risk what we know: Reflecting on the drug-using subject in harm reduction and its political implications. *Social Science and Medicine*, 62(12): 3035–47.

Nettleton, S., & Bunton, R. (1995). Sociological critiques of health promotion. In R. Bunton, S. Nettleton & R. Burrows (eds), *The Sociology of Health Promotion: Critical Analyses of Consumption, Lifestyle and Risk* (pp. 39–56). London & New York: Routledge.

Pach, I.A., & Gorman, E.M. (2002). An ethno-epidemiological approach for the multi-site study of emerging drug abuse trends: The spread of methamphetamine in the United States of America. *Bulletin on Narcotics*, 54: 87–102.

Perez, P., Dray, A., Moore, D., et al. (in press). SimAmph: An agent-based simulation model for exploring the use of psychostimulants and related harm among young Australians. *International Journal of Drug Policy*.

Perez, P., Dray, A., Ritter, A., et al. (2006). SimDrug: A multi-agent system tackling the complexity of illicit drug markets in Australia. In P. Perez & D. Batten (eds). *Complex Science for a Complex World: Exploring Human Ecosystems with Agents* (pp. 193–223). Canberra: ANU EPress.

Rhodes, T., & Moore, D. (2001). On the qualitative in drugs research: Part one. *Addiction Research and Theory*, 9: 279–99.

Rhodes, T., Stimson, G., Moore, D., & Bourgois, P. (2010). Qualitative social research in addictions publishing: Creating an enabling journal environment. *International Journal of Drug Policy*, 21(6): 441–4.

Siokou, C., & Moore, D. (2008). 'This is not a rave!': Changes in the commercialised Melbourne rave/dance party scene. *Youth Studies Australia*, 27(3): 50–7.

Siokou, C., Moore, D., & Lee, H. (2010). 'Muzzas' and 'Old Skool Ravers': Ethnicity, drugs and the changing face of Melbourne's dance party/club scene. *Health Sociology Review*, 19(2): 192–204.

Sussman, S., Stacy, A.W., Johnson, C.A., et al. (2004). Transdisciplinary focus on drug abuse prevention: An introduction. *Substance Use and Misuse*. 39: 10–12.

Townsley, M. & Johnson, S. (2008). The need for systematic replication and tests of validity in simulation. In L. Liu & J. Eck (eds). *Artificial Crime Analysis Systems: Using Computer Simulations and Geographic Information Systems* (pp. 1–18). London: IGI Global Publisher.

Wacquant, L.D. (1989). Towards a reflexive sociology: A workshop with Pierre Bourdieu. *Sociological Theory*, 7(1): 26–63.

PART 2

Drugs, health and the medicalisation of addiction

Beyond the 'potsherd'

The role of injecting drug use-related stigma in shaping hepatitis C

Suzanne Fraser

'Things that gather cannot be thrown at you like objects'.
Latour, 'Why has critique run out of steam?'

Hepatitis C constitutes a major health issue around the world. Despite some important variations, it is possible to trace a pattern in hepatitis C infection. It clusters among the most impoverished, disadvantaged and stigmatised members of almost any population, whether it be a national population in which injecting drug use is vilified or a global population in which some nations are underresourced compared to others. This clustering can be understood in a range of ways. The aim of this chapter is to formulate an approach to disease that is able to acknowledge the ways in which social and political forces, namely poverty, disadvantage and stigma, directly shape the disease hepatitis C. This will not, however, take the form of the fairly common-place argument that impoverished and disadvantaged people transmit and contract disease more freely than the privileged. An approach of this kind would suggest (at least) two assumptions: (1) that hepatitis C pre-exists the populations in which it manifests, and (2) that such populations should be enjoined to change their ways to reduce the freedom with which this pre-existing disease of hepatitis C moves between bodies. These ideas are insufficiently sophisticated to capture the interrelationship of bodies and viruses and the social in the making of disease. They can also lead to insufficiently careful and effective strategies for responding to particular formulations of the problem of disease.

This chapter offers an introduction to the construction of hepatitis C as disease and epidemic. Taking Australia and the changes it has seen in the provision of treatment for hepatitis C as a case study, it will analyse a key issue for hepatitis C – stigma – and explore its role in shaping the scale and form of the hepatitis C epidemic. It will argue that, contrary to conventional wisdom, diseases are not immutable objects 'lying around' waiting to be discovered. Instead they are emergent phenomena, constantly being made and remade by social forces such as stigma. Given this, the chapter concludes, it is necessary to scrutinise legal, policy and social responses to hepatitis C and their role in reinforcing or challenging stigma in new ways.

Theorising disease

Preventing hepatitis C transmission and dealing with the long-term effects of the disease are pressing concerns, yet, as Jacalyn Duffin has argued, from the point of view of medical knowledge, hepatitis C is still very much 'under construction'.[1] By this she means that, isolated as recently as 1989, the hepatitis C virus still presents many uncertainties to scientists. Hepatitis C is also very much under construction culturally and politically. Its close association with injecting drug use creates a powerful net of meanings that help shape understandings of the disease and of prevention and treatment options. These meanings are central to the shape and character of hepatitis C and its various epidemics around the world. According to Duffin, diseases should not be seen only to impact on society and culture. They are also partially constituted by society and culture. Speaking explicitly about hepatitis C, she asserts: 'Diseases are not immutable objects lying around waiting to be unearthed like potsherds in an archaeological dig. The so-called discoverer of a disease has actually "elaborated", "recognised", "described" or "invented" a new way of understanding a problem that has previously been overlooked or forgotten, possibly because it had not been considered a problem.'[2]

In Duffin's view, disease concepts theorise illness; its origins, location and the nature of its activity. Duffin notes, for example, that Western medicine is dominated by the organismic concept of disease, which understands disease as a discontinuous state located in the individual. It seems, then, that hepatitis C can be seen not as a corporeal 'potsherd' simply dug up and described by medical researchers, but as a socially constituted object our responses to which materially shape it over time. What are the implications of this? Most pressingly, seeing disease this way invites the recognition that phenomena such as stigma are part of this process of materialisation, even helping to create the very problems from which it is ordinarily taken to arise.

In taking up the question of the sufficiency of current theoretical approaches to disease and the need for greater sophistication in our concepts, this chapter could appear to direct focus away from the all-important material conditions of disease and the sometimes heartbreaking lived experiences of these epidemics. This would, of course, be far from my intention. My aim here is to demonstrate the direct links between concepts and materiality and to make an explicit contribution to practices that bear immediately on the lives of those affected by hepatitis C. This is not, of course, an easy task. Paula Treichler has attended closely to this issue in her highly influential 1999 book, *How to have Theory in an Epidemic: Cultural Chronicles of AIDS*. Treichler opens her book by asking, 'What should be the role of theory in an epidemic?' She goes on to note: 'The very mention of theory, cultural construction or discourse may be exasperating or distressing to those face to face with the epidemic's enormity and overwhelming practical demands.'[3]

Treichler's analysis begins from the now well-recognised view that material objects such as disease should be seen as constructed, rather than as ontologically stable or foundational, and their attributes as contingent upon rather than anterior to social relations. In this respect Treichler's work draws on science and technology studies (STS); indeed, it incorporates the early STS work of Bruno Latour and Steve Woolgar on the role of language and ideas in materialising objects: 'Interpretations do not so much inform as *perform*.'[4]

Treichler's focus is HIV, not hepatitis C, and it is important to bear in mind that her comments are made in relation to a life-threatening disease that goes untreated among the vast majority of those affected around the world. Mortality rates for HIV are extremely high in parts of Africa and elsewhere, and those who contract the disease can face very short futures when unable to access treatment. It would not do to conflate the circumstances of HIV with those of hepatitis C. This is not, however, to say that hepatitis C is not a serious disease warranting serious attention and resourcing. It can significantly limit quality of life and lead to severe liver disease, and treatment options are at present quite limited. While those able to access treatment for HIV cannot hope for cure, they can look forward to long lives with disease progression and symptoms very effectively managed. By contrast, those able to access hepatitis C treatment face the possibility of cure, but if this is not achieved through treatment (itself extremely onerous and debilitating) no medical treatment is available to manage symptoms and disease progression. Clearly the two diseases diverge markedly in their relationships to medicine, but both are serious health conditions and serious public health issues. It is in this sense that Treichler's work on epidemics informs the argument made here, especially given that HIV and hepatitis C are both diseases profoundly characterised by stigma and discrimination.

Just as Treichler unequivocally argues for the importance of theory in the face of HIV-related disaster, I argue for the importance of theory for engaging effectively with the scale and seriousness of hepatitis C incidence and prevalence. As Treichler asserts in countering the tendency to polarise 'theory' and 'real life': 'theory *is* about "people's lives"'. As she points out, we need to examine the representation of disease because representation is never less than part of the process of constitution: 'Language is not a substitute for reality; it is one of the most significant ways we know reality, experience it, and articulate it.'[5]

Treichler's book tells an important story of the discursive (and thus, in turn, material) constitution of HIV. Chapter 1, for example, traces the early epidemiological decisions that constituted HIV as a 'gay' disease even as transmission via injecting drug use remained common. Treichler notes that HIV scholars and advocates held the view that the constitution of the disease as 'gay' delayed public health and other responses in the United States. This is an interesting point to consider in light of what is known about responses to hepatitis C. While there is little doubt that the promulgation of the notion of the 'gay plague' affected public perceptions by shaping HIV as intrinsically moral – and simultaneously as largely sequestered within a marginal population – it is unlikely that clarifying its connection with injecting drug use would have altered this perception. In that people who inject drugs were just as stigmatised and marginalised as gay men at the time, greater recognition of their vulnerability to or place in the epidemic would not necessarily have generated faster, more committed or more effective responses. Still, there can be little argument that the construction of HIV as a gay disease shaped responses and still plays a part in the West's inability to fully engage with the worldwide (overwhelmingly heterosexual) epidemic and its implications. In these ways, Treichler's work reminds us of the importance of theory, concepts and language in the material enactment of disease.

In that Treichler's understanding of disease brackets the 'facts' of HIV as dependent upon the circumstances of the disease's constitution, it also raises questions about the status of facts themselves and the role of research in making facts. These issues are of central importance to this chapter. My argument concerns the making of facts about hepatitis C, so it would not do to simply posit alternative facts about the disease. If we do not speak of facts and their replacement, however, what should we speak of? Here Latour assists us by proposing a shift in focus from 'matters of fact' to 'matters of concern'. Writing in the aftermath of the attack on the World Trade Center, Latour laments what he sees as the unfortunate similarity between some forms of critique of science and its facts and the conspiracy theories sometimes used to explain or dismiss world events such as the attack. He mentions global warming and our need to mobilise to arrest it, and argues that without facts we are not able to act in urgently required ways. He questions the direction of critique and, in clarifying his own intentions, explains that in conducting research into scientific practice, he 'intended to emancipate the public from prematurely naturalised objectified facts' rather than to dismiss facts altogether as unnecessary or utterly without validity.[6]

Interestingly, given the subject of this chapter, Latour figures the role of the critic in the following terms: '. . . we behaved like mad scientists who have let the virus of critique out of the confines of their laboratories and cannot do anything now to limit its deleterious effects; it mutates now, gnawing everything up, even the vessels in which it is contained.' Here critique is a 'virus': an uncontrollable destructive force if not properly contained. It is an intrinsically dangerous phenomenon that if used as a tool, can generate knowledge, but can easily exceed this brief and become simply destructive. Against this destructiveness, Latour asserts that, 'The question was never to get away from facts but closer to them, not fighting empiricism but on the contrary, renewing empiricism.' He wants in turn to salvage realism, but to remake it in doing so. He argues, therefore, for a shift from a preoccupation with 'matters of fact' to one with 'matters of concern'. What is the difference? 'Matters of fact are only very partial . . . and very polemical, very political, renderings of matters of concern.'[7] I read Latour's aim here to be the expansion of our understanding of phenomena so that we see them as intrinsically political. Facts, he asserts, are made by social and political processes and can only ever describe issues, objects and events in very partial and shallow ways. The role of the critic, he says, is to develop new ways of addressing matters of concern rather than mobilising and creating more matters of fact. In doing so, critics should aim not to 'debunk' but, as Donna Haraway says, to 'protect and care'.[8]

These observations usefully address the issue this chapter tackles – how, that is, to frame disease more effectively so as to better understand and address the implications of stigma for hepatitis C. The disease can, I argue, be seen as a 'matter of concern' instead of a matter of fact. Speaking of the facts of hepatitis C in their pre-critical sense as though the facts as they are currently constituted, selected and communicated are all there is, will not do. Neither, however, will simply disposing of facts as though the disease, its implications and those affected by it have no material existence. Instead, following Latour, we might think of hepatitis C as a 'thing' in the Heideggerian sense – a gathering that exceeds any notion of simple fact or object. The word 'thing', Latour points out, has its origins in old Icelandic, which also uses it to refer to forms of parliament – to what he describes as 'the oldest of the sites in which our ancestors did their dealing and tried to settle their disputes'. The thing, then, is both 'an object out there' and 'an issue very much in here, at any rate, a gathering'. Things, in this sense, are as much made, or 'gathered', in culture and action as they are given prior to culture and action. If we are in any doubt as to the utility of this formulation of fact/concern, Latour asserts that 'Things that gather cannot be thrown at you like objects'.[9] Anyone who knows anything about the social and political status of injecting drug use and the stigma associated with hepatitis C will surely recognise the strategic merits of this kind of approach. If hepatitis C is made in practice, if it is gathered rather than given, if it has no essential nature (ordinarily taken to entail taint, degradation, blame), it cannot act as a stigmatising missile.

In focus

Gathering hepatitis C

As noted at the outset, hepatitis C is a pressing public health issue. In Australia, for example, 2007 saw approximately 11 760 new diagnoses, and an estimated 207 600 people (more than 1 per cent of the population) are now infected with the disease. These new infections are not evenly distributed throughout the population. Most (up to 91 per cent) occur among people who inject drugs. An estimated 10 per cent of Australian infections are believed to have been the result of blood transfusions or the use of blood products before 1990, when screening was introduced, but these have been almost eliminated since then. Elsewhere around the world incidence patterns vary. For example, in the United States co-infection with HIV is much more common than in Australia among people who inject drugs. In developing countries, iatrogenic transmission is more widespread than in Australia, and in Egypt, to take one especially pronounced case, the use of non-sterile needles and syringes for mass medical injection programs has led to infection in a large proportion of the population.[a]

a Frank, Mohamed, Strickland et al., 'The role of parenteral antischistosomal therapy in the spread of hepatitis C virus in Egypt'.

At present, hepatitis C is mainly seen in the West as the 'result' of injecting drug use. As Harris has noted, the two are 'virtually conflated' in the scholarly literature and in public health.[10] Of course, there is a strong association between injecting and infection. In a microbial sense this association can to some degree be seen as causal. Yet, as the case of Egypt shows, in that the epidemic is very much spread across the population and is in no way confined to any kind of stigmatised activity, the conflation of disease with injecting drug use is entirely circumstantial. From this point of view, hepatitis C can be seen as a matter of concern, or a 'thing' in the Heideggerian sense – both object and site of dealing and dispute, the facts entailed in which are constituted but no less real for this. In one place hepatitis C is synonymous with injecting illicit drugs and with a series of social ills assumed to go along with injecting drug use, in another with well-intentioned public health initiatives aimed at protecting the population from disease. It follows from this understanding of disease both that the facts of disease can be interpreted as socially produced and that they can then be reproduced differently. Reproducing these facts is important for a number of reasons, three of which, for the purposes of this chapter, are:

1 the perceived causal relationship between the stigmatised practice of injecting drug use and the harms associated with hepatitis C may be loosened, reducing the scope for blaming those who contract the disease

2 in turn this reduction in blame may allow responses more inclined to generosity and to broadly conceived networks of responsibility and action, and

3 where responses change, so does the disease itself. As has been argued already, diseases do not precede human action – they are made and remade within it.

In relation to this last point, Rosenberg points out that the modern approach to illness sees diseases as 'entities existing outside the unique manifestations of illness in particular men and women'. A related observation can be made by replacing 'men and women' with 'social and cultural contexts'. The essentialising of disease, argues Rosenberg, allows medicine to enact, intentionally and incidentally, a range of normalising functions: 'Everywhere we see specific disease concepts being used to manage deviance, rationalise health policies, plan health care and structure specialty relationships within the medical profession.'[11]

Disease concepts of hepatitis C do precisely this, particularly as they essentialise causal factors and the character of affected populations at the same time as they essentialise disease itself. What have been the effects of the particular ways in which hepatitis C has been conceptualised in the West? As I have said, my focus in this chapter is on the place of stigma in processes of conceptualisation. As Simmonds and Coomber argue in their analysis of stigma related to injecting drug use: 'In the public policy and health sphere the stigmatisation of specific populations may also result in the view that certain populations are less "worthy" and therefore "less eligible" or less "deserving" of services than other groups.'[12]

The stigma associated with injecting drug use and, by extension, with hepatitis C is well established in the literature.[13] This stigma can be found operating within policy, the media and, in particular, within health service delivery.[14] Noting the ubiquity of stigmatising responses to injecting drug use and hepatitis C in the media, Pugh notes:

> the media's classification of people with hepatitis C as 'innocent victims' or as guilty perpetrators perpetuates beliefs about injecting drug use as inherently bad and detrimental to the health of individuals and the community in general. Even seemingly straightforward news stories exclude injecting drug users in subtle ways and contribute to the maintenance of social inequalities between different groups of people.[15]

While Simmonds and Coomber's observations about stigma are highly relevant to this chapter, their formulation of the problem and its solutions tends to reproduce the approach this chapter aims to question. So, in considering how best to deal with stigma, they argue: 'The effects of stigma on IDU populations are sufficiently far-reaching for health-care providers and others whose remit it is to reduce the harms emanating from injecting drug use, to seriously consider its impact, its production and how best to address the problems it causes.'[16] If we proceed analytically in terms of 'matters of concern', the facts associated with which are constituted socially, and for which no *a priori* material basis can be assumed, it becomes problematic to position 'IDU populations' as anterior to stigma and the 'effects' of stigma as separate from 'health-care providers and others'. A matter of concern approach treats the 'facts' of the matter as emergent and contingent, and objects as 'things' – as always already sites of dealing and dispute. So the category 'IDU' and its characteristics do not meaningfully precede the operations of stigma, and the effects of stigma do not meaningfully precede the practices of health-care providers and others. Injecting drug use, health-care provision and stigma emerge continually in relation to each other, and hepatitis C too is produced through these phenomena, just as it contributes in turn to their production.

Stigma co-constitutes injecting drug use and hepatitis C in a range of material ways. Perhaps one of the most widely debated issues since the disease was named in 1989 is the question of whether current illicit drug users should be given treatment. In 1997 the United States National Institutes of Health produced a (now superseded) consensus statement, which included an extraordinary recommendation, taken up around the world, that hepatitis C treatment should not be offered to anyone consuming illicit drugs and should be offered only after they had stopped all such drug consumption for at least six months.[17] No clear reasons were given for this decision. Edlin and colleagues published an early commentary on the decision, considering the reasons for the decision and challenging each in turn. They speculate that the decision could have been motivated by concerns about:

1   adherence to treatment among injecting drug users
2   side effects of treatment and this group's ability to manage them
3   the potential for reinfection due to continued sharing of injecting equipment, and
4   undue haste where delay could allow injecting drug users to cease drug use before commencing treatment.[18]

The authors criticise each of these concerns in turn, showing that, in the case of (1), adherence is not a recognised reason for declining treatment in other populations and, indeed, general levels of treatment compliance across all health areas and social groups are low. In response to the second point the authors note that there is insufficient research to suggest that this group would be unable to respond to treatment side effects safely and effectively. In response to the third point the authors argue that reinfection should be minimised by effective provision of safe injecting equipment and education and that denying treatment is an inappropriate response to that concern. In relation to the last point they note that treatment for drug use must be readily available and effective if undertaking it and ceasing drug consumption are to be treated as threshold measures for access to hepatitis C treatment. They note that this is not usually the case. Overall they argue that withholding treatment is the product of stigma and prejudice and constitutes discrimination.

For our purposes, the issue serves as an exemplar of how stigma can shape disease. In refusing to treat people who consume illicit drugs, medicine discursively and materially produces those people as undeserving and illegitimate health consumers. It precludes those who would have achieved a cure from materialising that bodily state and in turn could potentially cause further infections. Withholding treatment, even in the case of a treatment of limited efficacy such as that for hepatitis C at the time, materialises disease and bodies in certain ways. Stigma, it can be said, helps materialise hepatitis C and the bodies of people who have the disease in these ways.

The role of stigma in shaping treatment responses to hepatitis C emerges again when we look at recent changes in policy and practice. In Australia at least this early parsimony in treatment provision has been replaced by a strong push to 'double' or even 'triple' the number of people in treatment. This push has developed as incidence rates for hepatitis C remain unsatisfactorily high and faith in the effectiveness of prevention education has to some extent waned. Speculation about the value of providing treatment in opioid pharmacotherapy clinics has arisen alongside debate about the benefits and otherwise of this blanket approach to treatment.[19]

In 2010 a report published by Hepatitis Australia, the peak body for Australian hepatitis organisations, argued strongly for the expansion of treatment. Given earlier policy, this approach would seem to be laudable. Now, we might argue, a better, more equitable approach to treatment is being advocated. This is of course a reasonable response to the initiative. Yet it is instructive to look closely at the report, in particular at the reasons it gives for advocating expansion and, by implication, for a radical shift in approach to illicit drug users. The report begins with a summary that lists the following as the first 'Action required': 'Treatment rates need to be at least doubled if we are to start reducing the burden of hepatitis C.' Elsewhere the report also argues for the tripling the number of people in treatment. The reasons given for this are worth exploring. They are alluded to in the opening section entitled 'Key points', in the observation that 'the personal, social and economic burden' of the epidemic in Australia is 'immense'.[20] Here, three separate areas of impact are listed in turn: personal (effects on the individual), social (effects on the social fabric and communities) and economic (effects on the economy and health budgets).

This report is not alone in indicating a preference for increasing participation in treatment. *The Third National Hepatitis C Strategy* emphasises the removal of barriers to treatment, implying a preference for increased participation in treatment:

> The introduction of pegylated interferon and the removal of liver biopsy as a criterion for access to subsidised treatment have resulted in immediate increases in the uptake of therapy but the number of people commencing therapy remains low (around 3500 per year). There is a need to make sure that people with hepatitis C are aware of the dramatic improvements to treatment efficacy over the past decade and that they can access treatment without structural health system barriers.[21]

The changes in policy indicated in these documents would, if effective, materially remake hepatitis C in several ways. First, although success rates for treatment vary significantly (they are regularly cited as ranging from approximately 30 per cent to as high as 70 per cent depending on genotype), it is probable that undertaking mass scale treatment would reduce to some extent the rate of infection and thus, eventually, the prevalence of the disease. Second, treatment is thought to reduce viral load and thus infectiousness at least for a time, and can also arrest liver damage for a time. Third, given treatment remains much more successful in some genotypes than others, widespread treatment would ultimately shape the spread and prevalence of genotypes, materially remaking the disease and its impact as it did so in that genotypes vary in terms of symptoms and effects. In all these ways, increases in treatment numbers would reshape the disease both as it materialises in individual bodies and epidemiologically. Returning to the focus of this chapter, it is also important to consider these recommendations and changes in relation to the operations of stigma.

As I have noted, the report describes several ways in which hepatitis C exacts costs: individual illness, social disruption and economic burden. These costs are presented as the rationale for action: in this context, for expanding treatment. Rather less clearly spelt out in the report, however, are the costs associated with treatment itself. For the purposes of this analysis of the role of stigma in materialising disease, I am interested in treatment side effects: the significant, extensively documented, costs to the health and well-being of patients as they undergo the standard period of 24 or 48 weeks of medication. Similar in impact to chemotherapy for cancer, current treatment medication (combination pegylated interferon and ribavirin) is recognised to be very debilitating and disruptive.[22] While some of the severe problems associated with treatment such as loss of vision or hearing, cardiac problems, induction or exacerbation of autoimmune diseases, suicidal thoughts and suicide, and panic attacks are rare (occurring in less than 1 per cent of patients), more than 30 per cent experience depression, anorexia, weight loss, irritability, hair loss, joint pain, nausea and insomnia. More than 50 per cent experience fatigue, headache and muscle aches. These side effects can undermine physical health, emotional well-being and capacity to function in everyday life, and are a major reason given for discontinuing treatment.[23]

In addition to these physical and mental side effects, there is also the possibility of stigmatisation and discrimination following disclosure of participation in treatment. Many people must reduce paid work while on treatment or stop altogether due to fatigue, depression and other problems. These changes often entail disclosure in the workplace as absences increase and explanations become necessary. Workplace responses to disclosure are not always positive and can lead to stigmatising and discriminatory practices. Intimate relationships also undergo serious strain, and treatment recipients can report spending months 'on the couch' at home while partners and other family members take on additional household burdens.[24]

The 'Key points' listed at the outset of the report make no mention whatsoever of these effects, focusing entirely on the reasons for encouraging people to have treatment. Reference to these issues appears only on page 7 (of the ten-page document), addressing them in extremely general terms: 'Many people with hepatitis C... delay treatment because of concerns about side effects and knowing treatment requires significant medical support.' Given the widely recognised problems associated with treatment, this vague remark and the broader silence in the document around side effects is extraordinary. Why would the peak advocacy organisation for hepatitis in Australia produce such silence? And what are its effects? Here we return to the operations of stigma.

Hepatitis C and its treatment are, as I have argued, both 'matters of concern'. They are things – both objects and sites of dealing and dispute. Hepatitis C has been materialised through stigma since its naming and, as 'non-A, non-B hepatitis', even earlier. The meaning of injecting drug use, the characteristics and attributes of people with hepatitis C and the appropriate way of addressing those people and the disease itself have long been in dispute, as we have seen so far. Indeed, this dealing and dispute includes another important element as well: the early association between hepatitis C and blood transfusion, and the dealing and dispute over deserving and undeserving victims of the disease.[25] This process, Duffin in effect argues, materialised hepatitis C in different ways. Where hepatitis C is materialised as the inevitable outcome of illicit and deviant behaviour, one materialisation occurs: that of an abject state indicating a non-functional subject unable to respond appropriately to the privilege and rigours of treatment. It is this materialisation, it seems, that the Hepatitis Australia report is attempting to overcome. Where side effects are emphasised and a view persists that people who inject drugs are unwilling or unable to cope with those side effects, expansion in treatment numbers, and in access to treatment for illicit drug consumers, would appear both difficult to achieve and unjustified. The report makes one or two references to the need to offer effective support during treatment, and this would seem to be an attempt to acknowledge the difficulty of treatment without presenting it as beyond the capacities of this poorly regarded group. In this way, advocacy opens up opportunities for otherwise marginalised people. Yet in doing so, in dealing with and disputing the materialisation of hepatitis C through stigma, another set of disputes and questions of equity arise. Here we must return to the list of effects of hepatitis C as presented in the report and ask how they relate to each other.

Elsewhere,[26] I have argued that implicit in this push to increase treatment can be the problematic assumption that even where it is not ideally suited to the patient's needs and circumstances, treatment is warranted as part of a strategy for helping to reduce overall incidence rates.[27] In other words, treatment is increasingly seen as a prevention measure: a strategy that helps directly reduce the burden of disease and new infections in the community where cure is achieved or, where it is not, reduces individual levels of viraemia and thus some new infections in the short term. As Moore and I argued, this approach risks treating affected people as epidemiological units bereft of individual differences and circumstances and their personal interests as indistinguishable from those of society as a whole, despite their evident exclusion from many of the rewards offered by society. Treatment, after all, is extremely difficult for anyone, but is perhaps especially burdensome for people on low incomes, with inflexible work conditions and inadequate housing, as are many people who inject drugs. When the report lists the costs of hepatitis C together, proposes expanding treatment and simultaneously understates the costs of treatment itself, it can be said to conflate the different orders of costs of disease and to collapse appropriate responses to them. These effects are worth examining. If people who inject drugs are not to be inappropriately responsibilised to enter treatment so as to reduce the 'economic burden' and 'social costs' of disease, it is necessary to communicate clearly about treatment risks and side effects. In this report, as in the earlier literature although in very different ways, hepatitis C materialises through the dealing and dispute between the interests and agencies of public health, the economy, advocacy, the stigma that would allow such responsibilisation and partial communication, and medicine.

Conclusion

To bring the issues canvassed here together for broader purposes, my key point is that treatment, stigma and the 'dealing and dispute' entailed in making injecting drug use as a social and political phenomenon all shape the 'thing' of hepatitis C and its effects. As Duffin makes clear, disease does not pre-exist its manifestation in bodies and societies.[28] Its attributes and effects are always made in process with such forces as economic, health and social policy, and various forms of stigma. Disease, this means, should not be taken for granted. It does not, as medicine tends to imply, lie in bodies passively awaiting discovery, description and mastery.[29] Indeed, as we have seen in the case of Egypt, it is at times actively *made by medicine* and related agencies.

This reframing of disease has important implications for our understanding of health, marginalisation and, specifically, drug use. The withholding and promotion of treatment both play a role in the shaping of hepatitis C. This role is complex and multivalent, yet this does not mean we should dismiss as too difficult the need to try to take part in this shaping. As my analysis of policies of treatment suggests, the shortcomings and inequities of one response cannot be overcome simply by reversing that response. Where disease is not fully recognised as a 'thing' – as always already both an object and a site of dealing and dispute – the importance and complexity of forces such as stigma in actually making disease and those who have it cannot fully be recognised. So long, as Paula Treichler has argued, as reality and theory are seen as separate, and reality is seen to occupy its own autonomous form of existence anterior to theory, we will proceed as though disease is largely a pre-determined matter the character and implications of which can only be addressed after its manifestation.

My point, ultimately, is that conventions, values and social practices such as health policy and stigma make the disease as much as microbes do. Disease is a gathering, a matter of concern that far exceeds the 'facts' by which it can be described. It is made in many moments and in many ways and, as such, is the responsibility – and the 'fault' – of many individuals, groups and forces, not just of those who have it. When we consider how to view treatment, how to provide it and whom to hold responsible for what ills, these ideas are indispensable. Things that gather cannot be thrown at you like objects.

Acknowledgements

I thank David Moore, kylie valentine and the anonymous reviewer for Cambridge University Press for their helpful comments on an earlier draft of this chapter. Some of the theoretical discussion included in the chapter also appears in the forthcoming book, Fraser, S., & Seear, K., *Making Disease, Making Citizens: The Politics of Hepatitis C*, Farnham, Surrey: Ashgate Press.

Notes

1. Duffin, *Lovers and Livers*, p. 83.
2. Ibid., p. 32.
3. Treichler, *How to have Theory in an Epidemic*, p. 3.
4. Latour & Woolgar quoted in ibid., p. 26; emphasis in the original.
5. Treichler, *How to have Theory in an Epidemic*, pp. 3 (emphasis added), 4.
6. Latour, 'Why has critique run out of steam?', p. 227.
7. Ibid., pp. 231–2.
8. Paraphrased in ibid., p. 232.
9. Ibid., pp. 233, 237.
10. Harris, 'Living with hepatitis C'.
11. Rosenberg, 'The tyranny of diagnosis', pp. 237, 238.
12. Simmonds & Coomber, 'Injecting drug users'.
13. Krug, 'HCV in the mass media'; Fraser & Treloar, 'Spoiled identity in hepatitis C infection'; Anti-Discrimination Board of NSW, *C-Change Report*; Harris, 'Living with hepatitis C'; Pugh, 'Hepatitis C and the Australian news media'.
14. Anti-Discrimination Board of NSW, *C-Change Report*.
15. Pugh, 'Hepatitis C and the Australian news media', p. 386.
16. Simmonds & Coomber, 'Injecting drug users', p. 128.
17. See Edlin, Seal, Lorvick et al., 'Is it justifiable to withhold treatment for hepatitis C from illicit drug users?'
18. Ibid.
19. Treloar & Fraser, 'Hepatitis C treatment in pharmacotherapy services'.
20. Hepatitis Australia, *Reducing the Burden of Hepatitis C*, p. 3.
21. Department of Health and Ageing, *Third National Hepatitis C Strategy 2010–2013*.
22. Hopwood, Treloar & Redsull, *Experiences of Hepatitis C Treatment and Its Management*.
23. Hopwood & Treloar, 2005. See above.
24. Fraser, 'Hepatitis C and the limits of medicalisation and biological citizenship for people who inject drugs'.
25. Duffin, *Lovers and Livers*.
26. Fraser & Moore, 'Harm reduction and hepatitis C'.
27. Also see, for instance, Martin, Vickerman & Hickman, 'Can HCV treatment of active injecting drug users (IDUs) lead to a reduction in HCV transmission?'; Department of Health and Ageing, *National Hepatitis C Strategy 2005–2008*.
28. Duffin, *Lovers and Livers*.
29. Fraser & Moore, 'Harm reduction and hepatitis C'.

References

Anti-Discrimination Board of NSW (2001). *C-Change: Report of the Enquiry into Hepatitis C Related Discrimination*. Sydney: Anti-Discrimination Board of NSW.

Duffin, J. (2005). *Lovers and Livers: Disease Concepts in History*. Toronto: University of Toronto Press.

Edlin, B., Seal, K., Lorvick, J., et al. (2001). Is it justifiable to withhold treatment for hepatitis C from illicit drug users? *New England Journal of Medicine*, 345(3): 211–13.

Frank, C., Mohamed, M., Strickland, G., et al. (2000). The role of parenteral antis-chistosomal therapy in the spread of hepatitis C virus in Egypt. *Lancet*, 355(9207): 887–91.

Fraser, S. (2010). Hepatitis C and the limits of medicalisation and biological citizenship for people who inject drugs. *Addiction Research and Theory*, 18(5): 544–56.

Fraser, S., & Moore, D. (forthcoming). Harm reduction and hepatitis C: On the ethics and politics of prevention and treatment. *Addiction Research and Theory*.

Fraser, S., & Seear, K. (forthcoming). *Making Disease, Making Citizens: The Politics of Hepatitis C*. Farnham, Surrey: Ashgate Press.

Fraser, S., & Treloar, C. (2006). 'Spoiled identity' in hepatitis C infection: The binary logic of despair. *Critical Public Health*, 16(2): 99–110.

Harris, M. (2005). Living with hepatitis C: The medical encounter. *New Zealand Sociology*. 20(1): 4–19.

Health and Ageing, Department of (2005). *National Hepatitis C Strategy 2005–2008*. Canberra: Australian Government.

—— (2010). *Third National Hepatitis C Strategy 2010–2013*. Canberra: Australian Government.

Hepatitis Australia (2010). *Reducing the Burden of Hepatitis C: The Case for Increasing Treatment Rates in Australia*. Sydney: Hepatitis Australia.

Hopwood, M., & Treloar, C. (2005). The experience of interferon-based treatments for hepatitis C infection. *Qualitative Health Research*, 15: 635–46.

Hopwood, M., Treloar, C., & Redsull, L. (2006). *Experiences of Hepatitis C Treatment and Its Management: What Some Patients and Health Professionals Say*. Sydney: National Centre in HIV Social Research, University of New South Wales.

Krug, G. (1997). HCV in the mass media: An unbearable absence of meaning. In N. Denzin (ed.). *Cultural Studies: A Research Volume*, vol. 2 (pp. 91–108). Greenwich, CT, & London: Jai Press.

Latour, B. (2004). Why has critique run out of steam? From matters of fact to matters of concern. *Critical Inquiry*, 30: 225–48.

Martin, A., Vickerman, P., & Hickman, M. (2010). Can HCV treatment of active injecting drug users (IDUs) lead to a reduction in HCV transmission? A modelling analysis. Presentation to Burnet Institute, Melbourne, Australia, 20 May 2010.

Pugh, J. (2008). Hepatitis C and the Australian news media: A case of 'bad blood'. *Continuum*, 22(3): 385–94.

Rosenberg, C. (2002), The tyranny of diagnosis: Specific entities and individual experience. *Millbank Quarterly*, 80(2): 237–60.

Simmonds, L., & Coomber, R. (2009). Injecting drug users: A stigmatised and stigmatising population, *International Journal of Drug Policy*, 20(2): 121–30.

Treichler, P. (1999). *How to have Theory in an Epidemic: Cultural Chronicles of AIDS*. Durham, NC: Duke University Press.

Treloar, C., & Fraser, S. (2009). Hepatitis C treatment in pharmacotherapy services: Increasing treatment uptake needs a critical view. *Drug and Alcohol Review*, 28: 436–40.

Drugs that work

Pharmaceuticals and performance self-management

Helen Keane

Psychoactive drugs have a complex and unstable status in contemporary culture. On one hand illicit drugs are believed to possess a unique ability to disable the user's self-control and thereby destroy physical, psychological and social well-being. On the other hand, the development, marketing and supply of a growing array of commodified psychoactive pharmaceuticals is a central activity of biomedicine and one of the most profitable sectors of global capitalism. As pharmaceutical consumers we rely on chemical effects to maintain our functioning as productive and healthy citizens, usually without being stigmatised as dependent drug users. This is despite the fact that substances on opposite sides of the dangerous drugs/beneficial medication divide frequently share common chemical structures, modes of action and psychoactive effects.

At the same time as the use of a wide range of pharmaceuticals has become normalised and domesticated, anxiety about the reliance of modern societies on chemical solutions has grown.[1] Within the general unease about the over-medication of society, psychoactive pharmaceutical drugs are the focus of particular anxiety. Publicity about problems of abuse and addiction seem almost inevitably to follow the adoption of a new medication. In addition, the mood-altering, cognitive and behavioural effects of psycho-pharmaceuticals are seen as potentially altering the self, raising ethical and personal questions about enhancement and identity.[2] As Emily Martin has observed, psychotropic pills are a *pharmakon*, a Greek term that means both 'remedy' and 'poison'. The meanings attached to their effects are both positive and negative, but this ambivalence does not prevent their consumption on a massive scale.[3]

One of the most productive ways of thinking about the pharmaceuticalisation of everyday life is through Nikolas Rose's notion of biological citizenship. Rose argues that as a result of the biotechnological advances of the past fifty years we have become 'somatic individuals', subjects who understand and judge ourselves, our actions, our rights and our obligations in biomedical terms.[4] Crucially, though, twenty-first-century styles of medical thought move beyond a concern with health and disease to the goal of optimisation. As biological citizens we are enjoined to monitor, manage and maximise our physiological and neuropsychological assets. The workplace is a key site for the elaboration of such projects of self-maximisation, a site where somatic individualism coalesces with the related ideals of entrepreneurialism and self-government.[5] As Colin Gordon has argued, the enterprising self is imagined as fundamentally manipulable, an agent 'who is perpetually responsive to modifications in its environment' and continually engaged in 'reconstructing his or her human capital'.[6] The intensified and accelerated work demands of the global economy, the emphasis on 'cognitive capacity' as 'the essential productive resource' and the model of enterprising biomedical selfhood encourage practices of pharmaceutical self-management.[7] Conversely, pharmaceuticals are both materially and discursively constructed to respond to the desires and needs of such responsive agents.

Of course, the use of psychoactive drugs to enhance work performance is neither new nor unusual. Caffeine and nicotine are enmeshed in the routines of office life, even in the era of the smoke-free workplace. In occupations with unusually extreme physical and mental demands, stronger stimulants such as amphetamines have been used to overcome fatigue, aid concentration and allow extended periods without sleep. On the other hand, drug and alcohol use are usually seen as antithetical to the self-control, seriousness and attentiveness required at work. As Gusfield has observed, industrial societies make a clear and oppositional distinction between leisure and work.[8] Because drinking and drug use mark the time frame of play, freedom and spontaneity, they are violations of the norms of work. The oppositional relationship between work and drugs is also seen in the assumption that work performance is one of the inevitable casualties of drug use. 'Failure to fulfil major role obligations at work' is one of the diagnostic criteria for substance abuse.[9]

In the United States, the eradication of drug and alcohol use in the workplace was one of the goals of the 'war against drugs'. The Drugfree Workplace Act 1988 led to widespread implementation of drug testing programs that aimed to identify and punish drug-positive employees. While couched as a reasonable response to the hazards and costs of workforce drug use, drug-free workplace policies can also be seen as a form of disciplinary surveillance that extends management gaze into the private and leisure time activities of employees.[10] As critics have pointed out, the standard tests do not measure intoxication or impairment; rather they screen for traces of past drug use through hair analysis.

Thus psychoactive drugs such as stimulants continue to have a suspect status in the workplace, even when they are medically prescribed. In addition, the notion of drugs as unnatural and harmful chemicals that suppress the authentic self and prevent the achievement of genuine health remains powerful and acts as a limit to the desire for biotechnologised self-enhancement. This chapter focuses on two cases that reveal the role of pharmaceuticals as mediators of the responsible, productive and self-managing worker while also demonstrating the ambivalent meanings attached to these drugs. The first case examines the constitution of sleep as a management issue and the concomitant construction of 'new generation' sleeping pills as restorative of enterprise and agency. The expert literature on sleep is a burgeoning field.[11] This case is based on analyses of articles on sleep disorders from medical and management journals; newspaper and magazine articles about sleep problems and their treatment; the information found on the websites of such organisations as the US National Sleep Foundation; and publicity material produced by pharmaceutical companies that market sleep medications. Medicalised sleep discourse legitimates the use of drugs as a rational response to a debilitating health problem, but also produces a counter-discourse of risks and adverse effects.

The second case focuses on the use of stimulant and other medications by adults diagnosed with Attention Deficit Hyperactivity Disorder (ADHD). Here the discussion draws on analyses of medical literature on ADHD, especially that which focuses on the role of executive function, and popular texts that played a major role in the publicising of adult ADHD. These texts are supplemented with data from a study of posts to a large and active online ADHD support forum. Adult ADHD has achieved medical legitimacy as a valid disorder, but it remains controversial in part because of suspicions about the use of stimulants as performance-enhancing drugs. Popular ADHD texts tend to reinforce these suspicions by presenting stimulant medications as an optional self-help tool for ambitious professionals. But posts to the online forum challenge the idea that ADHD treatment is a straightforward route to performance enhancement. Forum members do rely on medication in order to function in the workplace and eloquently acknowledge its benefits, yet their accounts of medicated selfhood are also full of ambivalence and struggle. The negotiation of dosages and brands, side effects, erratic results, tolerance and drug interactions make pharmaceutical self-management a demanding form of embodied labour, a burden and an obligation as well as an aid and entitlement.

Pharmaceutical self-government: Sleep and wake enhancement

In the new economic order characterised by globalised and deregulated markets, rapid information flows, competition and privatisation, the demands made on workers in many different industries and occupations have intensified.[12] Discourses of productivity and flexibility construct a regulatory ideal of an adaptable, alert, multitasking worker who is able to maintain attention and focus while calmly responding to heterogeneous demands and sources of information. At the same time the discourses of enterprise and excellence that have flourished in neoliberal economies emphasise the continual improvement of work performance, assessed through processes of formal performance appraisal.[13] One consequence of these trends is the problematisation and medicalisation of traits that interfere with optimum performance and efficiency.

A noteworthy example is sleepiness at work, previously understood as a relatively minor and private affliction. Lack of sleep now receives extensive attention as a costly public health problem and urgent issue for corporate management.[14] Sleep 'has a major impact on how well a business functions', states a recent article in a management journal. 'Poor sleep costs businesses directly through lost productivity, compromised physical or emotional health, impaired cognition, accident rates and absences and indirectly through factors such as poor morale, poor social relationships, and depression.'[15] The authors construct the sleepy worker as a deficient and dangerous subject; prone to flawed judgement and poor decisions, lacking motivation, slow to learn new tasks and at high risk of accidents and illness. The sleepy worker not only loses his or her entrepreneurial drive but also compromises the enterprise of the corporation and of the nation through losses in efficiency and increases in costs. While the article urges businesses to promote a culture that values sleep and to adopt policies such as limiting the workday (to no more than 12–16 hours!), the notion that workers are themselves responsible for ensuring they get sufficient sleep is also prominent. Individuals are urged to practise good 'sleep hygiene' and to be vigilant in detecting sleep disorders that might require treatment. The demands of the workplace thus encroach into the bedroom, and sleep itself becomes a duty and a skill that must be competently mastered in order to guarantee alert wakefulness on the job.

> **In focus**
>
> **Insomnia**
>
> Insomnia, defined as difficulty in falling or staying asleep, and more expansively described as poor-quality, insufficient or non-restorative sleep, is the most common sleep disorder. In publications such as the *Journal of Clinical Sleep Medicine*, the proliferating expert discourse on sleep constructs insomnia as a highly prevalent, chronic, underdiagnosed and undertreated disorder.[a] Insomnia is said to affect up to 40 per cent of adults, with 15 per cent suffering chronic sleep difficulties.[b] Websites of such organisations as the American Sleep Association and the American Academy of Sleep Medicine transmit medicalised sleep discourse to the general public, and encourage readers to take their sleep difficulties seriously as medical issues with harmful consequences both physical and psychological. Talking to a doctor followed by specialist testing is recommended for those experiencing problems.
>
> a Roth, 'Insomnia'.
> b Ringdahl, Pereira & Delzell, 'Treatment of primary insomnia', p. 212.

The standard medical advice recommends trying behavioural techniques, such as relaxation and cognitive therapies, before turning to medication, but medication is the most common treatment.[16] The market for hypnotics or sleeping pills has expanded dramatically in the past 10 to 15 years because of the development and aggressive marketing of new agents such as zopiclone and zolpidem, sold under brand names that include Lunesta, Imovane, Ambien and Sonata. Prescriptions have grown particularly rapidly among people younger than 45.[17] Pharmaceutical company Sepracor states in its 2005 annual report: 'Since the introduction of LUNESTA, the prescription sedative hypnotic market has progressed from year-over-year growth rates of 5 to 7 per cent to 28 per cent as of the week of February 24, 2006.'[18] In a similar pattern to the construction of SSRI anti-depressants as cleaner, smarter, safer and more scientific than earlier anti-depressants, the so-called Z-drugs are given a positive and modern image through comparison with benzodiazepam hypnotics such as Valium and Xanax. Unlike these old-fashioned sleeping pills, which knocked you out and left you hungover, depressed and possibly addicted, the 'new generation' drugs 'act only on specific receptors in your brain that are focused on sleep', have a low risk of dependence and do not produce morning grogginess.[19] Hence, according to Sepracor, physicians have developed a 'greater level of comfort in prescribing sleep medications'.[20]

The story of 'How I Faced Reality', originally found on the Ambien CR website, provides a vivid example of how the Z-drug hypnotics mesh with the desire of enterprising individuals to act on themselves to become 'the best they can be'. Ambien CR, an extended release version of zolpidem, is claimed by manufacturer Sanofi-aventis to have a unique combination of sleep-inducing and sleep-maintaining properties. The story is told in first person by Alice, 35 (who, the small print tells us 'is not an actual patient'):

> I've always been a go-getter. When it comes to my career, I like to give 100 per cent. But when my sleep problems started to affect me in the office, I felt powerless. Nothing seemed to help and I've never really been one for taking sleeping pills. Sleep is supposed to be natural, right? Well, I finally caved in and talked to my doctor. He soon made me realize that when sleep can't happen naturally, there's no point in suffering. Now I take AMBIEN CR when I need to. I sleep much better. I can concentrate better. And at work, I'm back to my 100 per cent and can concentrate on the day ahead.[21]

The accompanying image is of a slim, professionally dressed woman, standing face-on and smiling directly at the viewer. Behind her is an image of the same woman at work, smiling confidently and making a presentation to a business meeting (we can see the laptop and backs of two suited colleagues at the table). Alice's story does more than highlight the ability of Ambien CR to restore sleep and hence work performance. It is a conversion narrative in which taking the medication is itself a demonstration of agency. Before Ambien, Alice is powerless not only because she is sleep deprived and unable to perform at the office but also because her outdated beliefs about sleeping pills prevent her from taking steps to solve her problem. Despite being a 'go-getter', she believes that poor sleep is something that can only be endured. After Ambien, Alice is restored to full efficiency. Not only is she back to 100 per cent at work but also her identity as agentic 'go-getter' has itself been extended to include rational pharmaceutical self-management.

However, Alice's rhetorical question 'Sleep is supposed to be natural, right?' remains salient despite her conversion to neurochemical selfhood. The unnatural and uncanny properties of medication-induced sleep have been highlighted in the well-publicised stories of 'bizarre' nocturnal behaviour linked to the Z drugs. Reports of people walking, eating, having sex, making phone calls, doing housework and home repairs and even driving in their sleep after talking Ambien and other Z drugs prompted the US Food and Drug Administration to insist that manufacturers include stronger warnings on patient information.[22] While 'nocturnal wandering' on Ambien appears to be rare, its occurrence complicates the drug's relationship to sleep, as such activity is difficult to reconcile with the ideal of 'natural sleep' that 'restores your mind and body'.[23] The Ambien CR website itself reveals the darker side of zolpidem as a psychoactive *pharmakon* in the page devoted to side effects. As well as listing headaches, somnolence and dizziness as common side effects, it tells users that they 'should be aware that sleep medication may cause memory problems, tolerance, dependence, withdrawal, changes in behavior and thinking, and issues concerning pregnancy'. Because of the risks of tolerance and dependence it advises that 'Sleep medicines should, in most cases, be used only for short periods of time, such as one or two days and generally no longer than one or two weeks'. It warns that 'Withdrawal symptoms may occur when sleep medicines are stopped suddenly', that these may occur after only short term use and that 'rebound insomnia' is one of the possible withdrawal effects. Here on the mandatory warning page, the new and improved sleeping pill appears to be not so different from its predecessors. And while the positive effects of the drugs are distributed among a range of beneficiaries beyond the sleep-disordered individual, the negative effects are confined to the embodied experience of the pharmaceuticalised subject.

Adult ADHD: Underperformance and impairment

Another category of pharmaceuticals used both legally and illicitly to improve work performance are the stimulants methylphenidate and amphetamine, most commonly prescribed for the treatment of Attention Deficit Hyperactivity Disorder (ADHD). The spread of stimulant therapy from the schoolroom to the workplace occurred as a result of the reconfiguration of ADHD as a disorder that produced impairment in adults as well as behavioural problems in children. Until the mid-1980s ADHD was understood as fundamentally a disorder of childhood. In the DSM-IV, published in 1994 and revised in 2000, a positive diagnosis requires that the symptoms exhibit before the age of seven. The descriptions of symptomatic behaviour assumes a school-aged subject: he or she 'often fails to finish schoolwork', 'often leaves seat in classroom', 'often blurts outs answers'.[24]

The issue of ADHD in adults first emerged in follow-up studies of diagnosed children, which suggested that symptoms frequently persisted into adulthood. But in the early 1990s a new group of 'ADHD adults' gained visibility, those seeking diagnosis *as* adults. Popular texts such as *Driven to Distraction* raised the profile of the disorder, and parents began self-referring to clinics after their children were diagnosed with the condition.[25] Medical publications on adult ADHD constructed an under-treated population suffering from 'clinically significant impairment' and demonstrating characteristic inattentiveness, impulsivity and restlessness.[26]

In the most comprehensive text on adult ADHD, pre-eminent authority Russell Barkley and co-authors state that ADHD is 'a relatively common mental disorder in adults, affecting at least 5% of the US adult population'.[27] According to dominant medical discourse and patient advocacy groups, ADHD has clearly been established as a 'lifespan disorder'. However, the nature and validity of the condition remains contested.[28] For critics, the expansion of ADHD is a vivid example of the process of medicalisation and the elasticity of medical diagnoses, especially psychiatric diagnoses.[29]

The treatment of ADHD in adults has followed the protocols established for children. Stimulant drugs such as methylphenidate (e.g. Ritalin, Concerta) and amphetamine (e.g. Adderall) are the most commonly prescribed.[30] Adults are a lucrative growth market for ADHD medications. Prescriptions for 'people 19 years of age or older' of eight commonly used ADHD drugs increased by 90 per cent in the United States from 2002 to 2005. In 2006 it was reported that adults received about a third of all prescriptions for these drugs.[31] Although there is currently little research on the long-term effects of stimulant therapy on adults, pharmacological treatment is presented as particularly suitable for adults because they must manage their symptoms in a workplace setting. Taking a medication, especially a long-acting medication, is 'more convenient, effective and private' than behavioural treatment in this context.[32] The establishment and institutionalisation of adult ADHD thus produces a new form of 'pharmaceutical personhood' in which stimulants are incorporated into the production of the normal self from early childhood onwards.

As older ADHD medications such as Adderall and Ritalin come off patent and become available in generic versions, drug companies are marketing new formulations specifically to adults. A notable example is Vyvanse, an amphetamine 'pro-drug', which was approved for adult use in 2008.[33] Vyvanse is promoted as longer lasting than traditional formulations and therefore especially suited to adults who face the demands of a long working day. Shire, the company that developed Vyvanse, funded a 'simulated workplace environment study' in which subjects 'engaged in tests and activities that require a level of attention needed in many workplace settings'.[34] The finding that Vyvanse was effective in improving performance for up to 14 hours after administration was widely publicised and featured in an advertising campaign for the drug. The advertisements emphasised productivity and improved work performance as the outcomes of treatment. They featured brightly coloured images of adults posing with successfully completed projects: an executive with a Powerpoint display, an architect with a model of an impressive high-rise building, a dressmaker with a dress labelled SOLD and a cabinetmaker in a new kitchen.

Given the emphasis of popular adult ADHD texts on the hidden struggles of successful professionals and the broadness of the self-screening tests they promote, it is not surprising to find scepticism about the validity of the condition in public discourse. Stimulants improve concentration, memory and performance of problem solving tasks in individuals whether or not they have been diagnosed with ADHD. Thus, the dramatic rise in ADHD diagnoses and growth in prescriptions for stimulants can readily be interpreted as an example of neurocognitive enhancement, the use of psychopharmaceuticals by healthy individuals to improve functioning.[35] However, medical and psychological research challenges the discourse of adult ADHD as performance enhancement. In their major study of adults with ADHD, Barkley, Murphy & Fischer produce a comprehensive picture of 'impairment in major life activities' including education, work, finances and personal relationships.[36] Specific associations with ADHD include lower job status, more job losses and higher rates of substance use, risky driving, criminal activity, imprisonment and divorce. While such associations do not prove causality nor even the validity of the condition, they do point to a group of people suffering significant disadvantage and adversity. The struggle of living with ADHD as an adult is also vividly represented in the discussions found on the ADHD forums and support groups that are flourishing online.

Pharmaceutical self-management on the ADHD forum

The ADHD forum is a large and active online community with tens of thousands of members from several countries.[37] Most areas of the forum can be freely accessed, but posting requires registration. Some members are newly diagnosed or undiagnosed, others are veterans of long-term treatment. Members share personal experiences; ask for and give advice, sympathy and (rarely) criticism; reflect on the nature of their condition; and 'vent' about life with ADHD and the lack of understanding shown by 'normies' and society as a whole. Forum posts made between mid-2006 and mid-2010 related to work, career and medication were reviewed and analysed as part of a larger project on medicalisation.

Employment and its frustrations is one of the recurring themes of discussion. Members often wrote eloquently about the experiences of being reprimanded by a boss, of being classified as an underperformer and of being fired from jobs 'even though I always try my very best'. They linked their work problems closely to their symptoms of distractibility, disorganisation, difficulty completing tasks and poor awareness of time but also bemoaned the lack of freedom they were given to utilise their strengths and adopt the unconventional work styles that they felt would improve their productivity. Members frequently constructed themselves and other 'ADHDers' as fundamentally out of step with the norms and expectations of the average workplace. Several posts highlighted the discouragement produced by job advertisements, which inevitably seemed to list qualities opposite to those produced by the 'ADHD brain': 'self-starter', 'disciplined', 'punctual', 'organised' and 'independent worker with good follow-through'.

Indeed, the currently dominant theory of ADHD does present a vision of the ADHD subject as one who is uniquely ill-equipped to achieve the ideals of the productive worker as defined by discourses of enterprise and performance management. Developed by Russell Barkley, this theory posits ADHD as a deficit in executive function, the cognitive system often described as

analogous to the conductor of an orchestra or the chief executive of a corporation. As the corporate metaphor suggests, the theory of executive function
privileges qualities associated with organisation and the efficient achievement of goals. According to Barkley, it is executive function that allows individual behaviour to be controlled by 'hindsight, forethought, time, plans,
rules and self-motivating stimuli' that 'ultimately provide for the maximisa-
tion of future net outcomes'. Conversely, the deficiencies produced by ADHD
result in difficulties with 'goal-directed' persistence and produce an inability to maintain performance towards a task in the face of ordinary levels of
distraction.[38]

While resisting this exclusively negative view of ADHD as a list of inca-
pacities, forum members frequently described being overwhelmed by panic
and stress when faced with an ever-increasing pile of unfinished work, constant emails and conflicting demands. One poster described having to work
two to three times harder than her colleagues just to keep up, while another
described arriving at work one to two hours early in a vain attempt to get a
head start. Medication helped by improving focus and removing distracting
thoughts, thereby transforming work from 'torture' to 'almost bearable'.

Medication was discussed extensively on the ADHD forum, with each
brand of drug having a dedicated subforum. On threads addressing the general topic of the difference medication had made to their lives, members
often described their 'meds' with gratitude if not affection, as transformative
substances that had enabled a move from chaos and despair to a relatively
normal life. However, in the context of discussions focused on work, medication was spoken about in more instrumental and qualified terms. One
member bluntly stated that 'in order to make a living, I have to take Adderall', while another commented that 'with a high enough dose of medication
I can cope with this job'. In this context, medication was constituted as an
entitlement but not one that provided any form of reward or advantage. In
reply to questions from 'newbies' worried about stimulants showing up on
workplace drug tests, members pointed out that people with ADHD had as
much right to effective treatment as diabetics had to insulin. Medication was
not a 'magic bullet', but it was necessary for those 'with a clinically diagnosed
handicap'.

But as well as being a right, taking medication was constituted in some
posts as a burden, an imposition and a risk, even when the drugs themselves
were beneficial. In these posts, members voiced concern about the long-term
health effects of stimulants and expressed hopes of being able to manage
their symptoms 'meds-free' one day. Less frequently, members expressed
resentment that in order to be 'acceptable', 'normal' and to live up to other
people's standards they had to suppress or lose part of themselves. One
described a nagging unease resulting from not being able distinguish between
'what is part of me and what is just the meds'.

An ambivalent relationship with medication was, however, most strongly expressed in the numerous threads that detailed members' pharmacotherapeutic regimes, past and present. Long periods of trial and error 'cycling through meds' were the norm, with one member stating that it had taken her 15 years to work out which medications worked for her. This process of 'working out' is often a gruelling form of embodied labour focused on the identification and balancing of symptoms, positive effects, adverse effects and drug interactions. High hopes about a new medication were often disappointed. Dealing with side effects, such as dizziness, rapid heartbeat and excess sweating at work, could be as distressing as dealing with the symptoms of ADHD, especially for those who had not disclosed their diagnosis. The problem of tolerance, the gradual loss of efficacy of a previously effective medication, was another common complication. Because of the proliferation of ADHD medications – brand and generic drugs, stimulants and non-stimulants, sustained release and immediate release, high dose and low dose – the range of different combinations that can be tried is immense. Members sought advice on 'the best drug for inattentiveness' or 'a stim which won't make me angry and hostile', but the varied and contradictory replies to such queries demonstrated that the response of a particular body to a particular drug at a particular time could not be determined in advance. Medication histories such as the following were not unusual:

Vyvanse: No effect except insomnia
Strattera: Some improvement but feeling drowsy and depressed
Concerta: Only lasted a few hours, made me irritable and had a terrible crash
Adderall: No serious side effects but dose needed to be doubled in order to work all day.

Many ADHD forum members were managing complex poly-drug regimes that incorporated several different kinds of medication, including anti-depressants, anti-anxiety drugs, hypnotics, sedatives and anti-psychotics. Adults with ADHD are frequently diagnosed with 'co-morbidities' such as depression and anxiety, but as several posters observed it was almost impossible to work out whether a symptom, such as panic attacks, was a side effect of a medication or the result of an underlying condition. In other cases drugs, such as SSRI anti-depressants, which were prescribed to help with the anxiety caused by stimulants, also reduced the desired effects of the stimulant. See-sawing back and forth in an attempt to find a stable balance between stimulant and sedative effects was time-consuming, costly and frustrating.

The experiences with medication described on the forum are not claimed to be representative. Problems are much more likely to be posted than success stories and those experiencing good results without complications are less likely to seek advice or support. However, the posts do demonstrate that as 'technologies of the self' ADHD medications are not quick, clean or easy routes to enhancement. Rather the messiness of the interactions between drugs, bodies and selves meant that, for many forum members, a normal level of functioning was a hard-won and fragile achievement that could not be taken for granted but required daily vigilance. As well as being required in order to perform successfully as a worker, regimes of medication are themselves a form of work.

Conclusion

Psychoactive drugs have a long history as enhancers of work performance. This chapter has argued that the intensification of work demands, the rise of cognitive capacity as the most valued human resource and the prevalence of biomedical styles of thought have constituted pharmaceutical self-management as an attribute of the responsible worker. The possibilities of cognitive enhancement through smart pills produce excited speculation about a future where individuals will attain extraordinary abilities whenever required.[39] But the two examples discussed in this chapter present more everyday examples of pharmaceutical self-management at work. In the first, medical and management discourses combine to constitute somnolence as a major threat to the optimum functioning of individuals and corporations. The availability of a 'new generation' of sleeping pills allows the sleepy and underperforming worker to return to full capacity. In the second, workers diagnosed with ADHD are handicapped by the distractibility, disorganisation and temporal anomalies of the 'ADHD brain'. Stimulant medications, marketed to the relatively new target group of 'adults with ADHD', provide the clarity and focus required to make it through a demanding working day.

The cases demonstrate that biological citizenship is a varied and unevenly distributed phenomenon, even among those who depend on psycho-pharmaceuticals. The treatment of insomnia with hypnotic sedatives rarely involves the construction of a biomedicalised identity based on the malfunctioning brain. In Alice's Ambien story there is no diagnosis or mention of aetiology – there is simply a glitch to be fixed. In contrast, being diagnosed as an adult with ADHD usually involves a reconfiguring of the self as a neurological subject, one whose behaviour and experiences are linked directly to an idiosyncratic brain. Moreover, embarking on stimulant therapy requires reflection on the blurry boundaries between self, symptom and drug effect. As the posts to the ADHD forum demonstrate, this form of pharmaceutical self-management is an ambivalent experience that highlights the positive and negative sides of the *pharmakon*. Medication was viewed as life-saving and life-transforming, but the good effects were achieved through an often gruelling, messy and open-ended process of trial and error. Moreover, the unpredictability of drug effects when substances are ingested by actual bodies means that the promise of a clean and efficient elimination of symptoms is rarely fulfilled.

Notes

1 Fox & Ward, 'Pharma in the bedroom . . . and the kitchen'; Williams, Gabe & Davis, 'The sociology of pharmaceuticals'.
2 Kramer, *Listening to Prozac*.
3 Martin, 'The pharmaceutical person', p. 274.
4 Rose, *The Politics of Life Itself*.
5 Du Gay, Salaman & Rees, 'The conduct of management and the management of conduct'; Rose, 'Governing the enterprising self'.
6 Cited in Du Gay, Salaman & Rees, 'The conduct of management and the management of conduct', p. 269.
7 Bernardi, 'Schizo-economy', p. 76.
8 Gusfield, 'Passage to play'.
9 American Psychiatric Association, *DSM-IV-TR*, p. 199.
10 Warren & Wray-Bliss, 'Workforce drug testing'.
11 Kroll-Smith & Gunter, 'Governing sleepiness'.
12 Green, 'Why has work effort become more intense?'; Webb, 'Organizations, self-identities and the new economy'.
13 Billett & Pavlova, 'Learning through working life'.
14 Kroll-Smith & Gunter, 'Governing sleepiness'; Williams, 'Vulnerable/dangerous bodies?'
15 Gaultney & Collins-McNeil, 'Lack of sleep in the workplace', p. 132.
16 National Sleep Foundation, 'Sleep aids and insomnia'.
17 Gellene, 'Sleeping pill use grows as economy keeps people up at night'.
18 Sepracor, *Sepracor 2005 Annual Report*, p. 2.
19 Indeed Rozerem, one of a new class of sleep drugs that target melatonin receptors, is claimed to have zero side effects (Shaw, 'When counting sheep fails').
20 Sepracor, *Sepracor 2005 Annual Report*, p. 2.
21 Ambien CR, 'How I faced reality'. The Ambien CR website no longer features images and stories of ambien users, but simply reproduces the prescribing information required by the US Food and Drug Authority. For Alice's story, see Mack, 'Alice, 35, is not a real Ambien CR patient'.
22 Khamsi, 'Sleep medication linked to bizarre behavior'; US Food and Drug Administration, 'FDA requests label change for all sleep disorder drug products'.
23 Mayo Clinic, 'Insomnia treatment'.
24 American Psychiatric Association, *DSM-IV-TR*, p. 92.
25 Hallowell & Ratey, *Driven to Distraction*.
26 Faraone, Biederman, Spencer et al., 'Attention-deficit/hyperactivity disorder in adults'.
27 Barkley, Murphy & Fischer, *ADHD in Adults*, p. 25.
28 Zwi & York, 'Attention Deficit Hyperactivity Disorder in adults'.
29 Conrad, *The Medicalization of Society*.
30 Dodson, 'Pharmacotherapy of adult ADHD'.
31 Okie, 'ADHD in adults', p. 2638. Okie notes that these drugs are sometimes prescribed for indications other than ADHD.

32 Barkley, Murphy & Fischer, *ADHD in Adults*, p. 457.
33 A pro-drug is a drug that is administered in an inactive form, and only becomes activated once metabolised in the body.
34 E!Science News, 'Vyvanse CII provided significant efficacy at 14 hours in adults with ADHD'.
35 Conrad, *The Medicalization of Society*; Greely, Sahakian, Harris et al., 'Towards responsible use of cognitive enhancing drugs by the healthy'.
36 Barkley, Murphy & Fischer, *ADHD in Adults*.
37 To protect the privacy and anonymity of members the forum is not named and references to specific posts are not made. The quotes and examples are fictionalised composites based on actual posts. Due to the size of the group and the high activity level of the forums, threads and posts tend to repeat similar themes and experiences.
38 Barkley, 'Behavioral inhibition, sustained attention, and executive functions', pp. 75, 67, 77.
39 Hall, 'The quest for a smart pill'.

References

Ambien, C.R. (n.d.). 'How I Faced Reality'. Retrieved 15 July 2010. www.ambiencr.com/treating-sleep-problems.aspx.

American Psychiatric Association (2000). *DSM-IV-TR: Diagnostic and Statistical Manual of Mental Disorders* (4th edn). Washington DC: American Psychiatric Association.

Barkley, R.A. (1997). Behavioral inhibition, sustained attention, and executive functions: Constructing a unifying theory of ADHD. *Psychological Bulletin*, 121(1): 65–94.

Barkley, R.A., Murphy, K.R., & Fischer, M. (2008). *ADHD in Adults: What the Science Says*. New York & London: Guilford Press.

Bernardi, F. (2007). Schizo-Economy. *SubStance*, 36(1): 76–85.

Billett, S., & Pavlova, M. (2005). Learning through working life: Self and individuals' agentic action. *International Journal of Lifelong Education*, 24(3): 195–211.

Conrad, P. (2007). *The Medicalization of Society: On the Transformation of Human Conditions into Treatable Disorders*. Baltimore, MD: Johns Hopkins University Press.

Dodson, W.W. (2005). Pharmacotherapy of adult ADHD. *Journal of Clinical Psychology*, 61(5): 589–606.

Du Gay, P., Salaman G., & Rees, B. (1996). The conduct of management and the management of conduct: Contemporary managerial discourse and the constitution of the 'competent' manager. *Journal of Management Studies*, 33(3): 263–82.

E!Science News (2009). Vyvanse CII provided significant efficacy at 14 hours in adults with ADHD. Retrieved 22 March 2011. http://esciencenews.com/articles/2009/07/01/vyvanse.cii.provided.significant.efficacy.14.hours.adults.with.adhd.

Faraone, S., Biederman, J., Spencer, T., et al. (2000). Attention-deficit/hyperactivity disorder in adults: An overview. *Biological Psychiatry*, 48(1): 9–20.

Fox, N.J., & Ward, K. (2008). Pharma in the bedroom . . . and the kitchen: The pharmaceuticalisation of daily life. *Sociology of Health and Illness*, 30(6): 856–68.

Gaultney, J.F., & Collins-McNeil, J. (2009). Lack of sleep in the workplace: What the psychologist-manager should know about sleep. *Psychologist-Manager Journal*, 12(2): 132–48.

Gellene, D. (2009). Sleeping pill use grows as economy keeps people up at night. *Los Angeles Times*, 30 March. Retrieved 31 March 2011. http://articles.latimes.com/2009/mar/30/health/he-sleep30.

Greely, H., Sahakian, B., Harris, J., et al. (2008). Towards responsible use of cognitive enhancing drugs by the healthy. *Nature*, 456: 702–5.

Green, F. (2004). Why has work effort become more intense? *Industrial Relations*, 43(4): 709–41.

Gusfield, J. (1987). Passage to play: Rituals of drinking in American society. In M. Douglas (ed.), *Constructive Drinking*. Cambridge: Cambridge University Press.

Hall, S. (2003). The quest for a smart pill. *Scientific American*, 289(3): 54–7.

Hallowell, E.M., & Ratey, J.J. (1994). *Driven to Distraction*. New York: Touchstone.

Khamsi, R. (2007). Sleep medication linked to bizarre behavior. *New Scientist*. 6 February. Retrieved 19 July 2010. www.newscientist.com/article/dn11115-sleep-medication-linked-to-bizarre-behaviour.html.

Kramer, P. (1994). *Listening to Prozac*. New York: Penguin.

Kroll-Smith, S., & Gunter, V. (2005). Governing sleepiness: Somnolent bodies, discourse and liquid modernity. *Sociological Inquiry*, 75(3): 346–71.

Mack, J. (2008). 'Alice, 35, is not a real Ambien CR patient'. Retrieved 31 March 2011. http://pharmamkting.blogspot.com/2008/10/alice-35-is-not-real-ambien-cr-patient.html.

Martin, E. (2006). The pharmaceutical person. *BioSocieties*, 1(3): 273–87.

Mayo Clinic (2009). Insomnia treatment: Cognitive behavioral therapy instead of sleeping pills. Retrieved 19 July 2010. www.mayoclinic.com/health/insomnia-treatment/SL00013.

National Sleep Foundation (2009). Sleep aids and insomnia. Retrieved 17 July 2010. www.sleepfoundation.org/article/sleep-related-problems/sleep-aids-and-insomnia.

Okie, S. (2006). ADHD in adults. *New England Journal of Medicine*, 354(25): 2637–41.

Ringdahl, E.N., Pereira, S.L., & Delzell, J.E. (2004). Treatment of primary insomnia. *Journal of the American Board of Family Practice*, 17(3): 212–19.

Rose, N. (1992). Governing the enterprising self. In P. Heelas & P. Morris (eds). *The Values of the Enterprise Culture* (pp. 141–64). London: Routledge.

—— (2007). *The Politics of Life Itself*. Princeton, NJ: Princeton University Press.

Roth, T. (2007). Insomnia: Definition, prevalence, etiology and consequences. *Journal of Clinical Sleep Medicine*, 3(5 Suppl): S7–S10.

Sepracor Inc. (2006). *Sepracor 2005 Annual Report*. Retrieved 22 March 2011. www.corporatewindow.com/annuals/sepr05/cover.html.

Shaw, G. (2007). When counting sheep fails: The latest sleep medications. Retrieved 22 March 2011. www.webmd.com/sleep-disorders/guide/to-sleep-perchance-to-sleep-soundly.

US Food and Drug Administration (2007). FDA requests label change for all sleep disorder drug products. Retrieved 22 March 2011. www.fda.gov/NewsEvents/Newsroom/PressAnnouncements/2007/ucm108868.htm.

Warren, S., & Wray-Bliss, E. (2009). Workforce drug testing: A critique and reframing. *New Technology, Work and Employment*, 24(2): 163–76.

Webb, J. (2004). Organizations, self-identities and the new economy. *Sociology*, 38(4): 719–38.

Williams, S., Gabe, J., & Davis, P. (2008). The sociology of pharmaceuticals: Progress and prospects. *Sociology of Health and Illness*, 30(6): 813–24.

Williams, S.J. (2007). Vulnerable/dangerous bodies? The trials and tribulations of sleep. *Sociological Review*, 55(1): 142–55.

Zwi, M., & York, A. (2004). Attention Deficit Hyperactivity Disorder in adults: Validity unknown. *Advances in Psychiatric Treatment*, 10: 248–59.

From 'magic bullets' to medical maintenance

The changing meanings of medical approaches to drug use in US drug policy

Nancy D. Campbell

Multiple meanings are condensed in the term 'medicalisation'; these change over time in relation to the 'technologies of addiction' on offer. Technologies used to treat addiction have ranged from specific pharmacotherapies to drug-free 'therapeutic communities' (TCs) and recovery-oriented self-help groups. Recent medical approaches focus on specific pharmacotherapies that, in the language of medicalisation, target receptor sites in the brain, helping shift US drug policy away from the tenets of abstinence upon which it is premised. After a brief experiment with municipal morphine maintenance clinics in the first two decades of the twentieth century, abstinence from all illegal substances was adopted as the over-riding mark of individual morality and the goal of a moral society. US drug policy became profoundly anti-maintenance. Maintenance has been continually constructed not as a treatment modality but as tantamount to condoning drug use, being 'soft on addicts' and 'substituting' one addictive drug for another. Despite the anti-maintenance stance, hopes that pharmacotherapy could displace drug users' reliance on illegal substances have been embraced in the ethos of 'pharmacological optimism' that has pervaded four distinct eras in the development of drug policy in the United States (see 'Eras in US drug policy development' below).

This chapter tells the story of the recent convergence of 'medicalisation', medication and maintenance by focusing on prevailing forms of 'pharmacological optimism' – the idea that a pharmacotherapy could be developed to displace the problematic substance to which subjects are addicted. The dream of pharmacological optimism reconfigured social infrastructure and medical practice in each era.

In focus

Eras in US drug policy development

1 Morphine maintenance clinics – before the 1920s, the convergence of medicalisation and maintenance led to the establishment of clinics by entrepreneurial physicians and municipalities but gave way to criminalisation.

2 The first American approach to methadone – from the late 1940s to the mid-1960s, methadone was used in medically assisted detoxification during an anti-maintenance period in which criminalisation was dominant and drug development was geared towards re-engineering the morphine molecule to be less addictive.

3 The second American approach to methadone – from the 1960s onwards, a theory that methadone served as an effective 'narcotic blockade' formed the basis of the current treatment infrastructure of autonomous or 'free-standing' methadone clinics.[a]

4 Alternatives to methadone and the re-emergence of medical management – since the late twentieth century the US government has both scaled up methadone clinics and intensively searched for a treatment that would work 'better than methadone' (i.e. be less prone to overdose, diversion or tampering, and hence in less need of regulation). Proponents of 'medicalisation' used buprenorphine to return the United States to a legal regime of office-based medical management, allowing physicians to prescribe 'bupe' in primary health-care settings.

a Dole, Nyswander & Kreek, 'Narcotic blockade'.

Theoretical framework

Tracing the complex interrelationships between different regimes of 'medicalisation', subject formation and policy problematises the idea that medicalisation is simply an 'expansion of medical jurisdiction',[1] a social and political process by which 'non-medical' problems are redefined as 'medical' problems by social movements, patient advocates or the relevant professions. The history of medical approaches to drug use in the United States belies any simple account of the migration of responsibility from law enforcement to medical professionals. Groups seeking to reduce the public health consequences and social, economic and health effects of drug use via pharmacotherapies, the 'medical model', public health interventions, or other treatment technologies have coexisted within waves of criminalisation. As the social processes, specific practices and forms of knowledge that constitute individual 'addicts', criminalisation and medicalisation are co-constitutive, and they in turn co-produce the very forms of addicted subjectivity to which they are said to respond.

The term 'co-production' refers to how 'particular concepts for classifying or ordering social worlds – for example, selfhood, national identity, illness or wellness, professional standing, expertise, citizenship – gain or have gained, stability and coherence – along with equally particular expressions of knowledge' such as 'addiction'.[2] When 'addicts' categorise themselves as such, they inevitably draw from the medical, pharmacological and criminal registers through which contemporary social orders understand 'addiction', but embedded in these understandings are concepts based on the knowledge and conceptual practices of the past.

Actors within each of the historical moments explored in this chapter held specific ideas about the 'technologies of addiction therapeutics' most appropriate to the modal addicts of their time. The therapeutics available – and the scientific theories and hypotheses on which they were based – shaped the subjectivity and lived experience of addicted persons. Each 'technology of addiction' was in turn linked to 'technolog[ies] of care [that] operationalise [specific forms of] care of the self'.[3] The recent embrace of specific pharmacotherapies carries with it a set of notions about how the brain works, how drugs affect brain and behaviour, and what forms of medicalisation are appropriate. Each technological fix in the medicalisation of addiction creates new subjects and new modes of existence. Scott Vrecko usefully distinguishes between modernist 'social projects of "moulding individuals"' and technological or 'postsocial' projects of modulating specific subjective states. The prevailing forms of 'pharmacological optimism' traced in this chapter shift from modernist moulding to postsocial modulation in which there is 'constant monitoring and correcting only specific parts of (fragmented) subjects'.[4] The current emphasis on specific pharmacotherapies as 'technological fixes' for 'drug problems' dovetails with the perceived need for individuals to modulate their subjective states in accordance with social needs.

Pharmacotherapies arise in social spaces already densely populated with figures and images produced by the preceding technology. For instance, the dominant rendering of the historical experience with morphine maintenance clinics before 1923 made opiate maintenance an unlikely outcome of the 1950s debate between proponents of criminalisation and of medicalisation. By the 1970s, social conditions and political exigencies eased social acceptance of methadone maintenance. Therefore I argue that there have been multiple American approaches to methadone, each of which has constituted subjects differently and addressed different kinds of drug problems. Ongoing attempts to engineer a drug that would work 'better than methadone' accompanied the scaling up of methadone maintenance as a therapy. This chapter locates 'technologies of addiction therapeutics' within the political economy of subjectification in which drugs are constructed as 'good' or 'bad' depending on the specific meanings they enact in policy circles and political, medical and scientific discourse. Medicalisation is interpreted differently depending on whether it involves abstinence from or maintenance on morphine, heroin, methadone or buprenorphine. These pharmacotherapies are not interchangeable as they participate in different moral and political economies, are the fruit of different historical trajectories and constitute different formations of addict-subjects.

Morphine maintenance clinics give way to criminalisation in the United States

Public debate over the therapeutic and social implications of giving addicts 'another poison' in the form of morphine arose in the wake of the Harrison Act (1914), which criminalised narcotics. Municipal clinics were briefly established to maintain addicts on morphine in anticipation of returning morphine-addicted World War I veterans.[5] When few addicted veterans materialised, the clinics closed, but the nation's ongoing romance with opiates did not end as the contours of addict subjectivity shifted from that of hapless 'victim' to 'criminal'. By 1929 US prisons were so overcrowded with Harrison Act violators that Congress authorised construction of two very large, prison-like hospitals in Lexington, Kentucky, and Fort Worth, Texas, to treat and rehabilitate drug addicts.[6] Convicted felons comprised two-thirds of 'inmates' at the narcotic farms, but 'patients' voluntarily seeking treatment were also admitted if they performed their needs for care in accord with the larger society's notions of rehabilitation secured through abstinence. While the 'narcotic farms' were operated jointly by proponents of medicalisation in the United States Public Health Service (USPHS) and the federal Bureau of Prisons, they remained strictly anti-maintenance in philosophy and practice.

The first American approach to methadone: The 'medicalisation' of detoxification

Methadone was introduced into clinical use at the narcotic farms in 1948 to medically assist detoxification. Systematic investigation into various pharmacological agents for managing opiate withdrawal had been under-way at the National Academy of Sciences Committee on Drug Addiction and Narcotics (CDAN) since the 1920s, when it set out to re-engineer the morphine molecule to render it less addictive and thus prevent or 'cure' nar-cotic addiction.[7] This quest bore little fruit until the laboratory at Lexington established the efficacy of methadone in 1947. The CDAN recommended that USPHS scientists at Lexington undertake studies of its tolerance and addic-tion liability, in order to determine how methadone should be controlled. Finding that methadone alleviated the withdrawal symptoms associated with what was then called the 'morphine abstinence syndrome', researchers used methadone for the short-term clinical management of withdrawal on the detoxification wards at Lexington and Fort Worth.

Even as methadone was used to assist patients during detoxification, the USPHS researchers characterised methadone as a highly addictive, 'danger-ous' drug. Renamed the Addiction Research Center (ARC) in 1948, the Lex-ington laboratory was directed by Harris Isbell, an opponent of maintenance, from 1948 to 1963. Unsettled by early findings that former morphine addicts found methadone satisfying even at low doses and experienced euphoria that intensified with increases in dose, he concluded that 'narcotic drug addicts would abuse methadone and would become habituated to it if it were freely available and not controlled'.[8] The laboratory subjects' response to methadone resembled their response to other opiates; some could not differentiate between the effects of morphine and methadone. All subjects preferred the 'new synthetic drug' (methadone) to alcohol, barbiturates and cannabis, and one said, 'That was great stuff. I wouldn't have believed it was possible for a synthetic drug to be so like morphine. Can you get it outside? Will it be put under the narcotic law? I wish I could get some to kick my next habit.'[9] Such evidence convinced researchers that methadone could be abused; they were not surprised when primary methadone addicts began showing up for admission to the narcotic farms.

ARC researchers considered methadone's pharmacological profile that of an especially dangerous drug. They conveyed this conclusion to Amer-ican physicians, who first heard methadone characterised as an addiction-producing drug to be prescribed as cautiously as morphine. The notoriously anti-maintenance director of the Federal Bureau of Narcotics (FBN), Harry J. Anslinger, regularly attended CDAN meetings with Lexington researchers and argued for bringing so-called synthetics, including methadone, under international control. Regardless of whether such actors favoured bring-ing drug addiction under police or medical control, they were not propo-nents of opiate maintenance due to concerns about non-medical use. Hence American physicians steered clear of methadone, depriving addicted persons of medically assisted detoxification anywhere except the federal narcotic farms.

Mid-twentieth-century definitional disputes: Drug addiction – crime or disease?

During the 1950s a lively debate commenced in the United States as to whether drug addiction should be approached as crime or disease. Maintenance policy was reconsidered as an option by several professional associations and committees, but it was assumed that the maintenance agent would be morphine or heroin – not methadone. As a result of these public debates over maintenance, addicted persons began presenting themselves as 'sick' and explaining criminal activities as 'symptoms' of an 'illness' for which they needed 'treatment', not 'punishment'. Despite reconsideration of maintenance, law enforcement proponents of criminalisation prevailed in labelling it as 'foreign' to American values and mandated minimum sentences for narcotics offences in 1951. This incursion into judicial autonomy angered the American Bar Association (ABA), which requested a congressional review of federal drug policy. Organised medicine was also divided over maintenance. A 1955 report from the prestigious New York Academy of Medicine argued that addicts were 'sick' persons, rather than criminals, who should be allowed to maintain themselves through a system of low-cost dispensaries managed by the federal government. In 1961 the ABA and American Medical Association (AMA) jointly released a controversial report that advocated maintenance clinics.[10] USPHS clinicians and researchers, most of whom were physicians, distinguished their medical approach from medical maintenance by pointing to the failure of the morphine maintenance clinics and drawing negative associations with the so-called British system (i.e. heroin maintenance managed by physicians[11]). Neither law nor medicine united to favour maintenance, but both harboured prominent critics of the punitive direction of US drug policy.

Law enforcement was the most powerful constituency influencing the direction of US drug policy in the 1950s. In 1955–56 Senator Price Daniel (a Republican from Texas) convened senate hearings, called Illicit Narcotics Traffic,[12] in seven cities, staging the conflict between 'law enforcement' and 'medicine' before a national television audience. He assembled an imposing array of expert witnesses from the National Institutes of Mental Health (NIMH) and USPHS, who met in New York City in June 1955 to respond to the New York Academy of Medicine's controversial report. According to Daniel, the Academy advocated gratifying the desires of addicts through the provision of free drugs.[13] This system stood in stark contrast to the federal narcotic farms, which opposed dispensing narcotics beyond a brief period of detoxification.

Most of the nation's most prominent experts on drug addiction opposed maintenance, but favoured treatment by physicians. Robert H. Felix, NIMH director and chair of the AMA Committee on Narcotic Drugs, considered the addict to be an 'inadequately adjusted individual not radically different from his non-addicted fellows, who has at some time discovered that drugs either dulled the sense of discomfort produced by his difficulties, or gave him a subjective feeling of mastery over his situation'.[14] Felix argued there was a governmental obligation to rehabilitate the addict.[15] By contrast, Daniel wanted to lock up 'untreatables' and:

> take them off the streets, set up some place to have them go and get a chance for treatment, and then if they won't take it, and you cannot do anything with them, then, it seems to me, it is just as humane to put them into some kind of colony or some kind of farm or institution like you do mental patients. It is just as humane as the way we treat mental patients, it seems to me, after you have decided that there is just no way to help them any further; you cannot treat them any more.[16]

While Felix and colleagues believed that addicts were treatable – indeed Felix pointed out to Senator Daniel that treating the untreatable was his 'special hobby' – they also believed that most addicts were 'weak' people who made poor treatment prospects.[17] The USPHS remained committed to rehabilitation of the whole person and did not consider Daniel's proposal to warehouse 'untreatables' to be a humane course of action. Nor did they consider opiate maintenance to be a viable form of treatment.

Advocates of the medical model instead pursued research to find non-addicting analgesic that would prevent or 'cure' addiction – not maintain it.[18] Medicalisation in the 1950s often simply meant treating addicts with compassion.[19] However, the result of the Daniel hearings was the punitive Narcotic Control Act (1956), which guaranteed that by the end of the 1950s the subject formation of the addicted person remained that of the 'criminal'. In the wake of the punitive regime set in place by the late 1950s, the US medical community was left sharply divided over the question of maintenance.

An 'unending jam of drug addicts': Calls for a 'medical approach' in the 1960s

In 1962 the US Supreme Court ruled against the criminalisation of a condition, status or affliction: 'Prosecution for addiction, with its resulting stigma and irreparable damage to the good name of the accused, cannot be justified as a means of protecting society, where civil commitment [an approach adopted in the mental health field] would do as well.'[20] The decision paved the way for civil commitment laws passed in the 1960s, but was silent on the topic of maintenance. In 1963 the AMA defined maintenance as unethical on grounds that physicians who maintained patients on opiate drugs were not making a 'bona fide attempt at cure'. On 15 July 1964 President Johnson ordered that the full power of the federal government be directed towards destroying illegal trafficking, preventing drug abuse and the 'cure and rehabilitation of victims of drug trafficking'. Rehabilitation was defined to exclude maintenance – again, because maintenance was not considered curative.

Proponents of a 'public health approach' believed that the punitive approaches of the 1950s were failing. Police official Richard Kuh declared, 'We in New York law enforcement have not got used to the unending jam of drug addicts that fills our courts week after week, year after year. And we have decided to do something about it.'[21] The landmark federal civil commitment law passed in 1966 was understood as marking a fundamental move away from criminalisation. Speaking at a conference entitled 'The Institute on Rehabilitation of the Drug Addict', held at the Fort Worth Narcotic Farm in 1966, Earle V. Simrell of the USPHS pointed out that medicalising the drug problem was simply catching up with those who had authorised the narcotic farms in 1929: 'If a label is necessary for this new approach, perhaps a better one would be a "public health approach", since the basic philosophy of public health is harmonizing the science and art of medicine with the requirements and instruments of a social order.' Medicalisation was harnessed to the project of normalisation in order to give addicts 'maximum opportunity ... to achieve a normal life'.[22]

Despite the critiques of criminalisation and support for medicalisation, those working closely with addicts – administrators, clinicians and researchers at the federal hospitals – opposed both civil commitment and methadone maintenance. Dole and Nyswander's 1965 report on the successful rehabilitation of their initial 22 patients occasioned great distress in the rehabilitation community. Dole dispatched medical colleague Joyce Lowinson to publicise the positive results at the drug rehabilitation conference referred to above. Throughout the conference, methadone maintenance was criticised for failing to intervene in the addict's 'value system': 'How can a pill alter an addict's perception of himself in the world, provide him with the conscience our civilization demands, with a sense of responsibility that is required to function in our society?'[23]

Rehabilitation was understood as a technique for instilling self-governance and 'normal functioning' in addicted persons, who were constructed as lacking the precise modes of 'conscience', 'responsibility' and 'self-perception' deemed necessary for civilisation. Treatment providers doubted that a mere 'pill' could achieve this. Their exceedingly anti-maintenance stance was consistent with the tenets of abstinence central to US drug policy.

The 'narcotic blockade': The second American approach to methadone

Given the anti-maintenance sentiments of the 1960s, how did the second American approach to methadone – methadone maintenance – come to dominate by the mid-1970s? Redefining addiction as a metabolic disease or biochemical process, Dole and Nyswander presented methadone as a *medication* that worked to 'block the normal reactions of addicts to heroin and permit them to live as normal citizens in the community'.[24] They constructed addicts as 'functionally disabled' because they had little time to lead normal lives. Dole was a respected Rockefeller Institute specialist on appetite, hunger and satiation in obesity and metabolic disease, whose model of addiction was based on his knowledge of diabetes. He consulted Nyswander, a key figure in the transition between psychiatric constructions of addictive disease and metabolic, biochemical and behavioural constructions.[25]

Dole characterised the failure of the ARC researchers to see methadone's potential as a maintenance agent as arising from their failure to relate to *patients*. According to him, the ARC researchers took a 'guinea pig attitude' towards subjects that prevented them from establishing the 'cooperative relationships with patients' necessary for rehabilitation.[26] Those promulgating the view of the first American approach to methadone cast it as a dangerous drug, and were in turn represented by those advocating the second American approach to methadone as members of a conservative 'research establishment' that had missed an exciting opportunity to truly rehabilitate American addicts.

Dole and Nyswander billed methadone not only as an effective treatment for heroin addiction but also as a pragmatic tool for reducing crime. According to Joseph, 'methadone maintenance did not expand because society wanted to provide treatment for heroin addicts. To the contrary, the main concern was reducing the number of crimes committed by addicts.'[27] Methadone was seen by the Nixon administration as a solution to the anticipated problem of heroin-addicted Vietnam veterans returning to the States in the midst of a domestic crime wave. Such rapid expansion of free-standing methadone maintenance clinics was not Dole's plan: he felt that too many people adhered to abstinence rather than maintenance, and that the expansion of clinical competence was too incremental to support such rapid institutionalisation. Finally, he believed that methadone enabled the federal government to make an unprecedented entry into medical practice.[28]

Dole and Nyswander's maintenance regimes and the ideas and metaphors underlying it resonated with the new generation of American addiction researchers, who parleyed the second American approach to methadone into a forced sea change in how 'addiction' was viewed in the American political system. By the mid-1970s the use of methadone as a maintenance drug began to displace and stand in for all modes of *successful* rehabilitation in the drug policy and research community. At the same time, 'methadone maintenance' remained words unspoken in mainstream medicine, stigmatised almost from the outset.[29] Methadone reached US consumers outside routine medical practice; its regulation made it 'untouchable' for self-respecting physicians. To remedy this problem Dole and Nyswander proposed that medically stable and employed patients be treated routinely in private medical practice and removed from the 'rigid clinical reporting system that compromised their confidentiality': '[Long-term maintenance] is seen as suggesting a certain lack of personal integrity on the part of these clients as compared with clients who have become abstinent. It is as if "treatment" or "cure" is incomplete until the client is completely drug free.'[30]

The second American approach to methadone was rapidly transcended by criticisms issuing from multiple constituencies. Offered as a 'technological fix', its chief proponents saw it as the basis for a 'complex rehabilitation routine',[31] but this view was never widely held. While methadone maintenance was used by proponents of the second American approach to methadone to redefine heroin addiction as a medical problem, it was also seen as a quick fix focused merely on the addict's physiological needs, the most manageable parts of the complex problems represented by addiction. An early analysis of the limitations of methadone maintenance as a 'technological fix' noted that problems approached technologically had to be more precisely defined than was the case with the heroin problem.[32] Indeed, Nelkin came to consider methadone maintenance as a short-term form of management that failed to address less manageable, longer-term and more fundamental questions. The political will, trust and social acceptance required for methadone to be deployed as a technological tool for the remaking and ongoing modulation of addicted selves failed to materialise. Indeed, the second American approach to methadone enabled a modernist form of medicalisation that moulded its subjects only insofar as regulatory strictures permitted. A new mode of addicted subjectivity arose in which addicts were not 'criminals' but 'dysfunctional' in ways that could be 'managed' with methadone.

Alternatives to methadone: The re-emergence of medical management

Therapeutic goals had been deeply intertwined with drug development in the public health arena since the search for the 'bee without the sting' began (the phrase was used by founding ARC director Clifton Himmelsbach to refer to a 'morphine substitute' that would eliminate medical need for this most 'troublesome' compound). Treatment of addictive disorders involved notions of moral purity to which the promotion of abstinence replied. The quest for a non-addicting analgesic was both preventive and curative: to prevent new cases of narcotic addiction, to 'cure' existing cases and to deliver effective analgesia without risk of addiction or dependence. But the goal of the search for the 'bee without the sting' was at odds with abstinence.

During the 1960s addiction pharmacologists turned to a promising class of drugs called 'narcotic antagonists', known to combat respiratory depression consequent to opiate overdose. They theorised that opiates exerted their effects on the central nervous system by wholly or partially occupying brain 'receptors'. Hoping to find an addiction pharmacotherapy that did not simply 'blockade' effects but allowed some effects and not others, they had invested more than three decades of scientific resources in research activity by the time Dole and Nyswander advanced the second American approach to methadone. In the 1970s the search for a pharmacological agent to prevent or cure opioid dependence was implicated in molecular pharmacology.[33] Initially centred on modifications of the morphine molecule, the search migrated to notions that some magical mixture could be compounded along with an opiate. For instance, in the 1950s, Isbell had suggested that the narcotic antagonist nalorphine might be used for this purpose. The idea of treatment based on the concept of opiate antagonism took hold slowly. Taking over the ARC after Isbell's retirement in 1963, William R. Martin hypothesised the existence of multiple opiate receptors well before 'receptor theory' was widely accepted when he recognised that nalorphine worked differently from morphine, and advanced the concept of antagonist effects.

There was one big problem with narcotic antagonists such as naltrexone, cyclazocine and nalorphine: they were and are not well liked by human subjects. Searching for a compound to make narcotic antagonists more acceptable to patients, Martin persuaded Endo Products in Westbury, New York, to add the narcotic antagonist naloxone to cyclazocine, classified as a mixed agonist/antagonist. He thought that addiction treatment could potentially be based on the pharmacological concepts of 'receptor dualism' or 'competitive antagonism', in which a drug occupies a particular receptor and 'competes' with surrounding agonists. Simply 'blocking' psychoactive effects was insufficient 'treatment' for people actively seeking these very effects. For instance, naltrexone should have been the pharmacologically 'perfect' anti-addiction drug, but in retrospect 'turns out to be too non-addicting' for those prescribed it.[34]

The ethos of pharmacological optimism shifted towards mixed drug profiles – the 'partial agonists' or 'mixed agonist/antagonists' – and was reinforced as 'receptors' became more 'real' and efforts to find a 'magic bullet', to use Nobel Laureate Paul Ehrlich's term, intensified. Methadone was disclaimed as a 'magic bullet' almost from the outset of the institutionalisation of the second American approach to methadone. Pharmaceutical houses innovating in the analgesic area routinely supplied compounds to enable Martin and others to conduct basic explorations of the pharmacologic properties of antagonists, agonists, and partial and mixed agonist/antagonists, all of which they observed operating differently at the receptor level. The most promising candidate drug of the 1970s was buprenorphine (a partial agonist), which was found to produce a 'lesser maximal effect' than heroin or morphine – a ceiling preventing the 'high' but suppressing the discomfort of opiate abstinence.

Doubtless the first suggestion that buprenorphine had clinical application not simply as an analgesic but also as an addiction treatment came from Donald Jasinski, who began his career at the ARC in 1963 working with naloxone because of its 'pure competitive antagonism'. Aware that a compound could appear effective in theory but fail in clinical practice, Jasinski saw in buprenorphine a compound that did not have dysphoric effects while reducing euphoric effects. Most importantly for public health and unlike most opiates, buprenorphine did not depress respiratory function – as Jasinski said, 'everyone was fascinated that you could push the dose [of buprenorphine] and not kill people'.[35] He conducted the first direct addiction studies involving buprenorphine in 1977 at Lexington, hoping to show that it was 'a better drug than methadone, a longer-acting partial agonist with greater safety, relative non-toxicity, morphine-like subjective effects to act as a reinforcer, and an effective blocking agent'.[36] Such thinking propelled buprenorphine to its current pride of place as a global 'technology of addiction' central to re-engineering 'medical maintenance therapy' in the USA.

The concept of medicalisation embodied in medical maintenance therapy with buprenorphine was remodelled so as to avoid the perceived pitfalls of methadone maintenance. As shown above, the regulation of methadone maintenance was set up in ways that discouraged mainstream medical professionals from taking much interest in it. However, methadone maintenance therapy (MMT) helped shift the meaning of medicalisation to specific *medications* and away from holistic notions of rehabilitation. Today, the medicalisation of addiction therapeutics has narrowed to a conversation about molecules acting at receptor sites – methadone versus buprenorphine; the former heavy with the burdens of its past and the latter promoted as the bee without the sting.

Conclusion

New forms of subjectivity arose with each new technology of addiction. In the era of the morphine maintenance clinics, addicted persons were initially treated as 'needy' victims of unscrupulous physicians and drug traffickers. The first American approach to methadone helped turn them from unfortunate 'victims' to 'criminals', while prosecution turned their doctors into criminals and deterred physicians from treating them as patients. In the mid-twentieth century, addicted persons presented themselves as 'patients' who were 'sick' and in need of 'treatment' rather than 'punishment'. They were met with a mode of rehabilitation that emphasised their deviance from social norms. The second American approach to methadone came about as a way to restore human dignity and 'normal functioning' to 'patients' in drug treatment, but it was delivered in a form that magnified stigma and spoiled 'patient' identity formation. The major change wrought by methadone maintenance was entailed in its construction as a medication for a chronic illness, rather than as a 'cure'. As those subject to 'technologies of addiction' began to think of themselves not simply as 'patients' but as lifelong 'consumers' of a socially approved substance, medicalisation has transmuted into pharmaceuticalisation.

Office-based medical management through drugs other than methadone is the result of conceptual, methodological, legal and political shifts, as well as new technologies. The unmistakable emphasis on rehabilitating the whole person that prevails at the narcotic farms contrasts markedly with the fragmented subject of today, in which specific parts of the brain – not the 'person' – are targeted for modulation and the 'patient' is represented as a 'consumer' of legal pharmaceutical drugs.[37]

Will the United States witness the birth of a new American approach to methadone in which it is but one choice among many? What discourses, policies and practices will the globalisation of buprenorphine – either its 'pure' form, Subutex or mixed with naloxone, Suboxone – yield in terms of new subject formations, and how will they be positioned in relation to 'addiction'? What new addict subject formations will be produced through interaction with international harm reduction movements, human rights discourse or the pharmaceutical industry?

Acknowledgements

Nancy D. Campbell thanks the following for shaping her thinking on the history of medications development: Don Jasinski, Jerome H. Jaffe, Ed Johnson, Herman Joseph, John Lewis, Jewell Sloan and Jim Woods. For productive and ongoing conversations about the meanings of these medicines and the efforts to develop them, she thanks Helena Hansen, Anne Lovell, Todd Meyers, Samuel Roberts and Scott Vrecko. For time and space to think and write, she thanks Ned Woodhouse, Grace Campbell Woodhouse and Isaac Campbell Eglash.

Notes

1   Conrad, *The Medicalization of Society*, p. 7.
2   Jasanoff, *States of Knowledge*, p. 5.
3   Fraser & valentine, *Substance and Substitution*, p. 60.
4   Vrecko, 'Therapeutic justice in drug courts', p. 219.
5   Waldorf, Orlick & Reinarman, *Morphine Maintenance*.
6   Campbell, *Discovering Addiction*; Campbell, Olsen & Walden, *The Narcotic Farm*.
7   Acker, *Creating the American Junkie*.
8   Isbell, Wikler, Eddy et al., 'Tolerance and addiction liability of 6-Dimethylamino-4-4-Diphenylheptanone-3 (Methadon)', p. 892.
9   Ibid., p. 892.
10   ABA/AMA, *Drug Addiction*.
11   See Mold, *Heroin*.
12   US Congress, Senate Subcommittee on Improvements to the Criminal Code on the Judiciary, *The Illicit Narcotics Traffic* (hereafter 'US Congress, Senate Subcommittee').
13   Ibid., Part 4, p. 1966.
14   Felix, 'An appraisal of the personality types of the addict'.
15   US Congress, Senate Subcommittee, Part 4, p. 1479.
16   Ibid., p. 1496.
17   Ibid., p. 1487.
18   Acker, *Creating the American Junkie*.
19   For example Nyswander, *The Drug Addict as Patient*.
20   *Robinson v. California* 1962, p. 677.
21   Quoted in Simrell, 'New laws for drug addicts', pp. 31–2.
22   Ibid., p. 32.
23   Sells, *Rehabilitating the Narcotics Addict*, p. 378.
24   Dole, 'Thoughts on narcotics addiction'; Dole, Nyswander & Kreek, 'Narcotic blockade', p. 304.
25   Courtwright, 'The prepared mind'.
26   Courtwright, Joseph & Des Jarlais, *Addicts Who Survived*, p. 336.
27   Joseph, 'Medical methadone maintenance'.
28   Courtwright, Joseph & Des Jarlais, *Addicts Who Survived*, p. 341.
29   Joseph, 'Medical methadone maintenance'.
30   Ibid.
31   Nelkin, *Methadone Maintenance*, p. 4.
32   Ibid., p. 5.
33   See Keane, *What's Wrong with Addiction?* (p. 39), for an account of how 'addiction' has been bound to an addict's body and brain by medicoscientific texts presuming 'pharmacological determinism' as their starting point.
34   Ibid., p. 32.
35   Donald Jasinski, author's interview, 2003.
36   Ibid.
37   Vrecko, 'Therapeutic justice in drug courts', p. 219.

References

Acker, C.J. (2002). *Creating the American Junkie: Addiction Research in the Classic Era of Narcotics Control*. Baltimore, MD: Johns Hopkins University Press.

American Bar Association/American Medical Association (1961). *Drug Addiction: Crime or Disease?* Bloomington, IN: Indiana University Press.

Campbell, N.D. (2007). *Discovering Addiction: The Science and Politics of Substance Abuse Research*. Ann Arbor, MI: University of Michigan Press.

Campbell, N.D., Olsen, J.P., & Walden, L. (2008). *The Narcotic Farm: The Rise and Fall of America's First Prison for Drug Addicts*. New York: Harry N. Abrams.

Conrad, P. (2007). *The Medicalization of Society*. Baltimore, MD: Johns Hopkins University Press.

Courtwright, D.C. (1992). The prepared mind: Marie Nyswander, methadone maintenance, and the metabolic theory of addiction. *Addiction*, 92(3): 257–65.

Courtwright, D.C., Joseph, H., & Des Jarlais, D. (1989). *Addicts Who Survived: An Oral History of Narcotic Use in America, 1923–1965*. Knoxville: University of Tennessee Press.

Dole, V.P. (1965). Thoughts on narcotics addiction. *Bulletin of the New York Academy of Medicine*, 41(2): 211–13.

Dole, V.P., Nyswander, M.E. & Kreek, M.J. (1966). *Narcotic Blockade. Archives of Internal Medicine*, 118: 304–9.

Felix, R.H. (1944). An appraisal of the personality types of the addict. *American Journal of Psychiatry*, 100(4): 462–7.

Fraser, S., & valentine, k. (2008). *Substance and Substitution: Methadone Subjects in Liberal Societies*. Basingstoke, UK: Palgrave Macmillan.

Isbell, H., Wikler, A., Eddy, N.B., et al. (1947). Tolerance and addiction liability of 6-Dimethylamino-4-4-Diphenylheptanone-3 (Methadon). *Journal of the American Medical Association*, 135(14): 888–94.

Jasanoff, S. (2004). *States of Knowledge: The Co-Production of Science and Social Order*. New York: Routledge.

Joseph, H. (1995). Medical methadone maintenance: The further concealment of a stigmatized condition. PhD diss. City University of New York. Retrieved 30 March 2011. http://cdrwg.8k.com/stigma01.htm.

Keane, H. (2002). *What's Wrong with Addiction?* New York: New York University Press.

Mold, A. (2008). *Heroin: The Treatment of Addiction in Twentieth-Century Britain*. DeKalb, IL: Northern Illinois Press.

Nelkin, D. (1973). *Methadone Maintenance: A Technological Fix*. New York: George Braziller.

Nyswander, M.E. (1956). *The Drug Addict as Patient*. New York: Grune & Stratton.

Rose, N. (2007). Beyond medicalisation. *Lancet*, 369(9562): 700–2.

Sells, S.B. (ed.) (1966). *Rehabilitating the Narcotics Addict*. Washington, DC: US Department of Health, Education and Welfare.

Simrell, E.V. (1966). New laws for drug addicts, rehabilitating the narcotics addict. S.B. Sells (ed.). *Rehabilitating the Narcotics Addict* (pp. 31–48). Washington, DC: US Department of Health, Education & Welfare.

US Congress, Senate Subcommittee on Improvements to the Criminal Code of the Committee on the Judiciary (1955). *The Illicit Narcotics Traffic*. 84th Congress, 1st session. Washington, DC: Government Printing Office.

valentine, k., & Fraser, S. (2008). Trauma, damage and pleasure: Rethinking problematic drug use. *International Journal of Drug Policy*, 19(5): 410–16.

Vrecko, S. 2009. Therapeutic justice in drug courts: Crime, punishment and societies of control. *Science as Culture*, 18(2): 217–32.

Waldorf, D., Orlick, M., & Reinarman, C. (1974). *Morphine Maintenance: The Shreveport Clinic, 1919–1923*. Washington, DC: Drug Abuse Council.

Pharmacotherapy as social policy, or, the public and private worlds of welfare capitalism

kylie valentine

We begin with the apparent paradox of Sweden and Australia. Australian social policy researchers, especially those who are concerned with poverty, equality and population well-being, are used to hearing (and telling) a familiar story about the difference between Australia and Sweden. The story goes like this: Australia and Sweden are at two ends of the welfare state spectrum.[1] Sweden provides a universal system of cash and non-cash benefits, a system of contributory finance and extensive state intervention to maintain full employment. The most effective test of a commitment to equality and protection against poverty is a country's treatment of those without paid work – typically children, the elderly, people with illness and disability, and their carers. In Sweden, substantial resources are dedicated to these groups. Only 4 per cent of Swedish children live in poverty (3 per cent of households with children), compared to 12 per cent of Australian children (10 per cent of households with children).[2] Adult joblessness is a much greater risk for child poverty in Australia than in Sweden: 13 per cent of Swedish households with children and no working adult are poor, compared to 43 per cent of Australian households.[3] Parental leave after the birth of a baby is offered to Swedish workers for 480 days, the first 390 at 80 per cent of income.[4] Assistance for the elderly is based on an assessment of needs and ranges from home-based care to residential and institutional care, for which recipients pay according to their income and needs.[5]

In contrast, Australia is characterised by a tightly targeted and incomes-tested system of benefits. Universal paid parental leave will be introduced in Australia for the first time in 2011, at a far lower rate than in Sweden. Australia is a low social spender on family benefits and old-age pensions, and poverty rates for older people are among the highest in the OECD (only Korea, Mexico and Ireland have higher rates).[6]

In Gøsta Esping-Andersen's influential formulation, Sweden is a paradig-matic *social democratic* regime;[7] that is, it is egalitarian and universalistic, and labour is decommodified: standard of living is not dependent on labour market status. In contrast, Australia is a classic *liberal* welfare state. It encour-ages market provision of services and has very low decommodification. In welfare state terms, Sweden has long appeared (perhaps especially to the non-Swedish) as a bastion of social rights and equity, committed to alternatives to market labour and the well-being of those who are most vulnerable.

Australian researchers of illicit drug use, especially those concerned with access to services based on harm reduction principles (e.g. clean injecting equipment and pharmacotherapy treatment programs such as methadone), are used to a far different story about the difference between Australia and Sweden. Australia was an international pioneer in harm reduction when the AIDS pandemic emerged.[8] It remains committed, albeit with torturous logic and internal contradictions, to strategies that have been shown to reduce the harm associated with drug use and that do not require abstinence from drugs. Opioid pharmacotherapy (specifically methadone maintenance pro-grams) and needle and syringe programs prevented the social catastrophe of HIV that occurred elsewhere, especially in the United States. In contrast, Sweden has extremely limited pharmacotherapy programs, almost no nee-dle and syringe exchange program, coercive treatment and a zealous testing regime. Opponents of harm reduction in Australia cite Sweden, with weari-some frequency, as a model of drugs policy that Australia should adopt. The overarching drug policy framework is expressed through the Panglossian motto adopted by the Swedish parliament in the 1970s: 'Sweden, a drug-free society'.[9]

What analytics might be deployed to make sense of these two, seemingly contradictory, stories of Sweden and Australia? How can Sweden be, on the one hand, the dream of a social democratic state realised and, on the other, a regime in which drug users are far more likely to be sent to prison than offered a maintenance treatment program? By what logic is Australia, on the one hand, far more ruthless in its treatment of the vulnerable and, on the other, flexible and pragmatic in its treatment of that most maligned and vulnerable group, illicit drug users? This chapter is concerned with two primary tasks. The first is an exploration of these questions, although I make no attempt at answers, only to argue that drug researchers should be interested in them. The second is to consider why these questions are asked so rarely, and why analysis of drug treatment and broader social policies remains incipient at best.

The chapter is concerned with harm reduction, specifically opioid pharmacotherapy, viewed in a social policy context. I consider pharmacotherapy from relatively unusual vantage points. The first of these is scientist social policy and its relationship to research, or 'evidence-based' policy. The established effectiveness of pharmacotherapy in these terms, I argue, may have occluded consideration of other questions. One alternative to evidence-based policy is human rights, but the approach I take here is the more avowedly political and quotidian framework of feminist welfare state analysis. This framework points to the significance of the relationship between private and public concerns, and to the importance of participation and advocacy in public policy development. As all of these are critical to the delivery of pharmacotherapy, I argue that lessons from feminist analysis of work, care, markets and the state could be usefully applied to analysis of pharmacotherapy and to drug policy more broadly.

Social policy and pharmacotherapy

Intuitively, social policy, in its broadest terms, would seem to be important to the welfare of illicit drug users. The role of the state and market and the interlocking activities of both, in meeting their needs, matter enormously. Employment, income support, parenting and family payments, disability policies, carer payments and housing policies have a material influence on the well-being of users, many of whom occupy vulnerable positions in the labour market. Pharmacotherapy clients in particular exemplify the impact of a broad range of public policies to drug use. This chapter will focus on these clients, but most of its arguments could apply to other drug users as well.

In focus

Pharmacotherapy

Pharmacotherapy is drug-based treatment for drug dependence. The best known is methadone maintenance treatment, which is prescribed to people dependent on heroin and other opiods. The phrase is worth parsing: methadone is a synthetic opiate that is chemically similar to heroin but has a much longer half-life and so requires less frequent administration. Medications taken for maintenance treatment are consumed over a long period. In clinical contexts such as oncology, maintenance treatment may be used to keep the symptoms of a disease under control or to prevent its return. Methadone maintenance treatment, then, involves the prescription of opioid drugs to people who are identified as opioid-dependent, over a long period. In common with other maintenance programs, clients are given a prescription by a medical practitioner, dosed at community pharmacies or clinics, and pay for the drug.[a] Maintenance treatment is distinguished from drug-based detoxification programs, and other rehabilitation programs, in that the aim of the program is not to establish abstinence from drugs. Instead, it is designed to bring about relief from the symptoms associated with dependence such as craving, and improve social functioning and participation. Pharmacotherapy clients are expected to – and do – participate in paid work and education, raise their children safely without intensive support, and desist from any illegal activities in which they were previously engaged. As a treatment modality, pharmacotherapy is longstanding, effective and widely used[b] but also controversial.[c] Critics of harm reduction and advocates of abstinence argue against its use on the basis that treatment should make users 'free' of drugs. Other criticisms focus on its stigmatising and pacifying effects.[d] Methadone is sometimes diverted to unauthorised uses (street sale, injection, hoarding) which can lead to death from overdose,[e] and this also adds to the controversy associated with pharmacotherapy.

a See Fraser & valentine, *Substance and Substitution*.
b WHO & UNODC, 'Substitution maintenance therapy in the management of opioid dependence and HIV/AIDS prevention'.
c See chapter 7.
d Bourgois, 'Disciplining addictions'.
e Caplehorn & Drummer, 'Fatal methadone toxicity'.

Pharmacotherapy clients therefore occupy a unique position among drug users. They traverse the private and public spheres and the boundaries between illicit and legal drug use. Unlike those users of drugs (legal or not) who are untroubled by supply problems, dependence or other harms, pharmacotherapy clients have, by definition, experienced problematic drug use. As clients of health services, they do not rely entirely on the market but also have a relationship with state provision and regulation. Whereas illicit drug use is sometimes discussed as though it were primarily a problem of crime and policing, pharmacotherapy clients are clearly subject to health policy as well. As clients of health services, pharmacotherapy clients also have interests in the intersection of health and employment policies, in the quality of the treatment they receive from health practitioners and in the cost of their treatment. Despite this, they are most familiarly constructed under the fairly narrow rubric of risk (of relapse, overdose or crime). A growing number of studies examine specific policies, for example, the influence of welfare-to-work policies on methadone clients[10] and the difficulties of managing care and work responsibilities with methadone dosing regimes.[11] Sustained, systematic analysis of drug treatment as a question of social policy, however, is very rare. Equally, critical social research on pharmacotherapy emphasises the importance of privacy, relationships and choice to the experience of pharmacotherapy. These concerns are often neglected in social policy research, with the important exception of feminist research, a point to which I return shortly.

Integrated policies?

Two recent Australian policy documents illustrate the narrowness of policy frames within which illicit drug use and treatment are typically apprehended, and the difficulties that result. A consultation paper for the development of the next phase of the national drug strategy calls for a whole-of-government, cross-sectoral approach. Perhaps tellingly, however, no new cross-agency bodies or protocols are proposed to resource or monitor this ambition. Instead, the processes by which it would be achieved are the basis of consultation questions: 'How can structures and processes under the National Drug Strategy more effectively engage with sectors outside health, law enforcement and education? Which sectors will be particularly important for the National Drug Strategy to engage with?'[12] In its submission to the strategy, responding to the consultation paper, the Australian Injecting and Illicit Drug Users League (AIVL), the peak national body for illicit drug users and drug treatment consumers, supports the inclusion of expertise in human rights, health promotion, social policy, health literacy and cultural diversity in the strategy. AIVL also expresses alarm, however, at the specific current manifestations of inter-sectoral language in drug policy and treatment; that is, the importation of terms 'from the mental health and disability sectors'. Of particular concern is the increase in the use of the term 'carers' in AOD strategies.[13] AIVL argues that placing carers as central figures to drug policy is both misleading, as most users do not have or need carers, and concerning, as it indicates that policy responsibility for drug users may be shifting back to the mental health and disability service sectors and policy arenas.

These documents demonstrate, then, that policy-makers and peak bodies both recognise that drug users are affected by policies other than health and policing and illustrate the constraints on change. Even with the aspiration to broaden the scope of analytic focus to policy portfolios other than health and policing, the means by which this could be done remain, apparently, mysterious and subject to further inquiry. Where new language is used, and new agents and interests are incorporated into drug policy frameworks, it is based on borrowing from inappropriate domains.

What is behind this narrowness of focus? Why does this narrowness of focus fail even, for the most part, to be noticed? Why are social and drug policies so rarely in conversation with each other, and why are the kinds of questions that emerge from the Sweden–Australia paradox so rarely considered? One answer is the split between health and social policy, a split that is as important to academic disciplines as it is to policy portfolios. Harm reduction first emerged as a public health framework and remains most influential in these terms. In Australia at least, much of the traffic between policy-relevant research and government is directed through health departments. Social policy research, especially welfare regime analysis, has historically been influenced by disciplines other than health, especially economics. Much of Australia's social policy research circulates from and to government departments with responsibility for employment, welfare and families.

Analysing policy (1): Evidence-based policy

These disciplinary boundaries are not, however, the whole story. Probably the most important factor behind the failure of drugs research to take a broad policy view (and for social policy research to engage in drugs research in any meaningful way) is that both public health research and social policy research are dominated by a relentless empiricism and epidemiological thrust that has, in recent years, been strengthened by the rubric of evidence-based policy. The kind of research that tends to be highly valued for policy-makers gives specific, quantitative answers to a defined set of questions, constructed along the lines of portfolio responsibilities: crime to justice and attorneys-general departments, disease to health and so on. The questions that have been asked most often in recent terms about drug users include:

- Who commits crime?
- What prevents crime?
- Who is at risk of contracting illness x?
- What will prevent the transmission of illness x?

This sort of question requires, of course, certain assumptions: that terms such as 'criminal' are stable and objective, and that individual people and events can be isolated from their environment for the purposes of assessment and measurement. That these assumptions have been subject to sustained critique for more than 50 years is not so much disputed by policy-makers as entirely irrelevant to the interest they take in research.

In this context, harm reduction is important to policy formation because it provides such a robust answer to the 'what works' questions. Opioid pharmacotherapy meets the criteria for even the most stringent requirements of 'evidence-based' policy,[14] but important questions about autonomy, choice, privacy and the social meanings attached to pharmacotherapy clients are (deliberately) occluded by the methods associated with it. Because of this, and because of the continuing resistance in many quarters to pharmacotherapy despite its efficacy, alternative understandings are needed.

Analysing policy (2): Human rights

An alternative to this scientist social policy approach is that of human rights, which appears to be increasingly attractive to harm reduction advocacy, both as claim-making for individuals and for transnational, universal arguments.[15] To return to the Sweden–Australia paradox, it could be hypothesised that the human rights of drug users are taken more seriously in Australia than Sweden, and that this both acts as a brake on the introduction of the coercive policies Sweden favours and facilitates the availability of pharmacotherapy in Australia. There are, however, difficulties with this hypothesis. For one thing, the level of abstraction needed to consider the claim that Australia *overall* has a more serious approach to the human rights of drug users than Sweden *overall* is probably unworkable. Does (limited) choice of treatment and access to other harm reduction measures trump, in human rights terms, a modest but decent standard of living? Do egalitarian societies enable more authentic human rights for drug users than liberal societies?

Second, the rhetorical – as distinct from legal – power of rights discourse is always substitutable.[16] Every claim about the human rights of users to choose their treatment, or to take whatever drugs they wish, can be countered with an equally emphatic claim about the human rights of users to be drug-free. Insofar as human rights inhere in United Nations conventions and legal frameworks, exactly what the human rights of drug users *are* is always contestable. The incoherent position of the United Nations towards harm reduction exemplifies this: the International Narcotics Control Board routinely castigates governments for such harm reduction measures as medically supervised injecting centres, while other UN agencies, including UNAIDS, UNICEF and the World Health Organisation, accept harm reduction as an effective strategy.[17] Human rights discourses are, in short, very useful as a means to argue for entitlements that can be claimed as universal, apolitical and incontestable. They are less useful as an analytic approach.

Analysing policy (3): States, markets and privacy

A third alternative is expanding welfare regime analysis to incorporate critical insights into gender, agency, embodiment and the private sphere. Feminist critiques of Esping-Andersen's work have begun precisely this task.[18] Although these critiques have not been concerned with drug use, they provide a model for asking questions of a different order from those cited earlier:

- How do different policy spheres (health, education, employment, health, justice) work, individually and as interrelated networks, to construct drug use and users as policy concerns?
- On what basis, and from which standpoints, can drug users make claims on the state for services and policies?
- How do the needs of drug users for treatment services articulate with their entitlements as citizens?
- What is the role of the state in ensuring that pharmacotherapy clients receive quality treatment?

These questions are rarely addressed in either drugs research or welfare research, and neither harm reduction nor human rights seem to be promising vehicles for raising them. Yet these questions are central to the relationship between pharmacotherapy, the state and the market and also suggest a possible alternative to the current positions clients are authorised to adopt as public identities. These positions are something of a double bind in that users are expected to be either experts in harm reduction or mendicants who are defined by their trauma and harms. They are required to be more expert than most people,[19] or seen as so deeply damaged that they are not fully recognised as citizens.[20]

In this regard, welfare regime analysis offers promise in at least two respects. First, it could enrich our understanding of national frameworks by adding a comparative dimension and thereby expanding the frame of reference in which drug policies (and welfare policies) are understood. It could, for example, address questions about the processes behind policy decisions to implement opioid pharmacotherapy and decisions about the nature of that implementation: public expenditure, cost to clients, regulation of dosing, types of treatment services and so on. In the case of Sweden and Australia, this kind of analysis would require scrutiny both of the policy mechanisms by which the social-democratic and liberal regimes are maintained (for example systems of social insurance, protection from the market and investment in full employment) and, just as importantly, of the policy mechanisms by which citizens are constituted and represented (for example regulation and protection of privacy, entitlement to participation and individual choice). Second, it could provide a basis for assessing the influence of policies that does not rely either on special pleading for an exceptional group *or* on a unitary model of citizenship that neglects the particular differences and needs of drug users.

Lessons from 'difference vs equality'

Here is how it could do these things. Feminist welfare regime analysis, and feminist critique of welfare regime models, has shown that gender is a central experiential dimension of the organisation of public expenditure and services. It has also shown that women's position in relation both to the family (unpaid care work) and to the market (paid labour) are affected not only by those policies that are directly targeted at the family and the market, but also by institutional regimes and public services: for example, workplace equality laws, abortion laws and child care. Further, it has shown that the positions from which individuals and groups can make claims on the state are simultaneously constituted by policy frameworks and important in shaping policy frameworks. At different times and in different places, women have been positioned as mothers and as workers. These different positions have been the basis for different claims. Maternalists in the early twentieth century insisted on gender difference and made claims to citizenship based on their capacity to mother;[21] more recent 'femocrat' claims have focused on gender equality and women's economic independence.

These examples of different arguments and standpoints are useful for thinking about drug users and their relationship to the state not because the differences between them have been resolved (they have not) but precisely because they demonstrate, over and over again, the complexities and risks of making a claim on the basis of either difference or equality. Claims for women on the basis of their difference, notably their capacity to mother, are inevitably stratified on the basis of class and have always been stratified on the basis of race, because the children of the elite are valued more highly by states than the children of the poor.[22] Attempting alliances between women based on the fact that they are mothers not only excludes women who are not mothers but also founders on the enormous differences in power and privilege between mothers. On the other hand, claims for women's equality, notably on the basis of their entitlement to economic independence from their families, continue to be fractured by the unequal distribution of unpaid care work between women and men,[23] and by the extent to which unpaid care work props up the *soi disant* independent worker.[24] Attempting alliances between women based on their capacity to perform as equals in the labour market with men founders on the implausibility of a universal model of worker-citizen unencumbered by care responsibilities.

Whether women make claims on the basis of difference or equality, in other words, there will always be costs and risks, including the risk that the category of 'women' as a group will be fragmented by the differential positions of race, class and caring responsibilities. Nonetheless, women's interests are now recognised as central to the organisation of state services and policies. Despite the differences between women and their interests, and despite the ongoing tensions between informal care and economic independence, it would be unthinkable for any state, of any welfare regime type, to abandon policies for women as workers and mothers.

Lessons for drug treatment could be drawn from this. Policy recognition of drug users, especially those in treatment, tends to construct similar dilemmas of difference and equality. Pharmacotherapy clients are either recognised as different from typical workers and citizens and so requiring special treatment, or are enjoined to behave as though they are exactly the same as people not on drug treatment. In the former case, any shared vulnerabilities or service needs work to construct drug users as impaired and requiring particular attention from the state (the Australian government's emphasis on 'carers', which exasperates AIVL, is a current example) or, more commonly, as concatenations of risk: of overdose, of crime, of child abuse, of homelessness.

If, however, the specific needs of clients are not recognised, then there are few avenues for arguing for regulatory or administrative structures (such as privacy and anti-discrimination laws and drug subsidies) that protect their interests.

Feminist welfare regime analysis, and feminist social policy research more generally, demonstrates that these tensions – between equality and difference, and between universality and specificity – do not need to be resolved in order for claims to be made on the basis of interests and entitlements as citizens. (An emergent critical drug research literature demonstrates the same point from a different perspective.[25]) It demonstrates indeed that such resolution is a less urgent task than, on the one hand, advocacy for interests and, on the other, analysis of the risks, trade-offs and interrelationships produced by that advocacy.

The Sweden–Australia paradox: Reprise

In the case of Sweden and Australia, examining not only policies and regulatory frameworks but also participatory mechanisms and spaces for advocacy, begins to illuminate the tensions and interrelationships behind the apparent paradoxes with which this chapter opened. As noted at the outset, public provision of income and services is very important, especially for those who are most vulnerable in relation to the labour market. In these areas, Sweden has a much more egalitarian, universalist framework than Australia (and, it should be said, most other countries as well). In this sense, the entitlements of drug users as citizens are probably better recognised in Sweden because universalism is less stigmatising than residualism and because it produces better outcomes: less poverty, less psychiatric distress, lower infant mortality, higher educational attainment and so on.

Yet public provision is not the full story. When we turn to the question of participation and arguments for special needs as well as universal entitlements, the differences between Sweden and Australia take on a different sheen. Although illicit drug users are vilified in Australia as elsewhere, peer user groups in each state and territory are funded to advance the rights and democratic participation of users in policy-making and service delivery. Australia was one of the first countries to initiate publicly funded peer advocacy groups and remains an international leader in this field. Sweden, with a less developed liberal tradition than Australia and hence with weaker norms of individual rights to freedom from state strictures, has an arguably more authoritarian stance towards users. One consequence of this is that Sweden takes equality more seriously than freedom: the 'welfare state cannot allow people to hurt themselves' as the costs of treatment and economic support are too high, and it remains 'difficult to argue in terms of civil liberties, e.g.

of the limits of state powers in relation to citizens, [which] applies equally to the debate on drug policy'.[26]

When national traditions of participation, regulation and privacy are considered, in other words, the trade-offs and balances between liberal and social democratic regimes become more complex. Regimes like Australia's in which liberalism is firmly entrenched are arguably more serious than Sweden's about the limitations of the state on individual liberty and about civil participation. This is not to be sentimental about liberty, given its place in the same logic that limits the role of the state in providing a social safety net: freedom from the state is also freedom to starve. We need to remember also the elementary Foucauldian point that liberal states deploy a particular kind of governance, rather than simply governing less than other states. Within contemporary liberal states, such concepts as liberty have particular functions, and subjects of these states are 'obliged to be free'.[27]

Notwithstanding this, the emphasis placed on both privacy and participation – a space in which private preferences can be pursued and a space in which public claims can be made – is a distinguishing feature of liberalism, sometimes neglected in critical social research, which warrants consideration in assessing the treatment of drug users in different countries. (So out of favour is liberalism, in fact, that a founding text such as John Stuart Mill's *On Liberty* is cited as support for the *human* rights of drug users, rather than support for the individual's right, based on liberal principles, to be free of interference from the state.[28]) The concept of privacy relates to the domestic and familial sphere and to the domains of intimacy and embodiment. A central question for feminist welfare regime analysis is women's autonomy around reproduction, which also slants the usual opposition, in welfare terms, between Sweden and liberal regimes: 'although the United States has a safety net full of holes, it has been an innovator in asserting women's body rights'.[29]

Research with pharmacotherapy clients demonstrates that the significance accorded to personal dignity, privacy and choice exerts an enormous influence on the experience of treatment. This manifests in practical, material ways: whether clients are forced to be dosed at a clinic every day or can take a week's dose home, whether they are treated as a valued customer or an untrustworthy prisoner.[30] Given this, an important consideration for comparative analysis is the degree to which policy regimes treat personal privacy as a legitimate concern.

Conclusion

Feminist welfare regime analysis of drug treatment involves, then, study of a messy, large and internally contradictory field, in which well-being could be promoted in one domain and neglected in another. It emphasises agitation and agency and is concerned with claims-making and interests. The results of this agitation are likely to be imperfect, or at least impermanent. Existing evidence suggests that easy answers as to the 'best' arrangements for drug users are unlikely. Far from resolving the Sweden–Australia paradox, it suggests difficult choices and foundational contradictions: few would care to choose between a hole-filled safety net that respects body rights, and its opposite. The possibilities for this approach lie not in a watertight series of rights or entitlements, but in the scope for new, perhaps temporary, alliances and coalitions that could be formed in order to make claims on the basis of shared interests and experiences. Rigid work hours, workplaces that are inaccessible to shops and services, and shift work disadvantage many pharmacotherapy clients, and they also disadvantage other workers. Rather than simply using feminist critiques of the 'adult worker' as a model, pharmacotherapy clients could also take up this critique and point out that the unsuitability of many workplaces is not because there is something wrong with clients, but because workplaces are inappropriately designed. This critique could be the basis of an advocacy coalition with other workers who also experience the effects of inflexible workplace design, including people with disability, older workers and low-income workers.

One of the effects of these new coalitions could be the partial, temporary fracturing of the categories of 'drug user' and (more specifically) 'pharmacotherapy client'. Just as claims for women on the basis of difference and equality have underscored the differences between women, so too claims for drug users on the basis of entitlements and service needs is likely to highlight the differences between them. A proportion of pharmacotherapy clients have significant needs for services, a marginal connection to the labour market, or insecure housing. Conversely, other clients are financially secure and have no significant health or service needs. The strength of the social safety net and public provision of welfare services will be far more important to the well-being of the former group of clients than the latter. This diversity of needs and positions need not be a hindrance, as other social movements have demonstrated. Unified categories are not prerequisites for action. Indeed, the similarities and shared interests between drug users and other groups should be a base from which new kinds of activity can be generated.

I would emphasise, finally, that this kind of analysis and advocacy is not at all incompatible with harm reduction, or with human rights. Campaigns against a number of fundamental injustices, including judicial executions for drug trafficking, are in fact better supported by human rights frameworks than the kinds of advocacy for services and policies that have been my focus here. Analysis of policies and their interrelationships is not a replacement for existing research methods, only one that could supplement them. As I have argued here, policy analysis cannot provide the answers as to which policy arrangements work best for drug users and for pharmacotherapy clients in particular. At best, it may provide theoretical models that combine participatory opportunities, respect for private preferences, recognition of difference, public provision and egalitarianism. It may also, of course, provide answers as to which policy arrangements are *worst* for drug users, and these models may have troubling resemblances to certain actually existing examples of national regimes: no or little public provision of services combined with authoritarianism, disregard for privacy and social stratification.

Perhaps more valuable than these exercises in modelling, however, could be recognising pharmacotherapy clients' interests in a context that does not have their identity as drug user as a central referent. As noted earlier, one of the effects of evidence-based policy has been to lock users into policy portfolios and risk categories, an effect that is proving hard to undo. Rather than appealing only to drug users' needs as drug users, or arguing for services only on the basis of their vulnerabilities and needs, researchers and advocates could look to welfare analysis as a means of arguing for users' entitlements as citizens and the contributions that they could make if policy and service frameworks were more favourable.

Notes

1 Saunders, Hallerod & Matheson, 'Making ends meet in Australia and Sweden'.
2 Whiteford & Adema, 'What works best in reducing child poverty'.
3 Ibid.
4 Blaxland, 'Early childhood education and care policy audits: Australia'.
5 Larsson & Thorslund, 'Does gender matter?'
6 Saunders & Abe, 'Poverty and deprivation in young and old'.
7 Esping-Andersen, *The Three Worlds of Welfare Capitalism*.
8 Stimson & O'Hare, 'Harm reduction'; Wodak, 'Australia's response to HIV among injecting drug users'.
9 Tham, 'Swedish drug policy'.
10 Benoit, Young, Magura et al., 'The impact of welfare reform on methadone treatment'; Scott, London & Myers, 'Dangerous dependencies'.
11 Banwell, Denton & Bammer, 'Programmes for the children of illicit drug-using parents'; Fraser, 'The chronotope of the queue'.
12 NDS, 'Australia's National Drug Strategy beyond 2009', p. 7.
13 AIVL, 'Submission to the Ministerial Council on Drug Strategy', p. 8.
14 Mattick, Breen, Kimber et al., 'Methadone maintenance therapy versus no opioid replacement therapy for opioid dependence'.
15 Barrett, 'Security, development and human rights'; Byrne & Albert, 'Coexisting or conjoined'; Wodak, 'Australia's response to HIV among injecting drug users'.
16 Kennedy, 'The critique of rights in critical legal studies'.
17 Islam, Day & Conigrave, 'Harm reduction healthcare'.
18 Brush, 'Changing the subject'; O'Connor, Orloff & Shaver, *State, Markets, Families*; Orloff, 'Gendering the comparative analysis of welfare states'.
19 Fraser, 'It's your life!'

20   valentine & Fraser, 'Trauma, damage and pleasure'.
21   Orloff, 'Gendering the comparative analysis of welfare states'.
22   O'Connor, Orloff & Shaver, *State, Markets, Families*, p. 29.
23   Craig, *Contemporary Motherhood*.
24   Fraser & Gordon, 'A genealogy of "dependency"'.
25   Moore & Fraser, 'Putting at risk what we know'.
26   Tham, 'Swedish drug policy', pp. 409, 410.
27   Rose, *Governing the Soul*.
28   Hunt, 'Public health or human rights'.
29   Brush, 'Changing the subject', p. 171.
30   Fraser, 'The chronotope of the queue'.

References

Australian Injecting and Illicit Drug Users League (2010). Submission to the Ministerial Council on Drug Strategy: Australia's National Drug Strategy beyond 2009. Canberra: AIVL.

Banwell, C., Denton, B., & Bammer, G. (2002). Programmes for the children of illicit drug-using parents: Issues and dilemmas. *Drug and Alcohol Review*, 21(4): 381–6.

Barrett, D. (2010). Security, development and human rights: Normative, legal and policy challenges for the international drug control system. *International Journal of Drug Policy*, 21(2): 140–4.

Benoit, E., Young, R., Magura, S., & Staines, G. (2004). The impact of welfare reform on methadone treatment: Policy lessons from service providers in New York City. *Substance Use and Misuse*, 39(13): 2355–90.

Blaxland, M. (2008). Early childhood education and care policy audits: Australia. In D. Brennan (ed.), *Building an International Research Collaboration in Early Childhood Education and Care: Background Materials for a Workshop funded by the Australian Research Alliance for Children and Youth (ARACY)*. Sydney: Social Policy Research Centre, University of New South Wales.

Bourgois, P. (2000). Disciplining addictions: The bio-politics of methadone and heroin in the United States. *Culture, Medicine and Psychiatry*, 24(2): 165–95.

Brush, L. (2002). Changing the subject: Gender and welfare regime studies. *Social Politics: International Studies in Gender, State and Society*, 9(2): 161.

Byrne, J., & Albert, E. (2009). Coexisting or conjoined: The growth of the international drug users' movement through participation with International Harm Reduction Association Conferences. *International Journal on Drug Policy*, 21: 110–11.

Caplehorn, J., & Drummer, O. (2002). Fatal methadone toxicity: Signs and circumstances, and the role of benzodiazepines. *Australian and New Zealand Journal of Public Health*, 26(4): 358–62.

Craig, L. (2007). *Contemporary Motherhood: The Impact of Children on Adult Time*. Aldershot, UK, & Burlington, VT: Ashgate.

Esping-Andersen, G. (1990). *The Three Worlds of Welfare Capitalism*. Cambridge: Polity Press & Princeton, NJ: Princeton University Press.

Fraser, N., & Gordon, L. (1997). A genealogy of 'dependency': Tracing a keyword of the US welfare state. In N. Fraser (ed.), *Justice Interruptus: Critical Reflections on the 'Postsocialist' Condition*. New York & London: Routledge.

Fraser, S. (2004). 'It's your life!' Injecting drug users, individual responsibility and hepatitis C prevention. *Health: An Interdisciplinary Journal for the Social Study of Health, Illness and Medicine*, 8(2): 199–221.

—— (2006). The chronotope of the queue: Methadone maintenance treatment and the production of time, space and subjects. *International Journal of Drug Policy*, 17(3): 192–202.

Fraser, S., & valentine, k. (2008). *Substance and Substitution: Methadone Subjects in Liberal Societies*. Basingstoke, UK: Palgrave Macmillan.

Hunt, N. (2004). Public health or human rights: What comes first? *International Journal of Drug Policy*, 15(4): 231–7.

Islam, M., Day, C., & Conigrave, K. (2010). Harm reduction healthcare: From an alternative to the mainstream platform? *International Journal of Drug Policy*, 21(2): 131–3.

Kennedy, D. (2002). The critique of rights in critical legal studies. In W. Brown & J. Halley (eds), *Left Legalism/Left Critique* (pp. 178–228). Durham, NC: Duke University Press.

Larsson, K., & Thorslund, M. (2002). Does gender matter? Differences in patterns of informal support and formal services in a Swedish urban elderly population. *Research on Aging*, 24(3): 308.

Mattick, R.P., Breen, C., Kimber, J., et al. (2009). Methadone maintenance therapy versus no opioid replacement therapy for opioid dependence. *Cochrane Database of Systematic Reviews* (3), art. no. CD002209.

Moore, D., & Fraser, S. (2006). Putting at risk what we know: Reflecting on the drug-using subject in harm reduction and its political implications. *Social Science and Medicine*, 62(12): 3035–47.

National Drug Strategy (2009). Australia's National Drug Strategy beyond 2009: Consultation Paper. Canberra: NDS, Australian Government.

O'Connor, J., Orloff, A.S., & Shaver, S. (1999). *State, Markets, Families: Gender, Liberalism and Social Policy in Australia, Canada, Great Britain and the United States*. Cambridge & New York: Cambridge University Press.

Orloff, A.S. (2009). Gendering the comparative analysis of welfare states: An unfinished agenda. *Sociological Theory*, 27(3): 317–43.

Rose, N. (1989). *Governing the Soul: The Shaping of the Private Self*. London: Routledge.

Saunders, P., & Abe, A. (2010). Poverty and deprivation in young and old: A comparative study of Australia and Japan. *Poverty and Public Policy*, 2(1). Retrieved 28 March 2011. www.psocommons.org/ppp/vol2/iss1/art5.

Saunders, P., Hallerod, B., & Matheson, G. (1994). Making ends meet in Australia and Sweden: A comparative analysis using the subjective poverty line methodology. *Acta Sociologica*, 37(1): 3–22.

Scott, E., London, A., & Myers, N. (2002). Dangerous dependencies: The intersection of welfare reform and domestic violence. *Gender and Society*, 16(6): 878–97.

Stimson, G., & O'Hare, P. (2010). Harm reduction: Moving through the third decade. *International Journal of Drug Policy*, 21(2): 91–3.

Tham, H. (1998). Swedish drug policy: A successful model? *European Journal on Criminal Policy and Research*, 6(3): 395–414.

valentine, k., & Fraser, S. (2008). Trauma, damage and pleasure: Rethinking problematic drug use. *International Journal of Drug Policy*, 19(5): 410–16.

Whiteford, P., & Adema, W. (2007). What works best in reducing child poverty: A benefit or work strategy? *OECD Social, Employment and Migration Working Papers 51*. Paris: OECD Directorate for Employment, Labour and Social Affairs.

Wodak, A. (2005). Australia's response to HIV among injecting drug users: The band is still playing. In Australasian Society for HIV Medicine (ed.), *HIV and Hepatitis C: Policy, Discrimination, Legal and Ethical Issues* (pp. 33–42). Sydney: Australasian Society for HIV Medicine.

World Health Organization & United Nations Office on Drugs and Crime (2004). Substitution maintenance therapy in the management of opioid dependence and HIV/AIDS prevention: Position paper. Geneva: World Health Organisation.

PART 3

Drugs, crime and the law

Court-ordered treatment, neoliberalism and *Homo economicus*

Toby Seddon

The practice of courts ordering drug-using offenders to attend treatment has become a striking feature of criminal justice systems around the world. Although this development is in many respects of relatively recent origin, penal or criminal justice responses to drugs have a much longer history. In late nineteenth-century Britain, for example, legislation provided powers to the courts for the compulsory detention of criminal inebriates in specialist reformatories.[1] And, of course, the global drug control regime that was constructed in the first two decades of the twentieth century has been based since its inception on the use of the criminal law as a tool for regulating the manufacture, distribution and possession of 'dangerous drugs'. In the US, for example, the Harrison Narcotics Act of 1914, one of the earliest pieces of national 'prohibition' legislation, provided for fines of up to \$2000 and prison sentences of up to five years for violations of its regulations.

The connection, then, between drugs and criminal justice is not a recent invention. It is embedded in the foundations of drug control. Nevertheless, the type of fusion of drug treatment and criminal justice that I describe in this chapter represents a new line of development in this longer story. Perhaps the first step along this road was Robert Dupont's ill-starred 'Operation Tripwire' proposal in 1977 in the US.[2] Although never implemented, its key components – the use of drug testing as a screening tool and for the monitoring of compliance, coupled with the systematic integration of treatment and criminal justice – set the template for much of what followed and indeed continues to do so. Initiatives began to emerge in the 1980s, gathering pace in the 1990s, but it is in the first decade of the twenty-first century that the fusion of drug treatment and criminal justice has become a genuinely worldwide phenomenon.

This chapter is structured as follows. I begin by briefly explaining the basic premise of court-ordered treatment and setting out its general rationale and overall mode of operation, before turning to a conceptual examination of what I call the 'lexicon of force'. By this I mean the family of terms used to describe court-imposed pressure to enter treatment – such as 'compulsory', 'quasi-compulsory', 'coerced', 'mandated' and so on. Building on this conceptual map, I then examine the policy and practice of court-ordered treatment, focusing primarily on two British examples: the Restriction on Bail (RoB) and the Drug Rehabilitation Requirement (DRR). The discussion here will set out an analysis of how these specific interventions (re)produce a distinctive notion of the citizen-subject as a calculating choice-maker. In conclusion, I consider some implications of my analysis, not only for drug policy and practice but also more broadly for our understanding of how we govern ourselves and others in the early twenty-first century.

In focus

Court-ordered treatment

Rationale and approaches

Court-ordered treatment and the wider integration of drug treatment and crim-inal justice are based on several premises:

1. *Drugs cause crime.* The underpinning behavioural model is straightfor-ward: users of addictive drugs like heroin and crack-cocaine, who tend to have limited sources of legal income, are driven to commit income-generating property crime in order to fund their drug purchases. This is sometimes called the 'economic necessity' model. Its empirical basis is the well-established finding that there is a strong correlation or association between heroin/crack use and involvement in property crime.[a]

2. *Identification and targeting.* The second premise is that the criminal justice system is a good place to find these drug-using offenders. The assumption here is that a sufficiently high proportion of this group are apprehended at some stage and brought into the system. In many juris-dictions, drug testing is used as a tool for identifying this group. For example, in England and Wales, all individuals arrested for specific 'trig-ger' offences (such as property crimes and drug possession or supply offences) and brought to a police station are required to undergo a drug test. Refusal or failure to take the test is itself a criminal offence.

3. *Criminal justice leverage.* The third premise is that the courts (and other criminal justice agencies) can effectively apply pressure to individuals

to attend treatment services. Most often this pressure takes the form of making imprisonment the alternative option to attending treatment. In some models, notably drug courts, there is ongoing judicial supervision of attendance and progress.

4 *Treatment 'works'*. Lastly, and fundamentally, it is assumed that individuals who enter and then stay in treatment will reduce their level of offending. The supporting evidence for this assumption comes from a series of longitudinal studies of treatment outcomes that have been undertaken in several different countries.[b]

a Bennett, Holloway & Farrington, 'The statistical association between drug misuse and crime'; but cf Seddon, 'Explaining the drug-crime link', and 'Drugs, crime and social exclusion'.

b For example Gossop, Marsden & Stewart, *NTORS After Five Years*; Hubbard, Craddock & Anderson, 'Overview of 5-year follow-up outcomes in the Drug Abuse Treatment Outcome Studies (DATOS)'; Jones, Donmall, Millar et al., *The Drug Treatment Outcomes Research Study (DTORS): Final Outcomes Report*.

Based on the four premises of court-ordered treatment, a number of interventions and programs have been developed over the course of the last two to three decades, all sharing the overarching goal of reducing drug-related crime. Here, I briefly describe the key features of the two basic models for court-ordered treatment of drug-using offenders.

Drug courts

Perhaps the single best-known and most widely adopted model for court-ordered treatment is that of drug courts.[3] The first drug court was established in Miami, Florida, in 1989. In the following years, others were set up across the US and around the world, including in Australia, Canada, England and Scotland. There is no single drug-court model, but there are some common features:

1 *Specialism*. Drug courts are specialist courts that are designed to deal exclusively with drug-using offenders. The aim here is to ensure that those involved in the court process – such as judges, lawyers and clerks – develop high levels of expertise. In some versions, speeding up case processing is central to the operation of the courts.

2 *Integrated treatment*. Drug courts offer access to a range of treatment and related support services. Treatment and criminal case processing are integrated. This requires a significant degree of coordination and partnership between judges, court clerks, lawyers, probation officers, treatment workers and others.

3 *Drug testing*. Frequent testing is used to monitor participants' compliance. Rigorous testing procedures (e.g. direct observation of the collection of samples) ensure that the results can be used within the legal process.

4 *Judicial monitoring.* The judge takes a central role in reviewing progress and draws on information provided by others, notably the treatment agency that reports on attendance and drug-test results. The judge is also central in rewarding positive progress (e.g. by praise or suspending imprisonment) and punishing non-compliance (e.g. by warnings or increasing testing frequency). Some models also emphasise the importance of judicial continuity; that is, that the same judge maintains contact with an individual participant.

The evidence on the influence and effectiveness of drug courts is mixed. Some studies, and indeed some reviews of research, have found that drug courts reduce reoffending,[4] whereas others have suggested that their impact on reoffending is marginal or unproven.[5] Nevertheless, drug courts are the most widespread model for court-ordered treatment throughout the world.

Treatment sentences

The second basic model of court-ordered treatment for drug-using offenders is specific sentencing options that include a drug treatment component. These can operate within the framework of drug courts or simply as stand-alone sentences. Again, many varieties exist, but there are some common features:

1 *Attendance requirements.* At the heart of treatment sentences is a requirement by the court for the offender to attend appointments at a treatment agency.

2 *Supervision.* Offenders on these sentences are usually under the close supervision of probation or parole officers who manage and coordinate their case.

3 *Drug testing.* Testing is often used for the purpose of monitoring progress and compliance with treatment.

4 *Alternative to imprisonment.* Treatment sentences are typically intended to be community-based alternatives to imprisonment. Breaches for non-compliance often lead to incarceration.

Examples of this type of court-ordered treatment sentence are many and varied. In the US, TASC (Treatment Accountability for Safer Communities – previously Treatment Alternatives to Street Crime), which originated in the 1970s, is one of the oldest. Other US examples include DTAP (Drug Treatment Alternatives to Prison), established in New York in 1990, which involves referral to residential treatment in lieu of a prison sentence, and California's Proposition 36, initiated in 2001, which allows first- and second-time non-violent drug-possession offenders the opportunity to receive drug treatment instead of incarceration. Evaluations of TASC[6] and DTAP[7] show some evidence of positive influence on reoffending, although findings for TASC are a little more equivocal, reflecting the wide variations in local arrangements for case management and monitoring. The evaluation of Proposition 36 has found quite mixed outcomes for reoffending.[8]

A British example of a treatment sentence is the Drug Treatment and Testing Order (DTTO), now restyled as the Drug Rehabilitation Requirement (DRR), to which I return later in this chapter. DTTOs were found to have very poor completion rates and little or no influence on reoffending, apart from the small proportion (30 per cent) who finished their orders successfully.[9] More recent innovations have seen new court interventions introduced that mirror treatment sentences but which apply at the pre-sentence stage, typically making treatment attendance a condition of bail. This has been introduced, for example, in Australia with the CREDIT (Court Referral and Evaluation for Drug Intervention and Treatment) program and in England with the Restriction on Bail (RoB) program.[10]

The lexicon of force

In many quarters, there has been disquiet about the emergence and spread of court-ordered treatment. This has taken many forms, from instrumental critiques (treatment only works when people are 'ready' and motivated) to ethical and political ones (treatment mandated by a criminal court is an unethical abuse of state power). I do not revisit this well-trodden ground here and refer readers to some of the better discussions of these issues.[11] Instead, I focus on what I call the 'lexicon of force'; that is, the family of terms used to describe court-imposed pressure to enter treatment: 'compulsory', 'quasi-compulsory', 'coerced', 'mandated' and so on. I suggest that on both empirical and theoretical grounds, we need to move away from terminology that revolves around the idea of pure or strict force.

Let me begin with some definitions taken from the *Oxford Compact English Dictionary*:

Coerce (verb) Persuade (an unwilling person) to do something by using force or threats. [ORIGIN Latin *coercere* 'restrain'].

Compel (verb) **1** Force or oblige to do something. **2** Bring about by force or pressure. [ORIGIN Latin *compellere*, from *pellere* 'drive'].

Compulsory (adjective) Required by law or a rule; obligatory.

We can see then, first, that the idea of coercion breaks down into three component parts: (1) persuading someone to do something; (2) which they are unwilling to do; (3) by using force or threats. The first component, persuasion, implies a process of persuading or encouraging someone to undertake a particular course of action by setting out the benefits of following that course and the costs of not doing so. Central to this, therefore, is the communication of information to targeted individuals about the options on offer and their relative merits. Reference to options is a reminder that coerced individuals are understood as still retaining choice, however constrained. This marks the formal distinction between coerced and compulsory treatment, as the latter does not involve or require consent, consisting simply of the use of 'force or pressure'. This is an important distinction for several reasons. Policy-makers have often been at pains to stress that although the purpose of these initiatives is certainly to use the leverage of the criminal justice process to pressure individuals into entering treatment, nevertheless they remain free to say 'no'. In other words, they still have a choice. So, for example, one English initiative launched in 2005, and designed to extend the use of coercive measures, was called 'Tough Choices'. But for critics, this reference to choice is misleading, perhaps even dishonest. Can we speak of 'choice' when the alternative on offer is imprisonment? For this reason, the term 'quasi-compulsory' treatment is preferred by some,[12] to indicate that the choice implied by the term 'coercion' is largely illusory.

The idea of choice turns out to be pivotal in several ways. At an empirical level, a key paper by Marlowe, Kirby, Bonieskie et al. first established two critical points. First, they demonstrated that coercive pressures at drug treatment entry were 'operative in multiple life spheres'.[13] In other words, coercive pressures emanated from diverse sources, including family and financial concerns as well as the criminal justice system.[14] Second, and perhaps counter-intuitively, Marlowe and colleagues went on to show that 'legal pressures may exert substantially less influence over drug treatment entry than do informal, extra-legal influences'. Research subjects 'perceived treatment-entry pressures as stemming predominantly from psychological, financial, social, familial, and medical domains respectively'.[15]

Why is this significant? The conceptual implications are fundamental. Marlowe, Kirby, Bonieskie et al.'s research suggests that referral to treatment from a criminal court cannot be simply equated with coercion. Indeed, it cannot be assumed that those referred to treatment by courts feel under any greater pressure to enter it than others who are not court-referred, nor can it be assumed that they are necessarily uninterested or unwilling participants in treatment.[16] In this sense, the meanings of the terms 'quasi-compulsory' and 'coerced' may be less straightforward than they appear at first sight. By itself, this is a critical insight, not least because it challenges those policy and research analyses that attempt to compare or juxtapose 'coerced' and 'voluntary' treatment. The two may not always be so different in practice. This implies that our focus ought to be on *mapping* these multiple sources of pressure, building on Marlowe's work, and exploring how they inter-act with each other and with those internal pressures usually described as 'motivation'.[17]

But more than this, there is an important but unexamined theoretical issue at play here. The allusion to choice and options points us towards what is a distinctive feature of wider strategies for the exercise of power in recent decades. In a lecture given at Dartmouth College in 1980, Foucault provided a striking definition of the exercise of power: 'We must not understand the exercise of power as pure violence or strict coercion. Power consists in complex relations: these relations involve a set of rational techniques, and the efficiency of those techniques is due to a subtle integration of coercion-technologies and self-technologies.'[18]

What does he mean by 'coercion-technologies' and 'self-technologies'? The former refers to those techniques, devices and mechanisms that use force, violence or threats to govern or direct the behaviour of individuals. Examples in the criminal justice context include police 'stop and search', arrest, detention in police cells and imprisonment. They are, in other words, what we might understand in lay terms as techniques of 'brute power'. Self-technologies are rather different but no less important in terms of governing people. These refer to those mechanisms that seek to mobilise and enrol the self-regulating capacities of autonomous individuals and to align them with governmental objectives. A criminal justice example would be the use of cognitive behavioural therapy (CBT) programs for offenders on probation. CBT programs seek to reshape styles and habits of thinking and feeling associated with 'undesirable' behaviour and shift them to more 'pro-social' forms. They aim to change offenders' cognitive and affective processes so that they are better able to regulate their own behaviour and avoid criminal activity.

For court-ordered drug treatment, we can certainly see the deployment of both coercion-technologies and self-technologies: mandatory drug test-ing and the use of imprisonment representing the former, offers of drug treatment the latter. Adopting a Foucauldian perspective, we can see that talk of 'coerced' treatment potentially blinds us to the 'subtle integration' of the two techniques of power and, in particular, to the importance of self-technologies.[19] The discourse of 'coercion' alerts us to only one dimension of the exercise of power and implies that it can be understood in terms of a 'sim-ple logic of domination'.[20] The complementarity of these dual techniques is nicely captured in the following quotation, which is drawn from a factsheet published by the British Home Office explaining the naming of the 'Tough Choices' initiative mentioned above: 'Tough Choices was chosen as a name because it was felt to succinctly describe the change in the consequences drug misusers face if they do not take advantage of the opportunities for treatment and support that exist.'[21]

So there is both an empirical and a theoretical basis for moving away from the language of strict coercion when describing court-ordered treatment. I should make it clear at this point that there are, of course, criminal justice approaches to drugs that largely or solely operate through coercive-technologies – for example, the compulsory detention of drug users in prison-like institutions, as in Vietnam, Cambodia, China and several other countries[22] – but the types of court-ordered treatment that are my focus in this chapter are rather different.

If we look at court-ordered treatment from the perspective I have outlined, an alternative critical agenda opens up. Rather than seeking to evaluate whether court-ordered treatment works[23] or to debate its ethics,[24] we are encouraged to focus on *how* it operates. This ethos of investigation is, of course, distinctly and distinctively Foucauldian, and brings into the spotlight the issue of subjectivities. In other words, it prompts us to ask what conceptions of human subjects are created and deployed within practices of court-ordered treatment.[25] I consider this question in the next section.

Practices of court-ordered treatment

Two recent English examples of court-ordered treatment are the Restriction on Bail (RoB) and the Drug Rehabilitation Requirement (DRR). Adopting the Foucauldian lens described above, I focus on how these interventions produce, and at the same time rely upon, a particular conception of the human subject. In so doing, my aim is to attempt to open up an alternative critical agenda. First, I briefly describe the two interventions.

Restriction on Bail

The Restriction on Bail program was first established on a pilot basis in England in 2004 before being implemented nationally.[26] Under section 19 of the Criminal Justice Act 2003, amending the Bail Act 1976, the courts were given the power to apply the Restriction where the defendant:

- is aged 18 or over;
- has tested positive for opiates and/or cocaine; and
- the court has grounds to believe that the offending is drug-motivated.

Where these conditions apply, and the court grants bail, it is required to impose as a condition of bail that the defendant must undergo an assessment and/or participate in any relevant follow-up. Further, the usual presumption in favour of bail is reversed: bail may not be granted unless the court believes there is no significant risk of another offence being committed while on bail.

Drug Rehabilitation Requirement

The DRR program is a revamped version of the earlier Drug Treatment and Testing Order (DTTO), which was first piloted in 1998. The DTTO was a stand-alone sentence targeted at high-risk drug-using offenders. It required offenders to attend treatment and undergo a regime of regular drug testing, with periodic progress reviews being conducted by the court.[27] As noted earlier, the DTTO was associated with only limited reductions in reoffending rates.[28]

The DRR was introduced as part of a wider restructuring of community sentences in the Criminal Justice Act 2003. It retains the key features of the DTTO – a combination of treatment, testing and supervision – but gives sentencing authorities the opportunity to tailor generic community orders to individual cases. The DRR is one of 12 requirements that can be attached to an order (others include mental health treatment, curfew, residence requirement and unpaid community work). Whereas the DTTO mandated high levels of weekly contact with a supervising officer and/or treatment worker, the DRR can be applied with varying levels of intensity, depending on the needs of the offender and the seriousness of their offence.

Practices of subjectification: *Homo economicus*

Conceptually, RoB and the DRR are very similar programs. In both, targeted individuals are identified largely on the basis of positive drug-test results during detention at police stations after arrest. In court, they are then offered the opportunity to access drug treatment. Those who accept this offer have their attendance at treatment monitored by the court, and sanctions are threatened should they fail to comply. Those who reject the offer face an alternative criminal justice disposal, most often imprisonment, either on remand in the case of RoB or as a sentence in the case of DRR.

Both operate, therefore, within a framework of incentives and sanctions, which is structured to maximise the number of targeted individuals who engage with drug treatment. Such a framework resonates strongly with styles of thinking associated with the emergence of neoliberalism in recent decades, namely the extension of economic reasoning to the entire span of human behaviour. One of the intellectual pioneers of this development has been the Chicago School economist Gary Becker.[29] His approach is founded on the idea of choice, which, as we have already seen, is a crucial component of court-ordered treatment. He argues that human behaviour can be understood as the outcome of rational actors seeking to 'maximize utility from stable preferences as they try to anticipate the future consequences of their choices'.[30]

Interventions like the RoB and DRR operate by manipulating the costs and benefits associated with different choices in order to change behaviour. They aim to structure the cost–benefit distribution such that choosing to engage with drug treatment becomes the best way for most drug-using defendants and offenders to maximise utility. So, for example, a defendant in court who has tested positive at the police station, and who does not want to be remanded in custody while awaiting trial, will be inclined to accept the offer of RoB in order to be granted bail.

So what kind of human subject do these interventions create and reproduce? Conventionally, the addiction concept has always been based on understanding addictive behaviour in terms of 'loss of control' and 'compulsion'.[31] This perspective is also implicit in the economic necessity model of the drug–crime link that I described earlier as an underpinning assumption of court-ordered treatment. In this view, drug-using defendants and offenders need to be channeled into treatment via RoB or DRRs precisely because they cannot control their drug-motivated offending. But here we come up against a paradox. How can an individual be both a compulsive addict suffering from 'loss of control' and, at the same time, a rational actor making choices to 'maximize utility'?[32] Becker himself has addressed this question in a classic article, 'A theory of rational addiction',[33] and behavioural economists have further developed his position.[34] Becker's argument is, in essence, an empirical one: he simply shows that empirical observations of behaviour are consistent with the idea that addicts act rationally as forward-looking utility-maximisers. For Becker, then, *Homo economicus*, the rational choice-maker of neoliberalism,[35] occupies all domains of human behaviour, including addiction.

A slightly different way of looking at rationality and choice is suggested by Foucault. In his 1979 course of lectures at the Collège de France, Foucault discussed at some length what he called 'American neo-liberalism', providing a brilliant and prescient analysis of what at that time was still 'mainly just an idea' rather than a suite of actual policies or programs.[36] In the last four lectures of his course, he focused on Becker's work in particular. Referring to Becker's landmark 1968 article on crime and punishment, Foucault observes:

> All the distinctions that have been made between born criminals, occasional criminals, the perverse and the not perverse, and recidivists are not important. We must be prepared to accept that, in any case, however pathological the subject may be at a certain level and when seen from a certain angle, he is nevertheless 'responsive' to some extent to possible gains and losses, which means that penal action must act on the interplay of gains and losses or, in other words, on the environment.[37]

Within neoliberal control strategies, whether drug-using offenders have an impaired or attenuated faculty of will by virtue of their addiction is irrelevant, *provided* that they are still to some degree 'sensitive to changes in the balance of profit and loss', as Lemke puts it.[38] In this sense, court-ordered drug treatment produces, and operates through, a hybrid human subject: one who has an impaired will but yet retains sufficient rationality to be responsive to changes in environment.

Furthermore, we can see that, based on this conception of the human subject, neoliberal control strategies are no longer much interested in seeking to change the 'deep subjectivity'[39] of individuals: 'Action is brought to bear on the rules of the game rather than on the players [. . .] there is an environmental type of intervention instead of the internal subjugation of individuals.'[40] The coercion-technologies within both RoB and the DRR can be understood, then, as action to alter the 'rules of the game' for a particular governmental end. The offer of the opportunity to attend treatment becomes a form of self-technology in which individuals are cajoled and encouraged to take personal responsibility for their own care.[41] Failure to do so is then constituted as a personal failure – recall the Home Office explanation for the naming of the 'Tough Choices' initiative: 'Tough Choices was chosen as a name because it was felt to succinctly describe the change in the consequences drug misusers face if they do not take advantage of the opportunities for treatment and support that exist.'[42]

The tying together of these coercion-technologies and self-technologies is the hallmark of neoliberal control practices, which we also see within court-ordered drug treatment. In this sense, as I have argued, the language of 'coerced' or 'quasi-compulsory' treatment obscures more than it reveals or, to put it another way, illuminates only half the picture.

Conclusion

In debates about court-ordered treatment, terms like 'coerced' and 'quasi-compulsory' have an undoubted force and power as tools for critique. In this respect, my attempts to interrogate and destabilise these concepts may be viewed as unhelpful or even misguided. I want to conclude, however, by pointing to two implications of my argument that, I will suggest, potentially open up a different kind of critical agenda.

First, in order to challenge, resist or refuse power effectively, we need to have a clear picture of exactly how it operates in specific sites. We need, in other words, to build up what Foucault calls 'strategic knowledge'.[43] In relation to court-ordered treatment, I have argued that the central mechanisms of power involve the harnessing together of coercion-technologies and self-technologies.[44] It seems to me that this should encourage us to move away from forms of critique that are unduly focused on the idea of the state and its exercise of power. Instead, our critical engagement should be at the level of mechanisms of power as they actually operate in practice. This points to the need for a significant reorientation of both the terms of the policy debate and the research agenda. For example, we do not currently know nearly enough about how different individuals perceive and respond to the frameworks of incentives and sanctions that are involved in particular programs of court-ordered treatment. Yet this is essential both for the crafting of better policy and for the development of more incisive forms of critique.

Second, at a more general level, the concept of *Homo economicus* clearly provides a powerful analytical tool for investigating neoliberal control strategies. This implies that there are strong 'family resemblances' between contemporary control practices across diverse fields, and there is therefore much to be learnt potentially from different disciplines with which we may be unfamiliar.[45] But this does not mean that there is a single blueprint or paradigm for the exercise of power within neoliberalism from which we can 'read off' or deduce actual practice in any given area. Detailed empirical enquiry in specific sites of power remains essential to a critical research agenda. It is only through generating such local and particular understanding of the present that we can hope to transform the future. For a practice like court-ordered treatment, which raises such profound questions of ethics and human rights,[46] the urgency of this task cannot be overstated.

Notes

1 Garland, *Punishment and Welfare*, pp. 217–18.
2 See Dupont & Wish, 'Operation Tripwire revisited'.
3 See Belenko, *Research on Drug Courts*; Fischer, 'Doing good with a vengeance'; Wilson, Mitchell & MacKenzie, 'A systematic review of drug court effects on recidivism'.
4 Wilson, Mitchell & MacKenzie, 'A systematic review of drug court effects on recidivism'; Shaffer, *Reconsidering Drug Court Effectiveness*.
5 Granfield, Eby & Brewster, 'An examination of the Denver Drug Court'; McIvor, *Review of the Glasgow and Fife Drug Courts*.
6 Anglin, Longshore & Turner, 'Treatment alternatives to street crime'.
7 Belenko, Foltz, Lang et al., 'Recidivism among high-risk drug felons'.
8 Urada, Hawken, Conner et al., *Evaluation of Proposition 36*.
9 Hough, Clancy, McSweeney et al., *The Impact of Drug Treatment and Testing Orders on Offending*.
10 Heale & Lang, 'A process evaluation of the CREDIT (Court Referral and Evaluation for Drug Intervention and Treatment) pilot programme'; Hucklesby, Eastwood, Seddon et al., *The Evaluation of the Restriction on Bail Pilot*.
11 Stevens, Berto, Heckmann et al., 'Quasi-compulsory treatment of drug dependent offenders'; Caplan, 'Ethical issues surrounding forced, mandated or coerced treatment'; Seddon, 'Coerced drug treatment in the criminal justice system'.
12 For example Stevens, Berto, Heckmann et al., 'Quasi-compulsory treatment of drug dependent offenders'.
13 Marlowe, Kirby, Bonieskie et al., 'Assessment of coercive and noncoercive pressures to enter drug abuse treatment', p. 82.

14 See also Marlowe, Merikle, Kirby et al., 'Multidimensional assessment of perceived treatment-entry pressures among substance abusers'.
15 Marlowe, Kirby, Bonieskie et al., 'Assessment of coercive and noncoercive pressures to enter drug abuse treatment', p. 81.
16 Farabee, Shen & Sanchez, 'Perceived coercion and treatment need among mentally ill parolees'.
17 See Longshore & Teruya, 'Treatment motivation in drug users'.
18 Foucault, 'About the beginning of the hermeneutics of the self', pp. 203–4.
19 See also Vrecko, 'Therapeutic justice in drug courts'.
20 Miller & Rose, *Governing the Present*, p. 215.
21 Home Office, *DIP – Tough Choices Project FAQs*.
22 Open Society Institute, *Compulsory Drug Treatment*.
23 For example Stevens, Berto, Heckmann et al., 'Quasi-compulsory treatment of drug dependent offenders'.
24 For example Caplan, 'Ethical issues surrounding forced, mandated or coerced treatment'.
25 Miller & Rose, *Governing the Present*, pp. 7–8.
26 See Hucklesby, Eastwood, Seddon et al., *The Evaluation of the Restriction on Bail Pilot*.
27 Turnbull, McSweeney, Webster et al., *Drug Treatment and Testing Orders*.
28 Hough, Clancy, McSweeney et al., *The Impact of Drug Treatment and Testing Orders on Offending*.
29 See Becker, 'Crime and punishment', and *The Economic Approach to Human Behavior*.
30 Becker & Murphy, 'A theory of rational addiction', p. 675.
31 See Levine, 'The discovery of addiction'; Seddon, *A History of Drugs*.
32 See Reith, 'Consumption and its discontents'.
33 Becker & Murphy, 'A theory of rational addiction'.
34 For example Vuchinich & Heather, *Choice, Behavioural Economics and Addiction*.
35 See also Read, 'A genealogy of homo-economicus'.
36 Tribe, 'The political economy of modernity', p. 694.
37 Foucault, *The Birth of Biopolitics*, p. 259.
38 Lemke, 'The birth of bio-politics', p. 199.
39 Dilts, 'Michel Foucault meets Gary Becker', p. 87.
40 Foucault, *The Birth of Biopolitics*, p. 260.
41 See Lemke, 'The birth of bio-politics', pp. 201–4.
42 Home Office, *DIP – Tough Choices Project FAQs*.
43 Foucault, 'Power and strategies', p. 145.
44 See also Vrecko, 'Therapeutic justice in drug courts'.
45 Rose, 'Government and control', p. 185.
46 See Seddon, 'Coerced drug treatment in the criminal justice system', pp. 274–7; Stevens, Berto, Heckmann et al., 'Quasi-compulsory treatment of drug dependent offenders'.

References

Anglin, M., Longshore, D., & Turner, S. (1999). Treatment alternatives to street crime: An evaluation of five programs. *Criminal Justice and Behavior*, 26(2): 168–95.

Becker, G. (1968). Crime and punishment: An economic approach. *Journal of Political Economy*, 76(2): 169–217.

—— (1976). *The Economic Approach to Human Behavior*. Chicago: University of Chicago Press.

Becker, G., & Murphy, K. (1988). A theory of rational addiction. *Journal of Political Economy*, 96(4): 675–700.

Belenko, S. (2001). *Research on Drug Courts: A Critical Review, 2001 Update*. Alexandria, VA: National Drug Court Institute.

Belenko, S., Foltz, C., Lang, M., et al. (2004). Recidivism among high-risk drug felons: A longitudinal analysis following residential treatment. *Journal of Offender Rehabilitation*, 40: 105–32.

Bennett, T., Holloway, K., & Farrington, D. (2008). The statistical association between drug misuse and crime: A meta-analysis. *Aggression and Violent Behavior*, 13(2): 107–18.

Caplan, A. (2006). Ethical issues surrounding forced, mandated or coerced treatment. *Journal of Substance Abuse Treatment*, 31: 117–20.

Dilts, A. (2008). Michel Foucault meets Gary Becker: Criminality beyond *Discipline and Punish*. *Carceral Notebooks*, 4: 77–100.

Dupont, R., & Wish, E. (1992). Operation Tripwire revisited. *Annals of the American Academy of Political and Social Science*, 521: 91–111.

Farabee, D., Shen, H., & Sanchez, S. (2002). Perceived coercion and treatment need among mentally ill parolees. *Criminal Justice and Behavior*, 29(1): 76–86.

Fischer, B. (2003). 'Doing good with a vengeance': A critical assessment of the practices, effects and implications of drug treatment courts in North America. *Criminal Justice*, 3(3): 227–48.

Foucault, M. (1980). Power and strategies. In C. Gordon (ed.). *Power/Knowledge: Select Interviews and Other Writings, 1972–1977*. New York: Pantheon Books.

—— (1993). About the beginning of the hermeneutics of the self: Two lectures at Dartmouth. *Political Theory*, 21(2): 198–227.

—— (2008). *The Birth of Biopolitics: Lectures at the Collège de France 1978–1979*. Basingstoke, UK: Palgrave Macmillan.

Garland, D. (1985). *Punishment and Welfare: A History of Penal Strategies*. Aldershot, UK: Gower.

Gossop, M., Marsden, J., & Stewart, D. (2001). *NTORS After Five Years: Changes in Substance Use, Health and Criminal Behaviour During the Five Years after Intake*. London: National Addiction Centre.

Granfield, R., Eby, C., & Brewster, T. (1998). An examination of the Denver Drug Court: The impact of a treatment-oriented drug-offender system. *Law and Policy*, 20(2): 183–202.

Heale, P., & Lang, E. (2001). A process evaluation of the CREDIT (court referral and evaluation for drug intervention and treatment) pilot programme. *Drug and Alcohol Review*, 20(2): 223–30.

Home Office (2006). *DIP – Tough Choices Project FAQs*. June 9th version. London: Home Office.

Hough, M., Clancy, A., McSweeney, T., et al. (2003). *The Impact of Drug Treatment and Testing Orders on Offending: Two-Year Reconviction Results*. Research Findings 184. London: Home Office.

Hubbard, R., Craddock, S., & Anderson, J. (2003). Overview of 5-year follow-up outcomes in the Drug Abuse Treatment Outcome Studies (DATOS). *Journal of Substance Abuse Treatment*, 25(3): 125–34.

Hucklesby, A., Eastwood, C., Seddon, T., et al. (2007). *The Evaluation of the Restriction on Bail Pilot: Final Report*. Online Report 06/07. London: Home Office.

Jones, A., Donmall, M., Millar, T., et al. (2009). *The Drug Treatment Outcomes Research Study (DTORS): Final Outcomes Report*. Research Report 24. London: Home Office.

Lemke, T. (2001). 'The birth of bio-politics': Michel Foucault's lecture at the Collège de France on neo-liberal governmentality. *Economy and Society*, 30(2): 190–207.

Levine, H. (1978). The discovery of addiction: Changing conceptions of habitual drunkenness in America. *Journal of Studies on Alcohol*, 39(1): 143–74.

Longshore, D., & Teruya, C. (2006). Treatment motivation in drug users: A theory-based analysis. *Drug and Alcohol Dependence*, 81(2): 179–88.

McIvor, G. (2009). *Review of the Glasgow and Fife Drug Courts: Report*. Edinburgh: Scottish Government.

Marlowe, D.B., Kirby, K., Bonieskie, L., et al. (1996). Assessment of coercive and noncoercive pressures to enter drug abuse treatment. *Drug and Alcohol Dependence*, 42: 77–84.

Marlowe, D.B., Merikle, E.P., Kirby, K.C., et al. (2001). Multidimensional assessment of perceived treatment-entry pressures among substance abusers. *Psychology of Addictive Behavior*, 15: 97–108.

Miller, P., & Rose, N. (2008). *Governing the Present*. Cambridge: Polity Press.

Open Society Institute (2010). *Compulsory Drug Treatment*. Human Rights & Drug Policy Briefing No. 4. New York: Open Society Institute.

Read, J. (2009). A genealogy of homo-economicus: Neoliberalism and the production of subjectivity. *Foucault Studies*, 6: 25–36.

Reith, G. (2004). Consumption and its discontents: Addiction, identity and the problems of freedom. *British Journal of Sociology*, 55(2): 283–300.

Rose, N. (2000). Government and control. In D. Garland & R. Sparks (eds). *Criminology and Social Theory*. Clarendon Studies in Criminology. Oxford: Oxford University Press.

Seddon, T. (2000). Explaining the drug-crime link: Theoretical, policy and research issues. *Journal of Social Policy*, 29(1): 95–107.

—— (2006). Drugs, crime and social exclusion: Social context and social theory in British drugs-crime research. *British Journal of Criminology*, 46: 680–703.

—— (2007). Coerced drug treatment in the criminal justice system: Conceptual, ethical and criminological issues. *Criminology and Criminal Justice*, 7(3): 269–86.

—— (2010). *A History of Drugs: Drugs and Freedom in the Liberal Age*. Abingdon, UK: Routledge.

Shaffer, D. (2006). *Reconsidering Drug Court Effectiveness: A Meta-Analytic Review*. Las Vegas, NV: University of Nevada.

Stevens, A., Berto, D., Heckmann, W., et al. (2005). Quasi-compulsory treatment of drug dependent offenders: An international literature review. *Substance Use and Misuse*, 40: 269–83.

Stevens, A., McSweeney, T., van Ooyen, M., et al. (2005). On coercion. *International Journal of Drug Policy*, 16: 207–9.

Tribe, K. (2009). The political economy of modernity: Foucault's Collège de France lectures of 1978 and 1979. *Economy and Society*, 38(4): 679–98.

Turnbull, P., McSweeney, T., Webster, R., et al. (2000). *Drug Treatment and Testing Orders: Final Evaluation Report*. Home Office Research Study 212. London: Home Office.

Urada, D., Hawken, A., Conner, B., et al. (2008). *Evaluation of Proposition 36: The Substance Abuse and Crime Prevention Act of 2000. 2008 Report*. Sacramento, CA: California Department of Alcohol and Drug Programs.

Vrecko, S. (2009). Therapeutic justice in drug courts: Crime, punishment and societies of control. *Science as Culture*, 18(2): 217–32.

Vuchinich, R., & Heather, N. (eds) (2003). *Choice, Behavioural Economics and Addiction*. Oxford: Pergamon Press.

Wilson, D., Mitchell, O., & MacKenzie, D. (2006). A systematic review of drug court effects on recidivism. *Journal of Experimental Criminology*, 2(4): 459–87.

Cannabis in cultural and legal limbo

Criminalisation, legalisation and the mixed blessing of medicalisation in the USA

Craig Reinarman

Use of cannabis or marijuana is a cultural practice that is both common and criminalised. This contradiction has helped spark a growing drug policy reform movement in the USA. Reformers have successfully exposed the high costs and ineffectiveness of punitive prohibition as the dominant drug policy paradigm. As alternatives to criminalisation, reformers have advocated rights-based legalisation, which has not been adopted, and health-based harm reduction strategies, which have enjoyed growing acceptance. Drug policy reformers generally regard various forms of medicalisation as unequivocally positive, both more effective in terms of public health and more humane. These include syringe exchanges; medical marijuana; and addiction treatment in lieu of incarceration, including 'drug courts' that practice 'therapeutic jurisprudence'.

In this chapter, however, I suggest that medicalisation is not a conceptually coherent alternative to criminalisation and that medicalisation discourses are multivalent – as easily deployed by prohibitionists in support of continued criminal punishment for drug use as they are by drug policy reformers in support of legalisation. Shifting the frame around drugs from criminal law to public health has much to recommend it, but this move foregrounds addiction-as-disease and pushes normal drug use into the shadows as deviance, which paradoxically may constrain drug policy reform in the long run.

The first section offers a brief historical sketch of cannabis criminalisation in the US and the drug control industry that created and sustains it. The second section traces the rise of the drug policy reform movement and the harm reduction paradigm. The third section describes some of the forms and consequences of medicalisation and examines, in particular, recent medical research showing a link between cannabis and psychosis. The concluding section outlines the political conjuncture that holds cannabis criminalisation in place in the US – despite, and with the help of, medicalisation.

Criminalisation and the drug control industry

Medical preparations containing cannabis were widely used in many societies for centuries. Cannabis was prescribed in American medical practice for a variety of conditions from at least the mid-nineteenth century. It was admitted to the *United States Pharmacopoeia* in 1850 and listed as a medicine in the *National Formulary* and the US *Dispensatory*. Extracts of cannabis were sold as therapeutic agents by major pharmaceutical companies.[1]

The moral status of cannabis was transformed from medicine to vice in the context of the Great Depression. A 1934 US Bureau of Narcotics report claimed that 'fifty percent of the violent crimes committed in districts occupied by Mexicans, Turks, Filipinos, Greeks, Spaniards, Latin Americans and Negroes may be traced to the abuse of marihuana'. The report quoted a narcotics officer saying: 'Marihuana has a worse effect than heroin. It gives men the lust to kill, unreasonably, without motive – for the sheer sake of murder itself.'[2] The 1936 film *Reefer Madness* depicted young people taking a few puffs and then engaging in wild sex, assault and murder. *Reefer Madness* has come to be seen as clumsy propaganda, ironically now beloved by cannabis users as a parody. But it influenced public perception and policy for three decades. After the repeal of alcohol prohibition in 1933 and several years of budget cuts,[3] the Federal Bureau of Narcotics advocated cannabis prohibition, which Congress passed in 1937. This law criminalised possession of cannabis for the first time.

As cannabis use became widespread in the 1960s and earlier claims that it caused crime and violence lost credibility, advocates of criminalisation shifted the foundation of their argument to claim that cannabis was dangerous because it had the opposite effect, causing users to lose all motivation.[4] Since then, a variety of new claims in support of dangerousness and criminalisation have been added: rising potency, addiction and mental illness.

Since 1971, when the US government first declared 'war on drugs', drug control activities have expanded continuously into more agencies and levels of the state (see 'Major components of the US drug control industrial complex'). Drug arrests have become the largest category of arrests, helping to quadruple the US incarceration rate to the highest in the world.[5] The number of Americans imprisoned specifically for drug offences increased ten-fold between 1980 and 2006.[6] The US imprisons more citizens for drug offences than all original member states of the European Union combined imprison for all offences combined, despite the EU's larger population.

In 2008 American police arrested 847 864 Americans for cannabis offences, 754 224 (88.96 per cent) for possession alone.[7] This is half of all drug arrests. Most arrested cannabis users no longer go to prison but are usually held in jail overnight and pay a fine. But this still results in a criminal record that can prevent them getting financial aid for education and makes it more difficult to get jobs. Cannabis arrests also serve as a gateway to deeper legal trouble that does end in incarceration. People on probation or parole or those who have other convictions often are sent to prison for cannabis possession, and prosecutors frequently use cannabis charges as bargaining chips to obtain longer sentences for other offences.

The people who work in drug control agencies share intelligence, equipment, technical knowledge, professional lore and an anti-drug ideology. They also share material interests. The budgets of these agencies and the careers of the drug control agents who work in them depend financially on a perpetual threat of 'drugs' and on the inference that only more stringent criminalisation will finally stem the tide. The Federal Bureau of Narcotics helped create cannabis criminalisation, and cannabis criminalisation in turn helped create a drug control industry. Taken together, this network of interlinked agencies constitutes a *drug control industrial complex*.

In focus

Major components of the US drug control industrial complex

- Drug Enforcement Administration, US Department of Justice
- Office of National Drug Control Policy (Drug Czar), White House
- Federal Bureau of Investigation
- Central Intelligence Agency
- Bureau of International Narcotics Matters, US State Department
- Drug control units in the Army, Navy, Air Force, Coast Guard, National Guard
- Immigration and Customs Enforcement
- Federal and state prisons and prison guard unions
- State police drug squads
- Local police drug squads
- Narcotic officers' associations
- Private sector drug testing companies
- Drug Abuse Resistance Education, Inc.

The drug control industrial complex is the most important force sustaining the criminalisation of cannabis. After the crack cocaine scare faded in the early 1990s,[8] cannabis arrests skyrocketed to new records each year, doubling between 1980 and 2010.[9] This sharp rise was *not* caused by increased prevalence of use, which was stable or declining, but rather appears to have been driven by the increased capacity of drug law enforcement. The Reagan and Bush-I Administrations expanded and escalated the drug war. The Clinton Administration further increased drug war funding, contingent upon effectiveness as measured by drug arrests. With cannabis being the most commonly used illicit drug, cannabis users were the low-hanging fruit.

The Drug Enforcement Administration has continued to raid medical marijuana dispensaries in defiance of President Obama's statements and his Attorney General's policy of non-interference with such dispensaries.[10] When drug policy reform activists gathered enough signatures to get a marijuana legalisation measure on the 2010 ballot in California, the California Police Chiefs Association, the California Narcotic Officers' Association and police union lobbyists led the opposition. Whenever criminalisation has faced such threats, the drug control industry has defended it.

Legalisation and the drug policy reform movement

Despite the four-decade war on drugs and tens of millions of cannabis arrests, the US government's latest national survey found that 102 404 000 Americans – that is, 41 per cent of the population older than 12 years of age – have used cannabis at least once, a quarter of them in the past year.[11] There are hundreds of references to cannabis in all genres of popular music from Louis Armstrong through Bob Dylan, the Beatles, Willie Nelson and Dr Dre. Cannabis use is depicted in dozens of major films, including *It's Complicated, Wonder Boys, Eyes Wide Shut, The Big Chill, American Beauty, The Big Lebowski* and *How to Make an American Quilt*. Some anti-drug organisations claim that these references are a key cause of cannabis use. But it is just as likely that music and movies contain so many references to cannabis because widespread use has become inscribed in popular culture. In a major international review of cannabis policy, Room, Fischer, Hall et al. concluded that 'cannabis is an enculturated drug',[12] and survey evidence from Western societies shows that cannabis use has become 'normalised'.[13]

On top of the normalisation of cannabis, the escalating war on drugs has swelled American prisons without reducing American drug problems, leading more people to see punitive prohibition as a costly failure. This has given rise to a variety of drug policy reform efforts that have coalesced into a drug policy reform movement that takes legalisation or decriminalisation of cannabis as a central goal. This movement has grown in size, scope, institutional capacity and influence.[14]

Drug policy reform organisations emerged in the wake of the 1960s, but a drug policy reform *movement* did not develop until the 1980s, when evidence began to mount that the sharing of syringes among injection drug users was a vector of HIV/AIDS transmission. This deadly epidemic helped give rise to 'harm reduction', a set of pragmatic public health practices and policies that began in the Netherlands and in Liverpool, England, with syringe exchange programs. Harm reduction was not designed as a direct challenge to prohibition, but it explicitly avoids taking a moral position against all drug use, unlike 'zero tolerance' and other drug war policies whose objective is a 'drug-free America'. Rather, harm reduction aims at the less utopian goal of reducing the harms associated with illicit drug use – and with drug policy – whether or not it reduces drug use.[15] Harm reduction policies have spread to 70 countries in the past 25 years.

Medical marijuana ballot initiatives did not derive directly from harm reduction, but within the harm reduction paradigm, depriving patients of a medicine from which they derive therapeutic benefit is a harm of criminalisation. Local campaigns for medical marijuana became the most visible front in the drug policy reform movement in the 1990s. Since 1996, voters in 15 states and Washington, DC, have passed medical marijuana initiatives. A growing number of patients and their physicians have rediscovered the range of therapeutic uses that were widely known in medical practice before criminalisation.[16]

The drug policy reform movement has more organisations, activists, funding and media coverage than ever before. For example, the National Organization for the Reform of Marijuana Laws (NORML) was founded in 1970. By 2010 it had 128 chapters in 35 states and 14 400 paid members, up tenfold since 1990. Nearly a million people have donated to support its work. The Drug Policy Alliance was formed in a merger of two drug policy reform organisations in the 1990s and plays a leading role in a broad array of drug policy reform efforts, with offices in several states and 130 000 subscribers to its 'Action Alerts'. DPA holds regular conferences that attract more than a thousand activists from dozens of countries, knitting together the disparate drug policy reform organisations into a more coherent movement.

Other key organisations include Students for Sensible Drug Policy, which has grown since 1998 to more than a hundred chapters in 41 of the 50 US states. Medical marijuana patients and their caregivers founded local advocacy organisations that became Americans for Safe Access in 2002. By 2010 it had 30 000 active members in 40 states. Law Enforcement Against Prohibition (LEAP) was started in 2002 by former narcotics officers and other police whose experience of futility on the front lines of the drug war persuaded them that legalisation was the only solution. Approximately 10 000 former police have joined LEAP across the US and in 90 other countries. And for the first time, mainstream civil rights organisations have been moved by the extreme racial skewing of cannabis arrests to endorse legalisation.[17] So, too, have the National Black Police Association and a growing number of labor unions.

In focus

Major organisations in the US drug policy reform movement

- National Organization for the Reform of Marijuana Laws
- Drug Policy Alliance
- American Civil Liberties Union
- Harm Reduction Coalition
- Students for Sensible Drug Policy
- Americans for Safe Access
- Marijuana Policy Project
- Law Enforcement Against Prohibition
- North American Syringe Exchange Network

Shifts in public opinion and public policy

The drug policy reform movement has made headway. Opinion polls show greater public support for legalising marijuana in the US than ever before. An ABC News/*Washington Post* poll found that the percentage of Americans who favour legalisation had more than doubled, from 22 per cent in 1997 to 46 per cent in 2009.[18] A 2009 Zogby poll found 52 per cent of Americans agreed that 'marijuana should be legal, taxed and regulated'. A Gallup poll found that the percentage who favour 'making use of marijuana legal' rose from 31 per cent in 2000 to 44 per cent in 2009. Gallup (2009) characterised these results as 'the most tolerant in at least 40 years' and concluded, 'If public support were to continue growing at a rate of 1% to 2% per year, as it has since 2000, the majority of Americans could favor legalization of the drug in as little as four years.'[19]

When the question is marijuana for medical purposes, repeated polls show that a strong majority of Americans already favour legalisation.[20] This shift in public opinion has been mirrored in the media. In 2009 positive stories about the legalisation of cannabis have appeared in the *New York Times*, *Newsweek*, the *Washington Post*, the *Wall Street Journal*, *Forbes Magazine*, *Texas Monthly*, *National Review* and on numerous television news and talk programs.

The reform movement also has won incremental changes in drug policy aside from medical marijuana. In 2000 the Drug Policy Alliance mounted a successful ballot initiative in California to divert non-violent, first-time drug offenders to treatment in lieu of prison. In his 2008 election campaign, Barack Obama supported this idea, saying he wanted to move drug policy

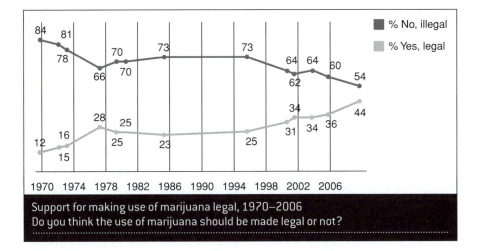

Support for making use of marijuana legal, 1970–2006
Do you think the use of marijuana should be made legal or not?

out of criminal justice and into public health. Although he does not support marijuana legalisation, he said he would not interfere with medical marijuana in states where voters have made it legal. Syringe exchange programs now operate in 160 US cities, and the Obama Administration has removed a long-standing ban on using federal funds for this purpose. In 2010 Congress passed the Fair Sentencing Act of 2009 (S. 1789), which reduced sentencing disparities between crack cocaine offences (for which mostly African Americans are arrested) and powder cocaine offences. The New York legislature repealed the notoriously punitive Rockefeller drug laws. Voters in 15 cities have passed ballot measures making marijuana possession the 'lowest law enforcement priority'. Denver has effectively decriminalised marijuana. In El Paso, Texas, the US city most affected by the violence surrounding Mexican drug cartels, the City Council unanimously passed a measure calling for a halt to the drug war and consideration of alternatives.

In the context of recession and state fiscal crisis, the mounting costs of imprisonment have strengthened the drug policy reform movement and given momentum to the shift away from criminalisation.

Medicalisations

Syringe exchange, medical marijuana, treatment in lieu of prison and other reforms march under the banner of medicalisation. Many drug policy reform activists, service providers and health professionals have been drawn to medicalisation because it seemed the only politically acceptable way to make US drug policy less harsh and to get help for those who need it. But defining drug issues within medicalisation discourse carries consequences.

The quintessential model for what became the harm reduction paradigm is syringe exchange, which is justified in terms of epidemiological evidence of its effectiveness in reducing the spread of HIV/AIDS and hepatitis C to the general population. Many lives have been saved, but this public health logic neither challenges the criminalisation that led to risky syringe sharing in the first place nor asserts the human rights of injecting drug users.

Medical research has shown a variety of therapeutic benefits from cannabis, and medical marijuana advocates have pushed for the legalisation of cannabis for such medical uses. This provides moral legitimation to those who suffer from medical conditions for which physicians are willing to recommend cannabis. Yet it also restricts a drug widely used for quotidian pleasures to the terrain of medicine, where such pleasures are pushed outside the bounds of moral legitimacy, leaving non-medical cannabis use either deviant or implicitly pathologised.

All modalities of drug treatment rest on the notion of addiction-as-disease. But this genre of medicalisation is a mixed blessing, too. First, most drug users, particularly cannabis users, are not addicts and neither need nor want treatment. Second, even for addicts, conceiving of their behaviour as caused by a disease individualises it and narrows the aperture such that the contributions of the social contexts of use fall out of view. Third, defining addiction as a disease that prevents addicts from controlling their drug use is often a self-fulfilling denial of their human agency.

Although labelling addiction a disease has justified expanded treatment, the same dreaded disease is then invoked to justify imprisonment.[21] Many treatment providers once imagined treatment as an *alternative* to criminalisation, but they lost this policy argument to the more politically powerful drug control complex. When treatment providers opposed criminalisation, they lost resources; when they supported criminalisation, they gained resources.[22] Addiction-as-disease has helped get services to many people who need them, but rather than leading to a fundamental shift of gaze towards public health approaches it has instead become an *adjunct* to criminalisation.

Similarly, under the heading of 'therapeutic jurisprudence', specialised 'drug courts' dispense a contradictory blend of treatment and punishment. Treatment is based on the assumption that addiction-as-disease prevents drug users from thinking rationally, but punishment is based on the assumption that they rationally weigh the consequences of their actions. In the context of a criminal court, this form of medicalisation coerces a guilty plea as a condition of getting treatment and deprives drug offenders of the procedural protections afforded other offenders. Drug court judges are not impartial arbiters who ensure that the state has proven its cases but leaders of 'treatment teams'. By defining drug use as disease, drug courts have helped many get treatment, but at the same time widened the net of criminalisation.

The case of cannabis and psychosis

The most recent instance of medicalisation supporting criminalisation is the claim that cannabis is associated with psychosis. Since 2000 an array of new, government-funded studies have reported evidence of such an association.[23] This research has been pressed into political service.[24] In a press conference on 3 May 2005, for example, Director of the US Office of National Drug Control Policy (or 'Drug Czar') John Walters claimed there was 'growing and compelling evidence... that regular marijuana use can contribute to depression, suicidal thoughts and schizophrenia'. He told of a 15-year-old whose marijuana use had driven him to suicide, and he brought the teen's grieving parents to the press conference. The parents later revealed on a radio talk show, however, that four drug tests in the months before their son's suicide and a toxicology test in the hospital afterward found no trace of cannabis, only alcohol.

Similarly, the day after a gunman in Tucson, Arizona, shot a Congress-woman in the head and killed a judge and five others, a conservative columnist wrote that the shootings 'should remind us why we regulate marijuana'. He cited research which he said showed that 'People who smoke marijuana are twice as likely to develop schizophrenia as those who do not smoke'.[25] A week later, another anti-drug crusader took the media to task for 'its tendency to overlook or underplay' the 'relationship of marijuana use to psychotic ill-nesses', implying that marijuana triggered the Tucson killings.[26]

Leaving aside its uses as propaganda, the association between cannabis and psychosis should not be dismissed. There are limitations in these studies and the strength of the correlations between cannabis use and psychotic symptoms varies, but the relationship persists across studies using different methods in different societies. Some show that the correlation becomes stronger with higher doses or longer use. Several knowledgeable researchers have argued that both the dose-specific response and the persistence of the association suggest the relationship is causal.

Given the history of politicised claims about cannabis, however, the nature of the evidence of a link to mental illness warrants critical reflection. The invocation of disease categories like 'psychosis' or 'schizophrenia' does a kind of 'cultural work'.[27] It brings questions about cannabis use into the realm of medicine and science, where experts are presumed to employ 'value-free' methods and measures. But certain values have been built into the methods and measures used to construct the indicators of the disease categories that are then linked to cannabis. These then become sedimented into 'statistical risk factors' and finally appear simply as 'facts' in the media and public discourse.

For example, authors of such studies tend to write of 'psychosis' as if it were a single, discrete disease entity that, once 'caused', a person 'has'. But that is not the case. Diseases 'are usually presented as if a disease were a constant, timeless biological entity uninfluenced by the larger social context' when it is usually impossible to 'directly apprehend the biological core of disease unadulterated by attitudes, beliefs, and social conditions'.[28] As Mol shows, even a common physical disease like atherosclerosis is constructed by the ongoing 'enactments' of various medical specialists in interaction with patients, each with different experiences of symptoms, which change over time.[29]

This is even more so with a disease category like 'psychosis'. Most of the cannabis/psychosis studies measure indirect indicators of psychosis that are interpreted as 'symptoms' of the underlying disease even when they are transient or without consequence. One frequently cited longitudinal study found that daily cannabis users were 1.6 times more likely than non-users to report psychotic symptoms that can indicate schizophrenia.[30] But in this study, as in several others, neither psychosis nor schizophrenia were actually diagnosed or directly measured; rather, survey respondents checked any of ten 'symptoms' they had experienced in the month before interview. The act of translation whereby responses to a self-administered questionnaire become 'psychotic symptoms' and then come to stand for 'psychosis' itself is camouflaged by the conventions of scientific presentation.

Such responses could indeed be symptoms, but they are open to other interpretations. 'Hearing voices that other people do not hear' could be a sign of psychosis, but one in five Americans describe themselves as born-again, fundamentalist Christians who regularly hear the voice of God. 'Feeling that you are being watched or talked about by others' could be a paranoid delusion, but many normal high school students would check this box, too. 'Having ideas and beliefs that are not shared by others' fits all contrarian characters and most great leaders in history.[31]

The measures of cannabis use in these studies also bear scrutiny. They vary markedly: having tried cannabis at age 18; any cannabis use at age 15; cannabis dependence at age 18; daily cannabis use at any point; even any cannabis use at all. The follow-up intervals range from one to 27 years, so it is impossible to control for all the events and influences other than cannabis use – in some studies a single use episode years ago – that might cause 'psychotic symptoms'.

Many of the studies statistically controlled for other possible causes, but the hypothesis that such symptoms and cannabis use share a 'common cause' cannot be ruled out.[32] A recent analysis of ten key prospective cohort studies found that after controlling for some other possible causes, only five showed a significant association between cannabis use and psychosis, and two did not determine 'whether the psychotic symptoms . . . occurred only whilst intoxicated, or whether they persisted'.[33]

Some researchers found that 'regular' cannabis use increased the probability of developing schizophrenia or schizophreniform symptoms.[34]

Schizophrenia is not generally understood as a disease one can 'catch' or cause by virtue of behaviour. A recent review of six longitudinal studies in five countries concluded that it is 'plausible that cannabis use precipitates schizophrenia' in those who are already 'vulnerable because of a personal or family history of schizophrenia'.[35] Precipitation of a disease one already has, however, is different from causation.

The notion that a psychoactive drug might trigger an acute episode of already-present mental illness is certainly plausible. However, the epidemiological evidence on mental illness does not support this. Lifetime prevalence of cannabis use has increased steadily from a few per cent before the 1960s to nearly half the adult population in 2009.[36] The hypothesis that cannabis causes psychosis or schizophrenia would predict a rise in the rates of these disorders. But population-level rates of psychosis and schizophrenia have not increased and do not generally correlate with cannabis use rates.[37]

One review of this research noted, 'The contentious issue of whether cannabis use can cause serious psychotic disorders that would not otherwise have occurred cannot be answered based on the existing data.'[38] Authors of studies suggesting an association between cannabis and psychosis carefully qualify their findings in scientific journals. But they have little control over the inferences drawn from their research by the media, politicians and the public as these findings find their way into the broader culture. As deployed in the drug war in support of the criminalisation narrative, correlation becomes causation.

Yet even if the evidence could establish that cannabis causes psychosis in those with no history of disorder, it does not follow that criminalisation is the appropriate policy. An analysis of the World Health Organization's Mental Health Surveys concluded, 'Globally, drug use is not . . . simply related to drug policy, since countries with stringent user-level illegal drug policies did not have lower levels of use than countries with liberal ones.'[39] The European Union sponsored a major assessment of the effectiveness of drug control policy between 1998 and 2007, when arrests and imprisonment of users had increased sharply. The authors concluded, 'We found no evidence that the global drug problem was reduced . . . In aggregate . . . the problem became more severe.'[40] It seems fair to say that the evidence may support warnings about an increased risk of 'psychotic symptoms' among those already vulnerable to psychosis, but it does not support the inference that criminalisation is an effective means of reducing that risk.

Conclusion

Medicalisation discourse is multivalent. It helped create the discursive space in which it was possible to legitimate syringe exchanges, medical marijuana licensing systems, expanded addiction treatment and other reforms that have made US drug policy less draconian. But this has come at the cost of putting the imprimatur of 'science' and the presumption of 'objectivity' on contested definitions of 'risk' and 'disease', which reinforce criminalisation and strand normal drug use in the realm of deviance.

Medicalisation also leaves certain key questions off the table. More than 200 studies have been funded on potential mental health *risks* of cannabis but almost none on the potential mental health *benefits* of cannabis. Yet when researchers on occasion have asked users what effects they get from cannabis, they far more frequently report 'relaxation', 'stress relief' and 'improved sleep' than symptoms of psychosis.[41] This is especially so for medical marijuana patients.[42]

Even the most rigorous medical research is designed, funded, conducted and interpreted in a cultural context dominated by criminalisation discourse. The new research on a cannabis–psychosis link is only the most recent form of medicalisation that has been marshalled in support of criminalisation. Despite the growing drug policy reform movement and public opinion that is increasingly disenchanted with the war on drugs, medicalisation has not developed into an alternative drug policy regime. A powerful conjuncture of pressures holds criminalisation in place:

- *Institutional.* As noted earlier, the drug control industrial complex zealously defends its ideological and material interests in criminalisation. Police departments use claims about the risks of drug use to justify budget requests and deploy drug laws as a means of social control of subaltern groups.[43] Cannabis arrests are used as evidence of effectiveness and therefore a warrant for continued drug war funding to fiscally strapped local police departments. The drug control complex remains the source of official, expert information about the nature and extent of America's drug problem for policy-makers.
- *Constitutional.* Article VI of the US Constitution states that federal law 'shall be the supreme Law of the Land'. Legal reforms in the US can most easily be made at the local level, and least easily at the more distant federal level. This is why medical marijuana initiatives arise at the state level. In 2010 California voters nearly passed a cannabis legalisation initiative. But when early polls showed it leading, the Attorney General in Washington asserted federal supremacy, warning that if it passed he would order all necessary law enforcement to ensure that national drug laws were fully enforced. A constitutional structure in which federal law trumps state law has been a brake on drug policy reform and a structural source of support for continued criminalisation.
- *Cultural.* When the Federal Bureau of Narcotics first pushed Congress to criminalise cannabis, it could rely on several widely shared cultural values, including the idea that ingesting a substance simply for pleasure

was sinful.[44] Americans tend to approach even therapeutic drugs with a kind of 'pharmacological Calvinism';[45] it is morally acceptable to take a drug to bring oneself up from illness to normal, but not to bring oneself up from normal to better-than-normal. When cannabis was initially criminalised during the Depression, Congress found it easy to condemn a practice that was depicted as cutting against the grain of the Protestant work ethic. The American middle class has long feared losing self-control or work discipline and falling into the lower classes.[46] Fear of downward mobility, particularly given the diminishing job prospects for young people, was only heightened in the recession of 2008. By this logic, drugs are especially feared because they are thought to 'cause' one to lose self-control or work discipline. Such deep cultural values have formed the backdrop for a series of drug scares, all of which bolstered the criminalisation narrative.[47]

Since 1990, the drug policy reform movement has gone some way towards dislodging criminalisation from its hegemonic position, forcing it to contend openly with medicalisation and legalisation. Reforms rooted in health-based discourse like medicalisation have been more successful than reforms rooted in rights-based discourse like legalisation. Perhaps because it does not directly challenge criminalisation but in some respects reinforces it, medicalisation remains more politically palatable than legalisation.

As such, medicalisation may be a necessary stage through which US cannabis policy must pass to get to something else. But the word 'stage' implies a teleological trajectory, as if cannabis policy had a clear direction and an ultimate end. I am not sure that this is true. If US cannabis policy can be said to be travelling a road from criminalisation to legalisation, it is a road riddled with potholes, drawbridges in the up position and long detours. Given the forces holding criminalisation in place, it does not seem safe to assume that US drug policy is moving inexorably towards some form of legalisation. The old shows signs of dying, but the new still cannot be born. Cannabis remains caught in a cultural and legal limbo in the US, entangled in conflicting webs of meaning from which it will not be easily extricated. The only thing safe to predict is increasing contestation.

Medicalisation will be of limited help in settling the debate over cannabis policy because the issues ultimately do not hinge on technical knowledge of health risks. Much of what Americans eat, a lot of the ways in which they play and many of the technologies of the self they use entail health risks. In the last instance, the debate is not about 'objective' assessments of such risks but rather the morality of pleasure seeking, a political issue about which medical science is mostly mute. Cannabis may be suspended in this contradictory space for a long time.

Acknowledgements

The author is grateful to Tom Heddleston, Harry G. Levine, Sheigla Murphy, Pat O'Hare, Freek Polak, Marsha Rosenbaum and Allen St Pierre, for helpful suggestions on an earlier draft and to Suzanne Fraser and David Moore for their theoretical insights and editorial patience. The flaws that remain are entirely the author's doing.

Notes

1 Brecher, *Licit and Illicit Drugs*.
2 Bonnie & Whitebread, *The Marijuana Conviction*, pp. 146–7.
3 Dixon, 'Bureaucracy and morality'.
4 Himmelstein, *The Strange Career of Marihuana*.
5 Cooney & Burt, 'Less crime, more punishment'; International Centre for Prison Studies, *Prison Brief*.
6 Bureau of Justice Statistics, 2007, table 4.1.
7 FBI, *Uniform Crime Reports*.
8 Reinarman, Cohen & Kaal, 'The limited relevance of drug policy'.
9 FBI, *Uniform Crime Reports*.
10 US Department of Justice, 'Attorney General announces formal medical marijuana guidelines'.
11 Office of Applied Statistics, *Results from the 2008 National Survey on Drug Use and Health*.
12 Room, Fischer, Hall et al., *Cannabis Policy*, p. 145.
13 For example Parker, Aldridge & Measham, *Illegal Leisure*; Johnston, O'Malley & Bachman, *Monitoring the Future*; Eisenbach-Stangl, Moskalewicz & Thom, *Two Worlds of Drug Consumption in Modern Societies*.
14 Nadelmann, 'An end to marijuana prohibition'.
15 See Heather, Wodak, Nadelmann et al., *Psychoactive Drugs and Harm Reduction*; Cheung, Erickson & Riley, *Harm Reduction*.
16 Grinspoon & Bakalar, *Marijuana, the Forbidden Medicine*.
17 Huffman, 'Marijuana law reform is a civil rights issue'.
18 ABC News, 'Changing views on gay marriage, gun control, immigration and legalising marijuana'.
19 Gallup, 'US support for legalising marijuana reaches new high'.
20 For example Pew Research Center, *Broad Public Support for Legalising Medical Marijuana*.
21 Reinarman, 'Addiction as accomplishment'.
22 Bertram, Blachman, Sharpe et al., *Drug War Politics*.
23 For example, Degenhardt & Hall, 'The association between psychosis and problematical drug use among Australian adults'; van Os, Bak, Hanssen et al., 'Cannabis use and psychosis'; Fergusson, Horwood & Swain-Campbell, 'Cannabis dependence and psychotic symptoms in young people'. For overall analyses of such studies, see Macleod, Oakes, Copello et al., 'Psychological and social sequelae of cannabis and other illicit drug use by young people'; Moore, Zammit, Lingford-Hughes et al., 'Cannabis use and risk of psychotic or affective mental health outcomes'; McLaren, Silins, Hutchinson et al., 'Assessing evidence for a causal link between cannabis and psychosis'.
24 For example, Walters, 'The myth of "harmless" marijuana'.
25 Frum, 'Did pot trigger Giffords' shooting?'
26 Califano, 'Tragedy in Tucson'.

27 Rosenberg, 'The tyranny of diagnosis', p. 246.
28 Aronowitz, *Making Sense of Illness*, pp. 12–13.
29 Mol, *The Body Multiple*.
30 Fergusson, Horwood & Ritter, 'Tests of causal linkages between cannabis use and psychotic symptoms'.
31 Studies of how specific and sensitive such questions are 'suggest that the psychosis and paranoid scales of the instrument do not identify psychotic patients in clinical samples, and that participants who are not psychotic may have elevated scores on this scale' (McLaren, Silins, Hutchinson et al., 'Assessing evidence for a causal link between cannabis and psychosis', p. 14).
32 Room, Fischer, Hall et al., *Cannabis Policy*, p. 36.
33 McLaren, Silins, Hutchinson et al., 'Assessing evidence for a causal link between cannabis and psychosis', p. 14.
34 For example, Arseneault, Cannon, Witton et al., 2004.
35 Degenhardt & Hall, 'Is cannabis use a contributory cause of psychosis?', p. 556.
36 Office of Applied Statistics, *Results from the 2008 National Survey on Drug Use and Health*.
37 For example Degenhardt, Hall & Lynskey, 'Testing hypotheses about the relationship between cannabis use and psychosis'; Frisher, Crome, Martino & Croft, 'Assessing the impact of cannabis use on trends in diagnosed schizophrenia'.
38 McLaren, Silins, Hutchinson et al., 'Assessing evidence for a causal link between cannabis and psychosis', p. 17.
39 Degenhardt, Chiu, Sampson et al., 'Toward a global view of alcohol, tobacco, cannabis, and cocaine use', p. 1053; cf. Reinarman, Cohen & Kaal, 'The limited relevance of drug policy'.
40 Reuter & Trauttman, *A Report on Global Illicit Drugs Markets 1998–2007*.
41 For example Reinarman & Cohen, 'Law, culture, and cannabis'.
42 Grinspoon & Bakalar, *Marijuana, the Forbidden Medicine*; Institute of Medicine, *Marijuana and Medicine*.
43 For example Levine & Small, *Marijuana Arrest Crusade*.
44 Becker, *Outsiders*.
45 Gaylin, 'Feeling good and doing better', p. 3.
46 Ehrenreich, *Fear of Falling*.
47 Reinarman & Levine, *Crack in America*, pp. 5–8.

References

ABC News (2009). Changing views on gay marriage, gun control, immigration and legalising marijuana. Retrieved 30 March 2011. http://abcnews.go.com/PollingUnit/Obama100days/story?id=7459488&page=1.

Aronowitz, R.A. (1998). *Making Sense of Illness: Science, Society, and Disease*. New York: Cambridge University Press.

Arseneault, L., Cannon, M., Witton, J., et al. (2004). Causal association between cannabis and psychosis: Examination of the evidence. *British Journal of Psychiatry*, 184: 110–17.

Becker, H.S. (1963). *Outsiders: Studies in the Sociology of Deviance*. New York: Free Press.

Bertram, E., Blachman, M., Sharpe, K., & Andreas, P. (1996). *Drug War Politics*. Berkeley: University of California Press.

Bonnie, R.J., & Whitebread, C.H. (1974). *The Marijuana Conviction: A History of Marijuana Prohibition in the US*. Charlottesville, VA: University Press of Virginia.

Brecher, E.M. (1972). *Licit and Illicit Drugs*. Boston: Little Brown.

Bureau of Justice Statistics (2007). *Sourcebook of Criminal Justice Statistics, 2007*. Washington, DC: US Department of Justice.

Califano, J. (2011). Tragedy in Tucson: Did marijuana play a part? Retrieved 30 March 2011. http://chairmanscorner.casacolumbia.org.

Cheung, Y., Erickson, P.G., & Riley, D.M. (eds) (1997). *Harm Reduction: A New Direction for Drug Policies and Programs*. Toronto: University of Toronto Press.

Cooney, M., & Burt, C.H. (2008). Less crime, more punishment. *American Journal of Sociology*, 114: 491–527.

Degenhardt, L., & Hall, W. (2001). The association between psychosis and problematical drug use among Australian adults. *Psychological Medicine*, 31: 659–68.

—— (2006). Is cannabis use a contributory cause of psychosis? *Canadian Journal of Psychiatry*, 51: 556–65.

Degenhardt, L., Chiu, W.-T., Sampson, N., et al. (2008). Toward a global view of alcohol, tobacco, cannabis, and cocaine use: Findings from the WHO mental health surveys. *PLoS Medicine*, 5(7): 1053–67.

Degenhardt, L., Hall, W., & Lynskey, M.T. (2003). Testing hypotheses about the relationship between cannabis use and psychosis. *Drug and Alcohol Dependence*, 71: 37–48.

Dixon, D. (1968). Bureaucracy and morality. *Social Problems*, 16: 143–56.

Ehrenreich, B. (1989). *Fear of Falling: The Inner Life of the Middle Class*. New York: Harper Collins.

Eisenbach-Stangl, I., Moskalewicz, J., & Thom, B. (eds) (2009). *Two Worlds of Drug Consumption in Modern Societies*. Farnham, UK: Ashgate.

EMCDDA Statistical Bulletin 2006 (2007). Lisbon, Portugal.

Federal Bureau of Investigation (2009). *Uniform Crime Reports: Crime in the United States, 2008*. Washington, DC: US Department of Justice.

Fergusson, D.M., Horwood, L.J., & Ritter, E.M. (2005). Tests of causal linkages between cannabis use and psychotic symptoms. *Addiction*, 100: 354–66.

Fergusson, D.M., Horwood, L.J., & Swain-Campbell, N.R. (2003). Cannabis dependence and psychotic symptoms in young people. *Psychological Medicine*, 33: 15–21.

Frisher, M., Crome, I., Martino, O., & Croft, P. (2009). Assessing the impact of cannabis use on trends in diagnosed schizophrenia in the United Kingdom from 1996 to 2005. *Schizophrenia Research*, 113(2–3): 123–8.

Frum, D. (2011). Did pot trigger Giffords' shooting? *FrumForum*, 9 January.

Gallup (2009). US support for legalising marijuana reaches new high. 19 October.

Gaylin, W. (1984). Feeling good and doing better: Introduction. In T. Murray, W. Gaylin & R. Macklin (eds). *Feeling Good and Doing Better: Ethics and Nontherapeutic Drug Use* (pp. 1–10). Clifton, NJ: Humana Press.

Grinspoon, L., & Bakalar, J.B. (1993). *Marijuana, the Forbidden Medicine*. New Haven, CT: Yale University Press.

Heather, N., Wodak, A., Nadelmann, E., O'Hare, P. (eds) (1993). *Psychoactive Drugs and Harm Reduction: From Faith to Science*. London: Whurr Publishers.

Himmelstein, J. (1983). *The Strange Career of Marihuana*. Westport, CT: Greenwood Press.

Huffman, A. (2010). Marijuana law reform is a civil rights issue. *Huffington Post*, 6 July.

Institute of Medicine (1999). *Marijuana and Medicine: Assessing the Science Base*. Washington, DC: National Academy Press.

International Centre for Prison Studies (2010). *Prison Brief*. London: King's College. Retrieved 30 March 2011. www.kcl.ac.uk/depsta/law/research/icps/worldbrief/.

Johnston, L., O'Malley, P., & Bachman, J. (2002). *Monitoring the Future: National Survey Results on Drug Use, 1975–2001*, vol. 2: *College Students and Adults Ages 19–40*. Bethesda, MD: National Institute on Drug Abuse.

Levine, H.G., & Small, D.P. (2009). *Marijuana Arrest Crusade: Racial Bias and Police Policy in New York City, 1997–2007*. New York Civil Liberties Union, 2009. Retrieved 30 March 2011. www.nyclu.org/files/MARIJUANA-ARREST-CRUSADE_Final.pdf.

McLaren, J.A., Silins, E., Hutchinson, D., et al. (2010). Assessing evidence for a causal link between cannabis and psychosis. *International Journal of Drug Policy*, 21(1): 10–19.

Macleod, J., Oakes, R., Copello, A., et al. (2004). Psychological and social sequelae of cannabis and other illicit drug use by young people. *Lancet*, 363(9421): 1579–88.

Mol, A. (2002). *The Body Multiple: Ontology in Medical Practice*. Durham, NC: Duke University Press.

Moore, T.H., Zammit, S., Lingford-Hughes, A., et al. (2007). Cannabis use and risk of psychotic or affective mental health outcomes. *Lancet*, 370(9584): 319–28.

Nadelmann, E.A. (2004). An end to marijuana prohibition: The drive to legalise picks up. *National Review*, 12 July, pp. 28–33.

Office of Applied Statistics, Substance Abuse and Mental Health Services Administration (2010). *Results from the 2008 National Survey on Drug Use and Health*. Tables G1–4. Rockville, MD: US Department of Health and Human Services. Retrieved 30 March 2011. http://oas.samhsa.gov/nsduhLatest.htm.

Parker, H., Aldridge, J., & Measham, F. (1998). *Illegal Leisure: The Normalisation of Adolescent Recreational Drug Use*. London: Routledge.

Pew Research Center (2010). *Broad Public Support for Legalising Medical Marijuana*. Washington, DC: Pew Research Center Publications.

Reinarman, C. (2005). Addiction as accomplishment: Discursive construction of disease. *Addiction Research and Theory*, 13: 307–20.

Reinarman, C., & Cohen, P. (2007). Law, culture, and cannabis. In M. Earleywine (ed.), *Pot Politics: Marijuana and the Costs of Prohibition* (pp. 113–49). New York: Oxford University Press.

Reinarman, C., Cohen, P., & Kaal, H. (2004). The limited relevance of drug policy: Cannabis in Amsterdam and San Francisco. *American Journal of Public Health*, 94: 836–42.

Reinarman, C., & Levine, H.G. (eds) (1997). *Crack in America: Demon Drugs and Social Justice*. Berkeley: University of California Press.

Reuter, P., & Trauttman, F. (eds) (2009). *A Report on Global Illicit Drugs Markets 1998–2007*. Brussels: European Commission.

Room, R., Fischer, B., Hall, W., et al. (2010). *Cannabis Policy: Moving Beyond Stalemate*. Oxford, UK: Oxford University Press.

Rosenberg, C. (2002). The tyranny of diagnosis: Specific entities and individual experience. *Milbank Quarterly*, 80(2): 237–60.

US Department of Justice (2009). Attorney General announces formal medical marijuana guidelines. Washington, DC: US Department of Justice, 19 October.

van Os, J., Bak, M., Hanssen, M., et al. (2002). Cannabis use and psychosis: A longitudinal population-based study. *American Journal of Epidemiology*, 156(4): 319–27.

Walters, J. (2002). The myth of 'harmless' marijuana. *Washington Post*, 1 May, p. A25.

Drugs, crime and the law in Australia

Ian Warren

Although prohibition is the dominant approach to regulating illicit drugs throughout much of the Western world, the criminal justice system is limited in minimising illegal drug supply and use. After outlining current Australian law enforcement statistics on illicit drug seizures, this chapter reviews a sample of cases decided between January and June 2010 to illustrate how criminal courts determine legal responsibility and sentences for drug trafficking and related activities. The case analysis highlights how a dominant focus on retribution and deterrence overrides the effects of various individual factors that contribute to many low-level trafficking offences. Although this emphasis might justify a criminal conviction and punishment, an alternative evidence-based strategy that aims to reduce drug-related harm appears to be more appropriate, particularly for low-level suppliers who also use illegal drugs. The supervised provision of cannabis or heroin to registered users will not necessarily eliminate all problems associated with illicit drug supply. However, these harm reduction methods can help contain the effects of questionable legal principles, harsh sentencing and law enforcement corruption under the criminal law and prohibitionist philosophy.

Trends in contemporary drug law enforcement

Since the late 1990s Australia's 'zero tolerance' policies have usually been examined in relation to the use of illicit drugs rather than the more complex issues associated with their supply.[1] The evils of drug trafficking appear beyond question, and calls for more intensive law enforcement activity and harsher criminal punishments aimed at those who 'prey on our children' or 'peddle death' frequently appear in the Australian media.[2] However, several intricate problems emerge when assessing whether current law enforcement strategies, court processes and criminal punishments genuinely reduce drug-related harm or the scale of the illegal drug trade.

Conservative estimates suggest the range of federal, state and customs drug law enforcement initiatives cost Australian taxpayers around $1.9 billion per annum.[3] The influence of these interventions is generally assessed by comparing the quantities of drugs seized by police or the number of charges laid for drug trafficking offences with estimates of the scale of illicit drug use throughout the community.[4] However, variations in data from different sources make it difficult to identify the extent of illegal drug supply or the availability and use of most illicit drugs at street-level.

Between June 2008 and June 2010 there was a slight decline in the number of prosecutions for cultivating, manufacturing and trafficking illicit drugs in the state of Victoria. Nevertheless, prosecution rates are relatively stable, with around 4300 offences being detected each year.[5] This contrasts with around 10 000 annual prosecutions for the possession and use of illegal drugs. Between June 2008 and 2009 the Australian Federal Police recorded 47 major seizures of illegal precursor chemicals, commonly used to manufacture various drugs including speed, weighing a total of 1816.7 kilograms. However, during the equivalent period in 2009 and 2010, only 343.2 kilograms of precursors were seized in 58 operations. The variable trend with illegal sedatives is more striking, with 53 seizures involving 3335.1 kilograms being detected between June 2008 and 2009, compared to 62 seizures involving 97.0 kilograms in June 2009–10.[6] During the same two-year period, heroin seizures increased from 327 cases involving 229.1 kilograms in 2008–09 to 392 cases involving 392.6 kilograms in 2009–10.

According to the Australian Customs and Border Protection Service,[7] more sophisticated methods of screening luggage and cargo, along with improved strategic cooperation between state, federal and overseas law enforcement agencies,[8] have resulted in greater numbers of people being detected while attempting to traffic smaller quantities of illegal drugs into Australia. Greater international vigilance in curbing the global production and distribution of different illegal drugs,[9] or targeted crackdowns on specific drugs considered to warrant closer attention by Australian law enforcement agencies, could also help explain these annual fluctuations in reported illicit drug seizures.

Despite these supply-reduction efforts, available research demonstrates that illegal drug distribution networks are highly resilient, evasive and persistent. Illicit drug use in Australia remains widespread, particularly among men and women aged between 15 and 29 years of age.[10] The street-level price and purity of most substances has also barely altered in the past decade.[11] When police target 'hot-spots' where drugs are sold or consumed, the market generally adapts by employing more 'careful and consistent' distribution and consumption methods[12] or relocating to other geographic regions.[13] When changes in price, purity and availability occur, such as the 2001 Australian heroin drought, suppliers and users commonly resort to other drugs such as cocaine. These market shifts can generate short-term increases in violent crime,[14] while the range of illicit drugs often diversifies once the drought subsides. Law enforcement agencies are also concerned about the influence of prohibition on their integrity. Considerable time and expenditure is devoted to specialist investigations directed at police, given potential incentives for the selective non-enforcement or outright contravention of drug laws.[15] Questions also emerge over the storage and destruction of illicit drugs once they have been seized by police and used as evidence in trafficking prosecutions.[16]

It is debatable whether current prohibitions on drug trafficking sufficiently deter, prevent or eliminate the demand for illicit drugs in Australia. It is also questionable whether the criminal justice system is a cost-efficient way of protecting the community from drug-related harm while respecting the rights of people suspected of drug trafficking.[17] Some Australian states recognise these problems and decriminalise minor 'personal-scale' offences[18] or adopt infringement penalty schemes to regulate the possession and use of illegal substances.[19] Others offer various therapeutic treatment options administered independently of the criminal justice system. These initiatives recognise that illicit drug users are often not deterred by criminal punishments.[20] However, such alternatives to criminal prosecution do not extend to those charged with drug trafficking, even if they have an extensive history of drug abuse. The remainder of this chapter outlines how Australian courts balance competing individual and social tensions when imposing a criminal conviction for drug trafficking or allied behaviour and determining appropriate punishments once a conviction has been recorded.

Method

LexisNexis Australia is the most systematic database of Australian intermediate and higher court rulings. As part of a broader study examining trends in imposing legal liability and criminal punishments in Australian drug trafficking cases, this chapter outlines the most significant rulings from a larger sample of 28 decisions handed down between 1 January and 30 June 2010. Each ruling was located using the key search term 'drug trafficking'. The judicial narratives reveal the background facts, enforcement strategies and legal arguments raised in each case.[21] The depiction of these issues below illustrates how criminal responsibility and sentences are determined under current Australian drug trafficking laws and how the context of each offence is framed in light of the broader prohibitionist philosophies that underpin contemporary drug regulation.

Liabilities for drug trafficking and allied crimes

Ten cases in the 2010 LexisNexis sample outline the requirements for imposing criminal responsibility for drug trafficking and related crimes. These include two applications for bail pending a forthcoming trial or sentencing review (*DPP v. Theodorellos*, 2010; *Re Marijancevic*, 2010), two alleged wrongful convictions linked to suspected police corruption (*Waldron v. WA*, 2010; *R. v. El Moustafa*, 2010) and an application to confiscate property acquired from the profits of illegal drug trafficking (*Pellew v. State of Western Australia*, 2010). All verdicts demonstrate how judges determine legal liabilities for the primary and secondary legacies of serious drug crime. Two cases documented in this section examine the contentious 'deemed possession' rule, which modifies the degree of proof required to support a conviction against people loosely associated with the illicit drug trade.[22] The final case highlights the collateral risks of prohibition on the integrity of police investigations.

Momcilovic (2010)

Vera Momcilovic owned and lived in an apartment in the Melbourne Central Business District. Her boyfriend, Velmir Markovski, confessed to organising regular methamphetamine sales from Momcilovic's home. A police search revealed 394 grams of speed in a bar fridge and freezer located in the kitchen. Police also discovered a shoebox in Momcilovic's wardrobe containing $169 000 in cash, a set of digital scales and several plastic bags.[23] Throughout, Momcilovic claimed no knowledge of the drugs or the use of her home 'as a base' for illegal drug supply. Markovski supported these claims and pleaded guilty to two counts of trafficking.[24] His sentencing hearing indicated that he developed extensive gambling, health, financial and alcohol problems after a serious car accident in 1984. Markovski was also convicted for trafficking heroin and possessing a drug of dependence in 1996.

Despite her denials, Momcilovic was also convicted by a County Court jury of one count of trafficking under Victoria's 'deemed possession' laws. This was because the large quantities of drugs found on her property raised a legal presumption that she was directly involved in drug trafficking.[25] Her appeal challenged the very legality of the deemed possession law, which appears to contradict established principles of fairness embedded in criminal law philosophy.[26]

Under section 25(1) of the Victorian *Charter of Human Rights and Respon-sibilities Act* (2006), all laws must ensure that people accused of a crime are *'presumed innocent until proven guilty according to law'*. The deemed possession law reverses this requirement because, 'unless the person satisfies the court to the contrary', they are 'deemed' by the law to possess any trafficable quantities of illegal drugs found on their property. This means that a person can be guilty of trafficking even if there is no evidence to prove they were aware the drugs were on their property or they intended to possess and supply them. Supporters of this law consider it a 'reasonable and proportionate' requirement to counter 'the evil of drug trafficking'.[27]

Although Momcilovic's argument seems compelling, the Victorian Supreme Court upheld her conviction and the legality of the deemed possession rule. This indicates that state courts are reluctant to overturn guilty verdicts in jury trials and valid laws enacted by state parliaments. It remains to be seen whether a forthcoming High Court appeal will take a different approach. However, the Supreme Court did question whether the deemed possession law increased Momcilovic's likelihood of conviction, or promotes fairness under a system normally requiring the prosecution to prove allegations of guilt 'beyond reasonable doubt':

> . . . [T]here is no reasonable justification, let alone any 'demonstrable' justification, for reversing the onus of proof in connection with the possession offence . . . [The effect of the 'deemed possession' law] is to presume a person guilty of the offence of possession unless he/she proves to the contrary. That is not so much an infringement of the presumption of innocence as a wholesale subversion of it.[28]

Deemed possession laws enable people who associate with drug traffickers to be guilty of a crime, regardless of their actual knowledge of or involvement in illegal drug distribution. Appeal courts can reshape these principles in individual cases, but appear reluctant to overturn these laws to promote fairness. Therefore, the 'evils of drug trafficking' supersede any countervailing due process requirements embedded in the conventional criminal law. Further, the dominant aim of suppressing the social harms and financial profits associated with illicit drug trafficking completely silence the complex gender and power issues in Momcilovic's relationship with Markovski. This raises further doubts over the fairness of this guilty verdict.

Dixon (2010)

Shell Dixon was convicted of two counts of trafficking that were upheld on appeal.[29] As with *Momcilovic* (2010), there was doubt over which cohabiting partner organised the illegal transactions. The only evidence found during a police raid on Dixon's property, where she lived with her two daughters, were three text messages on a mobile phone from people wishing to buy cannabis and other prescription medications from either Dixon or her partner Dale, who had moved out a week earlier. One of these text messages was reproduced in the verdict: 'Hi shelly, daz. was wondering if mite b able 2 get any things...ds or rs? – cash and bit smoko also if u camm [*sic*] help me...at hagley but b bak l8r or morn.'[30]

Most remaining phone correspondence was anonymous, making it difficult to pinpoint the identity of each sender or the intended recipient. However, various secondary factors indicated that Dixon was actively engaged in illegal drug trafficking. She was unwilling to explain small quantities of drugs and several syringes found in her bedroom, but admitted that two bags of cannabis and a smoking pipe discovered by police were hers. She was also undergoing methadone treatment at the time of the raid.

The three mobile phone transactions involved willing consumers actively wishing to buy illegal drugs. However, the social ills and personal gains associated with drug trafficking superseded the impact of Dixon's illicit drug use. As with *Momcilovic* (2010), the silenced gender relations between Dixon and Dale raise further doubts about the appropriateness of this circumstantial conviction or any likely deterrent effects of Dixon's punishment. This reinforces the limits of criminal prohibition in dealing with low-level drug trafficking, particularly where any financial gains are only likely to be enough to subsidise a problematic drug habit.

Buckskin (2010)

The illegal drug economy is a common source of police corruption.[31] *Buckskin* (2010) illustrates how a seemingly innocent association between a police officer and drug trafficker can undermine public confidence in the integrity of policing activities:

> During submissions I referred to you as a corrupt police officer. That is an accurate statement. You disgrace the many honourable men and women who serve in SAPOL [the South Australia Police]...you...had a complete disregard for the ethics and responsibilities of the position that you had sworn to uphold...it is vital that the community in South Australia has confidence in the integrity of the police department and members of that department. Your behaviour has eroded that confidence.[32]

Debra Buckskin was charged with unlawfully accessing confidential vehicle registration details from the South Australia Police computer system. This information was forwarded to a known drug trafficker who provided Buckskin with personal support during her volatile marriage separation. The leaked information posed a significant danger to witnesses involved in subsequent drug trials. However, a broader series of ethical questions associated with drug law enforcement emerged during an anti-corruption investigation into Buckskin's misconduct.

The information obtained by Buckskin was enmeshed in a broader feud involving two rival motorcycle gangs operating in South Australia. One of these gangs was declared an 'outlaw organisation' under anti-organised crime laws.[33] A separate investigation under these laws targeting a member of the outlawed gang revealed several documents with the photographs and addresses of up to nine rival gang members.[34] These documents were linked to Buckskin.

Understandably, the dominant emphasis situates Buckskin's activities within the broader mandate of public trust associated with police behaviour. Nevertheless, the collateral value of confidential information involving police investigations into drug-related activity feeds a broader problem of underground criminal organisations protecting their turf, at times through intimidation and violence, despite the objectives of criminal prohibition. Therefore, Buckskin's activities were considered an intolerable compromise in the broader police 'war' against drugs.[35] However, as with both *Momcilovic* and *Dixon*, an important gender dimension is overridden by the need to uphold the integrity of complex police anti-drug and organised crime investigations.

Sentencing rulings

Sentencing appeals replicate the contest embedded in the criminal trial. When determining an appropriate penalty, courts must balance the diverse range of personal factors leading to each offence against the broader social impact of the crime. Organisations such as the Victorian Sentencing Advisory Council monitor trends in the age and sex of those convicted for possession and trafficking offences,[36] as well as the type of drug involved and the frequency and length of each penalty. The weighting of these issues in such a wide variety of trafficking cases makes it extremely difficult to achieve proportionality and consistency in sentencing.

Sixty-four per cent of rulings in the current sample involve sentencing appeals. These rulings contain useful information about the personal histories of drug offenders before and at the time of the offence, including their prior criminal histories and degrees of cooperation with justice authorities. The types, quantities and purity of drugs involved, any links to violence or large-scale criminal conspiracies, the extent of illegal profits, as well as the methods employed by police to detect clandestine drug distribution, usually through authorised undercover sales, phone taps and organised raids, are also documented. These issues are the key 'signs' or 'signals' of the actual and symbolic power of the courts to formally punish a convicted offender.[37] The nature and length of each punishment is therefore determined by balancing the specific circumstances of each case against broader notions of deterrence and public safety.

Power (2010)

In April 2007 Michael Power's home was searched during an investigation targeting two other people. Police found 4.7 grams of methylamphetamine powder at 10 per cent purity and 8 grams of cannabis. Power readily admitted that these drugs were for personal use. Police also discovered a samurai sword, a loaded handgun and 2917 ecstasy tablets, analysed at 30 per cent purity and weighing 219.8 grams more than the 500-gram minimum for an illegal commercial quantity of ecstasy under Victorian law. Between 3 and 499 grams is classified as a non-commercial quantity that carries a lower imprisonment penalty.

Power pleaded guilty to possessing an unregistered firearm and the trafficking offence under the 'deemed possession' law. However, he claimed that a friend left these items at his home several days before the raid. He appealed his four-year-and-two-month sentence of imprisonment, arguing that the penalty for trafficking was manifestly excessive.

The appeal was partially upheld, and Power's minimum jail term was reduced from three to two years. This was due to his lack of prior convictions, his guilty plea, his good prospects for rehabilitation and lack of proof that he was directly responsible for trafficking the ecstasy tablets. The court noted that imprisonment is an appropriate punishment in serious drug trafficking cases to promote 'general deterrence, denunciation and protection of the public'. However, the deemed possession law also suggested that Power did not own or intend to sell the drugs, would not profit from their sale and was not continuously involved in the 'business of trafficking' ecstasy.[38] Despite his guilty plea, the court indicated that Power's involvement in drug trafficking was a circumstantial by-product of his troubled personal history:

> [T]he appellant was a slow developer who did not do well at school, was diagnosed with ADHD in 1985 and left school at the Year 9 level aged 15 . . . [when] he commenced a drug habit which had dictated the course of his life since. Soon after leaving school he left the family home in Canberra and went to a youth refuge where he was assaulted and returned home for six months but then left again. At age 17 he resumed his education and completed Year 11 but gave up Year 12 halfway through. In 1995 the applicant came to Melbourne and kept in work despite his drug addiction. In December 2002, his partner of two years died of an asthma attack which was not drug-related and which led to a worsening of the appellant's drug-taking.[39]

Michael Power's drug use gradually exposed him to higher levels of the illicit drug trade. However, Power remained a fringe player with good rehabilitation prospects, a relatively stable employment history and strong family support. He also successfully completed a detoxification program before sentencing. Nevertheless, this range of mitigating factors and the operation of the 'deemed possession' law could not displace the dominant emphasis on deterring others and denouncing the social harms of drug trafficking, which led to a significant prison term.

Duncan (2010), Velevski (2010), Skubevski (2010) and Vasic (2010)

When read in conjunction, this series of separate rulings illustrates the workings of a semi-organised drug trafficking network. Each narrative implicates George Cancer as the 'go-to' person, but no formal record of his apprehension or trial is available in current legal sources. All four defendants pleaded guilty to various degrees of commercial trafficking after police investigations using legal phone taps and coordinated property searches. The charges against each defendant documented in Table 1 show a clear gradation of lower- and higher-end offending. Minor adjustments to all bar Velevski's sentence demonstrate how courts balance specific aggravating and mitigating factors when multiple charges and imprecise estimates of persistent illegal activity characterise drug trafficking prosecutions.

Duncan (2010) rests at the lower end of the trafficking spectrum. Police intercepted a telephone call from Duncan to Cancer, requesting the sale of 4000 ecstasy tablets at $15 each to be on-sold for $15.50 each. Cancer provided Duncan with 1000 additional tablets on credit. When Duncan was arrested, police discovered 5026 ecstasy tablets, more than $11 000 in cash, a fake driver's license, two mobile telephones and a small amount of methylamphetamine for personal use.

Duncan managed to cease all drug taking and obtained full-time employment while on bail. These mitigating factors reduced his sentence for methylamphetamine possession. However, although the court viewed Duncan's transaction as an 'isolated episode' compared to Cancer's more systematic activities, the quantities of drugs and money involved warranted a lengthy aggregate jail term, which also sought to deter others from similar behaviour.

> In no way could you be described as a Mr Big of the drug trade . . . the potential profit, if indeed there was any profit at all, was to be modest. However, the offence seriousness remains high and the sentence imposed must be such as will send a loud and clear message to those who may be tempted as you were to deal in a large commercial quantity of a drug of dependence and that stern punishment is a likely consequence when apprehended.[40]

Telephone intercepts and other police surveillance indicated that Pepe Velevski engaged in several transactions involving unspecified quantities of ecstasy during a three-month period in 2005. The court examined Velevski's 'loose arrangement' with Cancer, who supplied the drugs and received payment once they were on-sold. Phone communications indicated that at one stage Velevski owed Cancer up to $50 000 for outstanding sales, but each transaction usually involved between $2000 and $5000.

Table 1: Summaries of charges in Duncan (2010), Velevski (2010), Skubevski (2010) and Vasic (2010)

Case	Charges	Outcome
Duncan	1 Trafficking 1561 grams of ecstasy (6 years) 2 Possession of 2.75 grams of methylamphetamine (6 months) 3 Using false documents to open a bank account (12 months) 4 Obtaining financial advantage by using a banking facility under a false name (12 months)	Total sentence of 6.5 years with 3-year minimum retained but Count 2 reduced from 6 to 2 months
Velevski	1 Trafficking a commercial quantity of ecstasy – precise amounts unquantifiable but 612 tablets and 23.7 grams of MDMA seized (4.5 years) 2 Trafficking a commercial quantity of pseudoephedrine – 8950 tablets or 525 grams (4.5 years) 3 Trafficking a commercial quantity of methylamphetamine – precise quantities undetermined; 5.6 grams seized on arrest and admitted to trafficking over a four-month period – (2 years)	Total sentence of 7 years imprisonment with 3.5 minimum reduced to 6 years with a 3-year minimum
Skubevski	1 Trafficking a large commercial quantity of ecstasy – precise amounts undetermined, but police seized large quantities of drugs, cash and other equipment including scales – (8 years) 2 Trafficking a large commercial quantity of methylamphetamine (5 years) 3 Trafficking methylamphetamine (1.5 years) 4 Trafficking ecstasy – 3.5 grams (12 months) 5 Possession of ecstasy (9 months) 6 Possession of methylamphetamine – several small bags seized during police raid – (6 months)	Total sentence of 10 years with 6.5 minimum reduced to 9.5 years with a 6-year minimum
Vasic	1 Trafficking a large commercial quantity of ecstasy – precise amounts undetermined – (9 years) 2 Trafficking methylamphetamine – 17.8 g (2 years) 3 Trafficking a large commercial quantity of cocaine – precise amounts undetermined but estimated in excess of 1 kg – (12 years)	Appeal refused and total sentence of 14 years with 9-year minimum retained

Velevski routinely participated in the 'nightclub scene' where he distributed the drugs and consumed up to 'a gram of ice' and '30 to 40 ice tablets per day'. However, he demonstrated good rehabilitation prospects by stopping all drug use, abandoning the nightclub scene and participating in several community activities while on bail:

> You were described . . . as a gofer or a sales agent for Mr Cancer. It would appear that you received no great individual profit from your operations apart from your own ability to consume drugs. You have not . . . acquired any great assets as happens sometimes to those higher up the chain. You were designated . . . essentially of one level up from street level.[41]

As with Duncan, Velevski's sentence was reduced on appeal to reflect his lower status within the illegal network. The initial sentence was considered too harsh because it gave insufficient weight to the limited financial gains associated with Velevski's 'gofer' role and wrongly equated his activities with the severity and persistence of Cancer's.

Bill Skubevski was linked to a separate distribution network that mailed large quantities of amphetamines and ecstasy from Melbourne to Tasmania, although his precise relationship with George Cancer is never clearly stated in his sentencing ruling. All charges against Skubevski arose after several raids on his property over a three-year period. Each search produced various trafficable quantities of drugs, which were hidden in his house and car. Evidence also supplemented telephone intercepts which indicated that Skubevski was a persistent trafficker who was caught 'red-handed'. He testified that most illegal profits subsidised his extensive drug and gambling habits:

> The police executed a number of search warrants [and] . . . located two clear plastic bags containing amphetamine which had fallen out of his girlfriend's pyjama pants . . . [and] about 2000 ecstasy tablets and 220g of amphetamine located in a bread box in the kitchen. In addition, inside hollow shelving on the wall of the study police located $16 200 in cash, approximately 427g of amphetamine and approximately 21 000 ecstasy tablets. Also located during the search was another $1150 in cash, six mobile phones, a large rear hydraulic meal press, digital scales and a vacuum sealer.[42]

Alexander Vasic was a major supplier at the high-end of the distribution chain who provided Cancer with significant amounts of ecstasy, cocaine and speed for on-selling to the likes of Duncan and Velevski. Vasic was exposed to drugs while working as a nightclub security guard, where he developed a cocaine habit costing 'between $12 000 and $16 000 per month'. He was apprehended after police surveillance involving 'about 40 000 legally intercepted telephone calls',[43] which identified numerous transactions with Cancer between March and August 2005. Vasic was also charged for arranging to purchase 10 ounces of cocaine for $100 000 in a separate operation targeting 16 other suppliers. While the true extent of Vasic's dealings with

Cancer remain unclear, the following quotation indicates the scale of his activities:

> On 22 March 2005, in a telephone conversation, Mr Vasic and Mr Cancer talked about the sale of packages of some 2500 ecstasy tablets. On the next day, in another telephone conversation, Mr Vasic told Mr Cancer that he would have 40,000 ecstasy tablets by Friday. Later that night Mr Vasic telephoned Mr Cancer and asked him whether he could get together $100,000 in one hour . . . On 7 April 2005, the two discussed by telephone the price of ecstasy tablets. That evening, Mr Vasic telephoned Mr Cancer and informed him that the best price his supplier would sell the tablets for was $150,000 for 10,000 tablets and Mr Cancer agreed to purchase the tablets at that price.[44]

The quantity of illicit drugs and sums of money involved highlight the seriousness of this case. These factors were magnified by the separate cocaine deal, which was arranged while Vasic was on bail for supplying ecstasy to Cancer. Any breach of a formal court order will negate the mitigating effects of a guilty plea or an extensive history of drug use. However, *Vasic* remains in the 'mid-range' for large-scale commercial trafficking, with the aggregate 14-year sentence being well within the statutory maximum of life imprisonment. In fact, the volume of ecstasy and cocaine in *Vasic* is extremely low compared to an organised shipment seized by federal authorities in July 2010, in which up to 240 kilograms of cocaine were hidden in paving stones imported from Mexico.[45] This case is more likely to attract a penalty of life imprisonment under current Australian state or federal laws.[46]

The discourses of drug trafficking

The criminal law aims to promote social cohesion by eliminating undesirable behaviour. However, the highly selective, reactive and inherently retrospective application of the criminal justice system limits its capacity to prevent or reduce social harm. Those who are easier to detect, usually because they have a visible street presence, are the main subjects of police attention.[47] Once a person is processed through the criminal courts, the state is entitled to impose a penalty if guilt is established. Criminal punishments are commonly justified as society's 'retribution' for the harms caused by the offence. Both individual and general deterrence is supposedly achieved by incapacitating convicted offenders. A term of imprisonment imposed in one case arguably sends a message to others that similar behaviour, if detected, will attract the same consequences.[48]

Cases involving the consumption of drugs have always created problems under this approach. As drug use erodes a person's 'vicious' or 'free use of their will', it is often difficult to prove the central requirement of intention to establish criminal responsibility. This reasoning has been a central element of criminal law philosophy since the mid-nineteenth century: 'In *intoxication*, where he has been deprived of... [free will] by the transient influence of a visible cause: such as the use of wine, or opium, or other drugs, that act... on the nervous system: which condition is indeed neither more nor less than a temporary insanity produced by an assignable cause.'[49]

In recent decades Australian laws and policies associated with illegal drugs have become more punitive.[50] For Bessant, this is due to confrontational language that frames illegal drug use as a social, moral and criminal 'problem'. This language often uses metaphors that highlight the 'threat and danger' of illicit drug use to justify zero tolerance responses that target the real or imagined harms associated with drug taking.[51] These zero tolerance discourses are extended in drug trafficking cases. Questionable principles of legal responsibility, such as the deemed possession law or convictions with circumstantial evidence, and lengthy retributive and deterrence-based punishments, are validated by a dominant focus on vague notions of social harm and the extensive profits associated with illicit drug distribution.

Each case presented in this chapter indicates that it is often difficult to separate problematic drug use from involvement in illicit drug supply. The legal separation of these issues is particularly harsh on those at the bottom of the distribution chain, such as Shell Dixon, Michael Power and Paul Duncan. The limited profits from their activities simply magnify their precarious lifestyles, by subsidising their illicit drug use and increasing their exposure to police surveillance. However, the scale, persistence and profits higher up the distribution chain in *Markovski*, *Velevski*, *Skubevski* and *Vasic* are more difficult to excuse. These cases demonstrate a clear gradation of sentences based on the scale, economic value and persistence of their illegal activities. Despite varied background circumstances, the quantity and value of illicit drugs seized provides a strong foundation for ensuring consistency in the sentencing process. The parity between *Power* and *Duncan* is particularly striking, producing only a 5.5 per cent difference between the amount of ecstasy tablets seized and the length of sentence imposed for their respective trafficking offences.

The deemed possession law and the circumstantial conviction in *Dixon* illustrate how low requirements of proof widen the punitive criminal justice net in drug trafficking cases. Even though there might be doubt over the credibility of their stories, Momcilovic and Power were also convicted with little evidence to establish their direct or persistent involvement in illegal drug trafficking. More challenging are the complex gender relationships in *Momcilovic*, *Dixon* and *Buckskin*, which remain suppressed by the prevailing focus on the evils of drug trafficking. This is extremely problematic in *Buckskin*, where tighter supervision or greater personal support from within the police organisation might have altered her behaviour. Invariably, the dominant emphasis on greed, profit, social harm or enforcement corruption outweighs the influence of any coercion, addiction, personal vulnerability or the need for drug or psychological treatment that underpins each of these cases. The consequences of a drug trafficking conviction are no doubt extremely damaging for these three women.

Alternative regulatory models

Each year Australian courts examine thousands of criminal cases involving illicit drug use, possession and trafficking. While much attention has been devoted to developing alternative ways of regulating illicit drug use, new approaches to 'managing' illicit drug supply remain at the fringes of contemporary Australian regulatory discourse.[52] Further, despite the persistence of underground drug supply markets involving people with extensive histories of drug use, those charged with trafficking offences are generally ineligible for most current alternatives to criminal prosecution.

Therapeutic jurisprudence enables individual users to undergo intensive non-custodial treatment penalties if they plead guilty to a restricted range of non-violent offences that attract no more than a 12-month prison term.[53] Rather than imposing a formal conviction and potential imprisonment term, these orders aim to promote desistence from both drug use and crime through intensive supervision, counselling, court visits and periodic urine testing. Similarly, partial decriminalisation allows users to possess or cultivate limited quantities of cannabis for 'personal consumption'. However, its influence in restricting illegal cannabis supply remains to be examined.

Ultimately, these regimes focus solely on managing illicit drug use, which inadvertently reinforces the dominance of prohibition as the prevailing method of managing illegal drug supply. While alternative models that simultaneously aim to reduce the harms from illicit drug use and supply will not eliminate illegal drug trafficking, they can contain its effects in ways that prohibition struggles to achieve. The 'compassionate laws' operating in 12 jurisdictions of the United States work in tandem with criminal prohibition, by allowing the medical prescription of cannabis to treat certain illnesses. Local governments can establish dispensaries to legally distribute cannabis to qualified patients, while criminal prohibitions against cultivation can be waived for authorised suppliers and primary caregivers.[54] The conventional criminal law still technically applies to all acts of supply and consumption occurring outside this model. However, public regulatory oversight has tempered the size of the criminal economy since the introduction of these laws.

Perhaps the most radical alternative involves the medically supervised administration of heroin to registered addicts. Since the late 1990s several clinical trials throughout Europe have demonstrated that this model can have considerable individual and social benefits.[55] Addicts receiving heroin under supervision are more likely to complete their treatment and report improved personal health, housing and employment stability. Most significantly, research from Switzerland indicates that almost 70 per cent of addicts undergoing supervised treatment lose their dependence on the criminal economy for day-to-day subsistence.[56] The longer an addict stays in supervised treatment, the less likely it is that she or he will re-enter the illegal drug scene.

Despite these impressive findings, political support for heroin-assisted treatments in most jurisdictions throughout the world remains limited.[57] The possible extension of any state-sanctioned approach to other illicit recreational drugs, such as speed or ecstasy, also appears politically unthinkable.[58] However, state-supervised supply goes beyond partial decriminalisation or offering treatment as an alternative to criminal punishment, by actively challenging the financial monopoly of underground drug supply networks. Therefore, any future legal strategies that seek to produce meaningful reductions in drug-related harm must simultaneously target the interconnected economic, health and social factors associated with both illicit drug supply and use.

Conclusion

The prevailing discourses associated with the prohibition of drug trafficking aim to punish an ill-defined series of social harms and illegal financial gains. This approach endorses the suspension of many conventional due process requirements under the criminal law, in a dubious 'war' on drugs that is mainly fought with increased law enforcement resources and harsher punishments.[59] However, those prosecuted and convicted of drug trafficking often have extensive drug problems, gain limited financial benefit or have little direct involvement in the illicit drug trade. While court decisions recognise many important background factors when determining legal liabilities and sentences for trafficking offences, dominant discourses that continually highlight the evils of illicit drug trafficking invariably prevail. The extent to which this approach substantively limits illicit drug supply in Australia remains questionable. Arguably, these problems can be minimised only through a major shift in regulatory philosophy which recognises that many who engage in drug trafficking often do so to subsidise their own extensive drug use and are more responsive to treatment than to punishment. Further research into the power and limits of these dominant legal and enforcement discourses and how alternative regulatory models might help to offset or contain these problems is clearly necessary.

Notes

1 Bessant, 'From "harm minimization" to "zero tolerance" drugs policy in Australia'.
2 Wilkinson, 'Quarter of criminals convicted of drug trafficking not sentenced to jail'.
3 Homel & Willis, *A Framework for Measuring the Performance of Drug Law Enforcement*.
4 McFadden, 'The Australian Federal Police Drug Harm Index'.
5 Victoria Police, *Annual Report 2009–2010*, p. 18.
6 AFP, *Australian Federal Police Annual Report 2009–10*, p. 31.
7 Australian Customs and Border Protection Service, *Australian Customs and Border Protection Service Annual Report 2009–10*, p. 54.
8 James & Warren, 'Australian police responses to transnational crime and terrorism'.
9 UNODC, *World Drug Report, 2009*.
10 AIHW, *Statistics on Drug Use in Australia 2006*.
11 Jenkinson & Quinn, *Victorian Drug Trends 2006*.
12 Van Nostrand & Tewksbury, 'The motives and mechanics of operating an illegal drug enterprise', p. 79.
13 Aitken, Moore, Higgs et al., 'The impact of a police crackdown on a street drug scene'; Wood, Spittal, Small et al., 'Displacement of Canada's largest public illicit drug market in response to a police crackdown'.
14 Degenhardt, Day, Hall et al., 'Was an increase in cocaine use among injecting drug users in New South Wales, Australia, accompanied by an increase in violent crime?'
15 Office of Police Integrity, *Ceja Task Force*.
16 Ombudsman Victoria, *Whistleblowers Protection Act 2001*.
17 Bentham, *On Utilitarianism and Government*, p. 257.
18 Brereton, 'The history and politics of prohibition', p. 98.
19 Sutton & Hawks, 'The cannabis infringement notice scheme in Western Australia'.
20 Indermaur & Roberts, 'Drug courts in Australia'; Wundersitz, 'Criminal justice responses to drug and drug-related offending'; Bessant, 'From "harm minimization" to "zero tolerance" drugs policy in Australia'.
21 Toolan, *Narrative*, pp. 249–55.
22 Brereton, 'The history and politics of prohibition'; Brown, Farrier, Egger et al., *Brown, Farrier, Neal and Wesibrot's Criminal Laws*, pp. 929–71.
23 *Re Momcilovic*, 2008.
24 *Markovski, Moir & Sheen*, 2009.
25 *Drugs, Poisons and Controlled Substances Act* 1981, Vic, sections 5 and 73(2).
26 Brereton, 'The history and politics of prohibition'.
27 *Momcilovic*, 2010, para 24.
28 Ibid., paras 152–3.
29 *Dixon v. Lusted*, 2010.
30 *Dixon*, 2010, para 3.
31 Office of Police Integrity, *Ceja Task Force*.
32 *Buckskin*, 2010, para 9.
33 Bartels, *The Status of Laws on Outlaw Motorcycle Gangs in Australia*.
34 *Buckskin*, 2010, para 67.
35 Bessant, 'From "harm minimization" to "zero tolerance" drugs policy in Australia'.
36 Sentencing Advisory Council, *Possessing Heroin*, and *Trafficking Heroin*.
37 Innes, 'Crime as a signal'; Hodder, 'The interpretation of documents and material culture'.
38 *Power*, 2010, paras 18, 14.
39 Ibid., paras 9–10.
40 *Duncan*, 2010, para 12.
41 *Velevski*, 2010, paras 7, 17.

42 *Skubevski*, 2010, para 9.
43 *Vasic*, 2010, paras 9, 15.
44 Ibid., para 10.
45 AFP, *Australian Federal Police Annual Report 2009–10*, p. 32; AAP & Staff, 'Four charged'.
46 ALRC, *Same Crime, Same Time: Sentencing of Federal Offenders*.
47 Dixon, *Law in Policing*.
48 *Sentencing Act,* 1991, section 5.
49 Bentham, *On Utilitarianism and Government*, p. 252.
50 Rowe, 'Evidence, expedience, and the politics of marijuana'.
51 Bessant, 'From "harm minimization" to "zero tolerance" drugs policy in Australia', p. 201.
52 Rowe, 'Evidence, expedience, and the politics of marijuana'.
53 Popovic, 'Court process and therapeutic jurisprudence'.
54 McCabe, 'It's high time'.
55 Haasen, Verthein, Degkwitz et al., 'Heroin-assisted treatment for opioid dependence'; Van Den Brink, Hendriks, Blanken et al., 'Medical prescription of heroin to treatment resistant heroin addicts'.
56 Rehm, Gschwend, Steffen et al., 'Feasibility, safety, and efficacy of injectable heroin prescription for refractory opioid addicts'.
57 Fischer, Rehm, Kirst et al., 'Heroin-assisted treatment as a response to the public health problem of opiate dependence'.
58 Rowe, 'Evidence, expedience, and the politics of marijuana'.
59 Bessant, 'From "harm minimization" to "zero tolerance" drugs policy in Australia'.

References

AAP & Staff (2010, 13 July). Four charged. Sydney police seize Mexican cocaine shipment worth $84m smuggled into Melbourne port. *Herald Sun*. Retrieved 28 March 2011. www.heraldsun.com.au/news/victoria/four-charged-sydney-police-seize-cocaine-shipment-worth-84m/story-e6frf7kx-1225891177144.

Aitken, C., Moore, D., Higgs, P., et al. (2002). The impact of a police crackdown on a street drug scene: Evidence from the street. *International Journal of Drug Policy*, 13(3): 193–202.

Australian Customs and Border Protection Service (2010). *Australian Customs and Border Protection Service Annual Report 2009–10*. Canberra, ACT: Commonwealth of Australia.

Australian Federal Police (2010). *Australian Federal Police Annual Report 2009–10*. Canberra, ACT: Commonwealth of Australia.

Australian Institute of Health and Welfare (2007). *Statistics on Drug Use in Australia 2006*, Drugs Statistics Series no. 16. Canberra, ACT: AIHW. Retrieved 28 March 2011. www.aihw.gov.au/publications/index.cfm/title/10393.

Australian Law Reform Commission (2006). *Same Crime, Same Time: Sentencing of Federal Offenders*, Report no. *103*, April. Canberra, ACT: ALRC. Retrieved 25 March 2011. www.alrc.gov.au/report-103.

Bartels, L. (2010). *The Status of Laws on Outlaw Motorcycle Gangs in Australia* (2nd edn). Canberra, ACT: Australian Institute of Criminology. Retrieved 28 March 2011. www.aic.gov.au/publications/current per cent20series/rip/1-10/~/media/publications/rip/rip02_v2.pdf.

Bentham, J. (2001). *On Utilitarianism and Government*. Ware, UK: Wordsworth.

Bessant, J. (2008). From 'harm minimization' to 'zero tolerance' drugs policy in Australia: How the Howard government changed its mind. *Policy Studies*, 29(2): 197–214.

Brereton, D. (2000). The history and politics of prohibition. In G. Stokes, P. Chalk & K. Gillen (eds), *Drugs and Democracy: In Search of New Directions* (pp. 85–99). Carlton, Vic.: Melbourne University Press.

Brown, D., Farrier, D., Egger, S., et al. (2006). *Brown, Farrier, Neal and Wesibrot's Criminal Laws: Materials and Commentary on Criminal Law and Process in New South Wales* (4th edn). Leichhardt, NSW: Federation Press.

Degenhardt, L., Day, C., Hall, W., et al. (2005). Was an increase in cocaine use among injecting drug users in New South Wales, Australia, accompanied by an increase in violent crime? *BMC Public Health*, 5: 40–50.

Dixon, D. (1997). *Law in Policing: Legal Regulation and Police Practices*. Oxford, UK: Clarendon Press.

Fischer, B., Rehm, J., Kirst, M., et al. (2002). Heroin-assisted treatment as a response to the public health problem of opiate dependence. *European Journal of Public Health*, 12(3): 228–34.

Haasen, C., Verthein, U., Degkwitz, P., et al. (2007). Heroin-assisted treatment for opioid dependence: Randomised controlled trial. *British Journal of Psychiatry*, 191: 55–62.

Hodder, I. (1994). The interpretation of documents and material culture. In N.K. Denzin & Y.S. Lincoln (eds), *Handbook of Qualitative Research* (pp. 393–402). Thousand Oaks, CA: Sage.

Homel, P., & Willis, K. (2007). *A Framework for Measuring the Performance of Drug Law Enforcement*. Trends and Issues in Crime and Criminal Justice, no. *332*, February, Australian Institute of Criminology, Canberra. Retrieved 28 March 2011. www.aic.gov.au/en/publications/current%20series/tandi/321–340/tandi332. aspx.

Indermaur, D., & Roberts, L. (2003). Drug courts in Australia: The first generation. *Current Issues in Criminal Justice*, 15(2): 136–54.

Innes, M. (2004). Crime as a signal, crime as a memory. *Journal for Crime, Conflict and the Media*, 1(2): 15–22.

James, S., & Warren, I. (2010). Australian police responses to transnational crime and terrorism. J.A. Eterno & D.K. Das (eds). *Police Practices in Global Perspective* (pp. 131–72). Lanham, MD: Rowman & Littlefield.

Jenkinson, R., & Quinn, B. (2007). *Victorian Drug Trends 2006: Findings from the Illicit Drug Reporting System*. NDARC technical report no. 274. Randwick, NSW: National Drug and Alcohol Research Centre. Retrieved 28 March 2011. http://ndarc.med.unsw.edu.au/NDARCWeb.nsf/page/NDARC%20Technical% 20Reports.

McCabe, T.L. (2004). It's high time: California attempts to clear the smoke surrounding the *Compassionate Use Act*. *McGeorge Law Review*, 35(3): 545–60.

McFadden, M. (2006). The Australian Federal Police Drug Harm Index: A new methodology for quantifying success in combating drug use. *Australian Journal of Public Administration*, 65(4): 68–81.

Office of Police Integrity, Victoria (2009). *Ceja Task Force: Drug Related Corruption, Third and Final Report*, Melbourne, Vic.: OPI.

Ombudsman Victoria (2009) *Whistleblowers Protection Act 2001: Investigation into the Handling of Drug Exhibits at the Victoria Police Forensic Services Centre*. Melbourne, Vic.: Victorian Government Printer.

Popovic, J. (2006). Court process and therapeutic jurisprudence: Have we thrown the baby out with the bathwater? *elaw (Murdoch University Electronic Journal of Law)*, 1: 60–77. Retrieved 28 March 2011. https://elaw.murdoch. edu.au/archives/special_series.html.

Rehm, J., Gschwend, P., Steffen, T., et al. (2001). Feasibility, safety, and efficacy of injectable heroin prescription for refractory opioid addicts: A follow-up study. *Lancet*, 358(9291): 1417–20.

Rowe, J. (2004). Evidence, expedience, and the politics of marijuana. In P. Mendes & J. Rowe (eds), *Harm Minimisation: Zero Tolerance and Beyond* (pp. 11–19). Melbourne: Pearson Education Australia.

Sentencing Advisory Council (Victoria) (2009a). *Possessing Heroin. Sentencing Snapshot: Sentencing Trends for the Magistrates' Court of Victoria 2004–05 to 2007–08, no. 67*, February. Melbourne, Vic.: Sentencing Advisory Council. Retrieved 1 July 2010. www.sentencingcouncil.vic.gov.au/content/publications/ possessing-heroin-magistrates-court-sentencing-snapshot.

—— (2009b). *Trafficking Heroin. Sentencing Snapshot: Sentencing Trends for the Magistrates' Court of Victoria 2004–05 to 2007–08, no. 71*, February. Melbourne, Victoria: Sentencing Advisory Council. Retrieved 1 July 2010. www.sentencingcouncil.vic. gov.au/content/publications/trafficking-heroin-magistrates-court-sentencing-snapshot.

Sutton, A., & Hawks, D. (2005). The cannabis infringement notice scheme in Western Australia: A review of policy, police and judicial perspectives. *Drug and Alcohol Review*, 24(4): 331–6.

Toolan, M.J. (1988). *Narrative: A Critical Linguistic Introduction*. London: Routledge.

United Nations Office on Drugs and Crime (2009). *World Drug Report, 2009*. Vienna: Policy Analysis and Research Branch, UNODC.

Van Den Brink, W., Hendriks, V.M., Blanken, P., et al. (2003). Medical prescription of heroin to treatment resistant heroin addicts: Two randomised controlled trials. *British Medical Journal*, 327(7410): 310–16.

Van Nostrand, L.-M. & Tewksbury, R. (1999). The motives and mechanics of operating an illegal drug enterprise. *Deviant Behaviour: An Interdisciplinary Journal*, 20(1): 57–83.

Victoria Police (2010). *Annual Report 2009–2010*. Melbourne, Vic.: Victoria Police. Retrieved 28 March 2011. www.vicpolannualreport.net.au.

Wilkinson, G. (2010, 7 July). Quarter of criminals convicted of drug trafficking not sentenced to jail. *Herald Sun*. Retrieved 28 March 2011. www. heraldsun.com.au/news/quarter-of-criminals-convicted-of-drug-trafficking-not-sentenced-to-jail/story-e6frf7jo-122588870 2235.

Wood, E., Spittal, P.M., Small, W., et al. (2004). Displacement of Canada's largest public illicit drug market in response to a police crackdown. *Canadian Medical Association Journal*, 174(10): 1551–6.

Wundersitz, J. (2007). Criminal justice responses to drug and drug-related offending: Are they working? Australian Institute of Criminology, Technical and Background Paper Series, no. 25. Canberra, ACT: Australian Government. Retrieved 28 March 2011. www.aic.gov.au/documents/9/C/F/%7B9CFCC5DC-A6E3-4321-84AB-4B6210862954%7Dtbp025.pdf.

Legislation

Charter of Rights and Responsibilities Act 2006, Vic.
Drugs, Poisons and Controlled Substances Act 1981, Vic.
Sentencing Act 1991, Vic.

Legal cases

Buckskin v. R (2010) SASC 138.
Dixon v. Lusted (2010) TASSC 16.
DPP v. Theodorellos (2010) VSCA 21.
Duncan v. R (2010) VSCA 92.
Pellew v. State of Western Australia (2010) WASCA 103.
Power v. R (2010) VSCA 139.
R v. El Helou (2010) NSWCCA 111.
R v. El Moustafa (2010) VSCA 40.
R v. Markovski; R v. Moir; R v. Sheen (2009) VSCA 65.
R v. Momcilovic (2010) VSCA 50.
Re Marijancevic (2010) VSC 122.
Re Momcilovic (2008) VSCA 183.
Skubevski v. R (2010) VSCA 91.
Vasic v. R (2010) VSCA 89.
Velevski v. R (2010) VSCA 90.
Waldron v. WA (2010) WASCA 63.

Reconceptualising harm reduction in prisons

Karen Duke

Harm reduction, as a framework to reduce drug-related harm, has a long history in some countries. However, it was not until the arrival of HIV in the 1980s that harm reduction began to be re-emphasised in drug policy debates throughout the world. Harm reduction was increasingly framed in public health and social justice terms. As part of the wider public health movement to protect individual and population health, the prevention of HIV transmission and drug-related deaths through harm reduction techniques became a high priority.[1] Harm reduction initiatives, such as needle exchange and drug consumption rooms, represented major transformations in dealing with problem drug users. Stimson points to the globalisation of harm reduction and its 'indispensable place in the way in which societies can respond to drugs problems'.[2] In Europe, joint strategies and action plans were developed to tackle problematic drug use and public health issues. A clear convergence towards harm reduction occurred as it became more mainstreamed and accepted.[3] This consensus also has been achieved in other countries.

The mainstreaming of harm reduction has not been successful in some settings. A good example is the prison environment where there has been a history of resistance to its implementation. The policies in prisons in many countries have failed to fully embrace the concept of 'harm reduction' and the public health agenda that operate successfully in the community (see 'Definition of harm reduction'). Within analyses of drug and penal policy, the complex relationship between medical and penal forms of control is a potent theme. The drug user is the subject of various forms of control and regulation, including medical, legal and moral, which are often in conflict with each other.[4] The discourses of rehabilitation, welfare and harm reduction frequently clash with those of punishment, security and justice, and these conflicts and contradictions manifest themselves most acutely within the prison environment.[5] This has had a significant effect on the historical development of harm reduction in prisons.

Drawing upon published research and national and international reports and guidelines, this chapter will explore the various ways in which prisons can be defined as high-risk environments for drug-related harm. Employing the risk environment framework developed by Rhodes,[6] it will provide a critique of current approaches to harm reduction in prisons, including health promotion and education, methadone maintenance therapy, bleach and disinfectant distribution, and needle exchange. It will examine critically the key dilemmas surrounding harm reduction within prisons and the principle of equivalence, with reference to the increasing pressure from the World Health Organization (WHO) and United Nations Commission on Human Rights (UNCHR) for governments to incorporate harm reduction measures in prison equivalent to those found in the community. Historically, the preoccupation of policy reform has centred on human rights and public health arguments. However, this focus has taken the debate only so far and has ignored the structural constraints to claiming rights to harm reduction. It will be argued that more attention needs to be paid to creating enabling environments for harm reduction in prison that seek to tackle the structural factors associated with risk, disadvantage and vulnerability.

In focus

Definition of harm reduction

Harm reduction has been defined in a variety of ways for a range of different purposes, settings and contexts. WHO defines harm reduction in relation to injecting drug use as follows: 'In public health "harm reduction" is used to describe a concept aiming to prevent or reduce negative health consequences associated with certain behaviours. In relation to drug injecting, "harm reduction" components of comprehensive interventions aim to prevent transmission of HIV and other infections that occur through sharing of non-sterile injection equipment and drug preparations.'[a]

However, the WHO Health in Prisons Project has argued that within the prison setting harm reduction needs to be conceptualised more broadly to incorporate all the negative health effects arising from imprisonment including the impact on mental health, risk of suicide and self-harm, risk of drug overdose on release, and the harms associated with the lack of facilities/provision within prisons or in overcrowded prisons. They have recommended the following definition of harm reduction within the prison environment: 'In public health relating to prisons, harm reduction describes a concept aiming to prevent or reduce negative health effects associated with certain types of behaviour (such as drug injecting) and with imprisonment and overcrowding as well as adverse effects on mental health.'[b]

a WHO, *Status Paper on Prisons, Drugs and Harm Reduction*, p. 5.
b Ibid., p. 6.

Prisons as high-risk environments for drug-related harm

Rhodes has developed the concept of the 'risk environment' and explores the ways in which drug-related harms are shaped by environmental factors. He defines the risk environment 'as the space – whether social or physical – in which a variety of factors interact to increase the chances of harm occurring'.[7] (See 'Risk environment'.) It consists of a number of types, including physical, social, economic and policy environments, and interacts with various levels of environmental influence at micro, meso and macro levels. In the prison setting, environmental factors operate at the micro level of interpersonal relationships between prisoners through their negotiations regarding the use of drugs and injecting equipment. At the meso level, the focus is social and group interactions within the prisons and how group norms influence patterns of drug use and injecting behaviour. It also includes the institutional response to drugs and injecting at the local level. The macro level of analysis includes structural factors, such as national and international laws, policies, economic conditions, social inequalities and wider cultural beliefs. These large-scale systems interact with micro and meso level factors to '"structure" the risk environments in which HIV risk and harm is produced and reproduced'.[8] This framework is useful in understanding how drug-related harm in prison is shaped by the various levels and types of environmental influence.

In focus

Risk environment

Rhodes argues that the history of harm reduction has been dominated by a focus on individual risk factors and modes of behaviour change. The risk environment framework is an important corrective in overcoming the limits of this individualism and shifting the focus towards structural factors. It is neither a causal model nor a theory, but a generative framework which gives primacy to context. The aim is to explore the reciprocal relationships between individuals and environments and their impact on the production and reduction of drug-related harm. 'A "risk environment" framework envisages drug harms as a product of the social situations and environments in which individuals participate. It shifts responsibility for drug harm, and the focus of harm reducing actions, from individuals alone to include the social and political institutions which have a role in harm production.'[a]

a Rhodes, 'Editorial essay: Risk environments and drug harms', p. 193.

Prisons are extreme settings in which a unique combination of factors is present that amplify drug-related harm and contribute to the development of the risk environment. For example, prisons throughout the world contain populations that suffer multiple disadvantages in relation to poor health, poverty and deprivation, mental health problems, unemployment, inadequate social support and lack of access to appropriate medical provision.[9] Many prisoners enter prisons with existing drug problems. Experience of a prison sentence is common for injecting drug users.[10] On admission to prisons where drug substitution therapy is not offered, prisoners who have been receiving drug substitutes in the community may experience severe withdrawal symptoms, which increase the risk of self-harm, suicide and violence.[11]

The physical environment of the prison is often unsanitary and overcrowded, and there are very few private spaces. This can lead to stress, violence and unrest among prisoners. Moreover, the prison population is transient in the sense that it is constantly changing with transfers in and out due to sentencing and release decisions. The instability of this context produces tensions that can initiate certain forms of 'escapism', including drug use and sexual activity.[12] Illicit drugs are available in most prison systems throughout the world. Research has shown that a high proportion of prisoners are initiated into drug use in prison.[13] For many prisoners, drugs are a way of coping with the overcrowding, boredom, violence and inadequate conditions, or the 'pains of imprisonment'.[14] Cannabis and heroin are the drugs of choice in custody as they help prisoners to relax, sleep and cope with mental health problems. Due to their sedative effects and aid in promoting sleep, these drugs also help prisoners to manipulate and suspend their experience of time in relation to their sentences.[15]

Injecting is common within prisons.[16] HIV prevalence is higher in prison populations, than in the general population.[17] Prisons have been associated with HIV outbreaks among injecting drug users in several countries.[18] Furthermore, hepatitis B and C have become growing problems for injecting drug users in prisons.[19] The restricted drug market in prison limits the type of drugs and the equipment available to prisoners. When injecting does occur in prisons, it is carried out in a more high-risk fashion than in the community due to the scarcity of clean injecting equipment. Sharing syringes and constructing syringe substitutes from other items, such as plastic and ballpoint pens, are common practices that increase the risk of venous injury, scarring, bacterial and viral infections.[20] For example, research conducted by Sarang,

Rhodes, Platt et al. found a culture of syringe sharing within Russian penitentiaries, which had become normalised and routine.[21] Even when harm reduction techniques are available in prisons, such as bleach and disinfecting tablets, prisoners may not be able to take advantage of them due to the contextual constraints operating within prison environments. Due to the lack of private space in prisons, they may inject in a hurry without taking proper care in terms of cleaning equipment. They may also forego the harm reduction on offer in prisons due to fears of detection, stigmatisation and punishment for their drug use.

The drugs market within prison also increases drug-related harms, particularly when drugs become the dominant currency within the informal economy. Research conducted by Crewe uncovered complex networks of trade and affiliation between prisoners around the drugs market. For those at the top of the prison drugs hierarchy, dealing confers status, prestige and power as they focus their efforts on the acquisition, smuggling, sale and financing of drugs.[22] However, drug markets and the culture of debt that surround them have the potential to lead to violence, bullying and intimidation of vulnerable drug dependent prisoners at the bottom of the drugs hierarchy, which can expand outside the prison walls. Prison staff often need to strike a balance when they tackle the issues surrounding the drugs trade as they risk destabilising the prison regime and losing legitimacy.[23]

Drug policies themselves can also exacerbate drug-related harm and limit the capacity of injecting drug users to access harm reduction in prisons. For example, mandatory drug testing programs in prisons underpinned by punitive sanctions are criticised on a number of different fronts, including that they transgress the right to privacy; cause switching from cannabis use to heroin use, which is less easily detectable in urine samples; lead to riots, violence and disorder; discourage drug using prisoners from presenting for treatment or accessing harm reduction due to fears of being targeted or additional searches, surveillance and punishment; and lead to drug-free urine becoming a currency.[24] Supply reduction and security measures, including the use of sniffer dogs, CCTVs, fixed furniture, supervised visits and intensive searching of prisoners and visitors, can lead to a number of unintended consequences such as swallowing packets of drugs, thus increasing the risk of overdose and death, and carrying drugs and injecting equipment internally to avoid detection, thus increasing the risks of injury and transmission of HIV and hepatitis. The lack of opioid substitution therapy or low dosages of opioid substitutes in prisons can also increase the risk of death among prisoners through overdose.[25]

There are also structural and institutional divisions that help to amplify drug-related harm within prisons. In many countries, health care in prison is the responsibility of the Ministry of Justice. Their prime concern will be matters of justice, security and control rather than health-care issues. In the community, drug users are more likely to be conceptualised and treated as 'patients', whereas in the prison they are treated as 'prisoners'.[26] Moreover, the goals and underlying philosophies of treatment also differ between the prison and the community.[27] Many prison systems have adopted a hard-line abstinence-based or zero tolerance approach to drug use. For example, drug substitution therapy is often seen as controversial within the punitive setting of the prison because it is not achieving immediate abstinence and viewed as simply replacing one drug with another. In the community, there is more likely to be a hierarchy of goals with harm reduction as the underlying philosophy. The focus of policy development and resourcing in prisons has been eradicating the drug problem through increased security, surveillance, testing and punishment, rather than reducing the harms associated with drug use. The abstinence-based regimes adopted in the UK have set the scene for conflicts between the prison administration and drug workers who may be working within a harm reduction framework. In many cases, drug agencies have been left working behind the scenes ensuring that harm reduction techniques are being delivered without the support of the institution, adequate resources or an 'official' policy framework.[28]

Prison staff and management have also played key roles in contributing to the prison risk environment by opposing and blocking the introduction of harm reduction measures.[29] For example, the prison officers' union in Australia was strongly opposed to the introduction of needle and syringe programs in prisons due to fears for their own safety (i.e. needles being used as weapons against staff) and arguments that they would encourage drug use.[30] Some prison authorities and governments have refused to contemplate a harm reduction approach because they believe that this would appear as if they are condoning two illegal activities in prison (i.e. drug use and sexual activity), which would be politically untenable. This links to the debates around the 'new punitiveness' or the ways in which penal policy has taken an increasingly punitive turn in many Western countries. These developments refer to the growth of imprisonment and the proliferation of expressive and symbolic penalties that have occurred despite declining crime rates.[31] This has led to the deterioration in prison conditions, overcrowding and the introduction of new austerity measures. Perceptions of politicians and the general public have become important in determining the balance between treatment and punishment and the place of harm reduction in the design and implementation of drugs policy in prison.[32]

Historically, the discourse of less eligibility, which aims to ensure that prisoners do not receive services, benefit and conditions that are not available to the working classes in the community, has also contributed to the development of the risk environment in prison.[33] When this discourse is transformed into practice, it has often meant that prisoners receive a standard of service provision well below that offered in the community. This discourse relates particularly to health care and has a long history in relation to drug treatment and harm reduction services for prisoners. In Britain, for example, the Rolleston Committee report of 1926 defined addiction as a 'disease' and legitimised maintenance prescribing for drug users in the community. However, the Rolleston consensus was not extended to drug-using prisoners, who were forced to undergo abrupt withdrawal.[34] These incongruencies between harm reduction in the community and prison have persisted in Britain and other countries.

Reconceptualising harm reduction in prisons

In many countries, following the HIV crisis of the 1980s, a liberal consensus surrounding harm reduction was achieved in the community based on the principle that HIV was more of a threat to public health than drug use.[35] Harm reduction can be viewed as a 'combination intervention', which consists of a 'package of interventions tailored to local setting and need that give primary emphasis to reducing the harms of drug use'.[36] The evidence base shows that harm reduction is more effective when it is provided as a package of care or in combination, rather than a stand-alone approach.[37] However, in the prison environment the range and combination of interventions are often limited. In most prison systems, there is a continuum of approaches within a harm reduction framework, including health promotion and education; detoxification and substitution therapy; needle exchange and disinfection facilities; and abstinence as a possible outcome.[38] Although the evidence base has demonstrated few problems with the introduction of harm reduction measures in prisons, the reality has been a series of compromises and 'second line strategies' and fragmented, piecemeal implementation that has failed to fully embrace the principles of harm reduction.

For the last 25 years, harm reduction in prisons has been conceptualised in human rights and public health terms. The preoccupation of policy debate has focused on the human rights of prisoners in accessing harm reduction measures. Ezard argues that human rights relate to drug-related harm and harm reduction in two ways.[39] First, violations of human rights can contribute to drug-related harm. Second, human rights instruments underline the responsibilities of governments to respond to drug-related harm. Within a rights-based analysis, governments have an obligation to honour the 'principle of equivalence'. (See 'The principle of equivalence and harm reduction in prisons'.) Various international instruments indicate a consensus that health care provided to prisoners, including harm reduction initiatives, must be comparable to that available in the community.[40] Although not legally binding, guidelines, principles and standards are important as they express moral and philosophical standards that should guide national administrators and courts.[41]

In focus

The principle of equivalence and harm reduction in prisons

The principle of equivalence has its roots in human rights theory and is based on the argument that individuals in prisons have a right to a standard of health-care provision equivalent to that available in the community and that they should not be subjected to inadequate health care simply because of their status as prisoners.[a] In the context of HIV and other blood-borne viruses, equivalent health services include providing prisoners with the means to protect themselves from HIV and HCV. However, it is rare to find the principle of equivalence in relation to harm reduction applied universally across and within prison systems.

For example, although there is increasing evidence that substitution treatment in prisons reduces drug-related harm and recidivism,[b] a consistent finding of studies in various countries is the incongruence between substitution treatments offered inside prisons compared to the community. If substitution therapy is available in prisons, it is mainly employed as a form of short-term detoxification. Longer-term maintenance treatment is provided in only a few prisons internationally. Stover, Hennebel & Casselmann point to the inadequacies in terms of the availability, implementation, clinical management and evaluation of substitution treatment in prisons.[c] Since 1993, WHO has argued that prisoners who have been on methadone maintenance treatment programs in the community before imprisonment should be allowed to continue their treatment in prison and have access to equivalent services.[d]

Similarly, needle exchange is considered to be the 'cornerstone of harm reduction' and the 'single most important factor in preventing HIV epidemics among IDUs'.[e] WHO has consistently argued for the provision of sterile needles and syringes in prisons.[f] However, in many countries with well-established exchange schemes operating successfully in the community, there is a reluctance to introduce them in prisons. As alternatives, bleach and other disinfectants have been introduced in a number of prison systems throughout the world. Bleach is not as effective as needle exchange in reducing hepatitis infection and therefore creates a false sense of security.[g] WHO has argued that it should be viewed as a 'second line strategy' and introduced only as a temporary measure where there is objection to needle and syringe exchange programs or in addition to them.[h]

a Lines, Jurgens, Betteridge et al., *Prison Needle Exchange*.
b See Stallwitz & Stover, 'The impact of substitution treatment in prisons' for a review.
c Stover, Hennebel & Casselmann, *Substitution Treatment in European Prisons*.
d WHO, *WHO Guidelines on HIV Infection and AIDS in Prisons*.
e Kerr, Wood, Betteridge et al., 'Harm reduction in prisons', p. 352.
f WHO, *WHO Guidelines on HIV Infection and AIDS in Prisons*.
g Hagan & Thiede, 'Does bleach disinfection of syringes help prevent hepatitis C virus transmission?'
h WHO, *Status Paper on Prisons, Drugs and Harm Reduction*.

The debates surrounding harm reduction in prisons have been dominated by a focus on risk factors, behaviour change and human rights at the individual level. For example, the development and delivery of health promotion and educational materials outlining the dangers of injecting drug use and unsafe sex and the importance of reducing risk behaviour is the most widely applied approach to harm reduction. This is mainly because such initiatives are easy to implement and the least controversial measures to introduce politically within prison settings.[42] Even when health promotion efforts have been combined with the practical tools of harm reduction such as syringe exchanges, they depend on human agency or individuals' abilities and capacities to change their harmful practices surrounding drug use. The provision of simple advice not to use drugs and share needles ignores the lure of drugs and the pleasures derived from their use in the brutality of the prison setting. As we have seen above, the various types of micro-, meso- and macro-environmental influences on prisons have constrained and limited the ability of drug-using prisoners to make changes to their behaviour to reduce drug-related harm.

Within the current public health and human rights framework, harm reduction has adopted a neoliberal perspective of the drug user who is viewed as autonomous, rational, independent, active and calculating and positioned as equivalent to other citizens.[43] We can see this clearly in the debates that have developed regarding prisoners and their equal rights to harm reduction initiatives. A neoliberal model views drug users as responsible for their own health care and as active collaborators in the design and development of services. Although such a perspective can encourage a sense of empowerment and resilience, it may ignore the disadvantage, stigma and inequality experienced by many drug users. This is particularly significant within the prison setting where there has been the assumption that if harm reduction initiatives are offered to prisoners, they will automatically make use of them.

Fraser, Hopwood, Madden et al. argue that there is a need to think beyond human rights at the individual level as advocated by the neoliberal approach towards examining rights at the community level and the structural barriers to claiming rights to harm reduction.[44] The social, cultural and economic contexts of drug use that mitigate against self-regulation, responsibility and autonomy need to be considered.[45] Within harm reduction discourses, the social context is often assumed to be stable, constant and ordered.[46] However, prisons are particularly unpredictable and unstable environments, and a more dynamic analysis is needed. Within the prison environment, there is a need to look at the various social, cultural and economic contexts that help to shape and structure drug use, injecting and responses to harm reduction.

The risk environment approach adds a crucial dimension to these arguments. Rhodes sees drug harms 'as a product of the social situations and environments in which individuals participate'.[47] He argues that the risk environment approach enables harm reduction in a number of ways. First, it provides a critique of public health initiatives that view harm reduction as a primary determinant of individual action and responsibility. It shifts the focus for change from the individual to social, political and economic situations and structures. The emphasis is on creating 'enabling environments' for harm reduction. Second, such an approach avoids blaming individuals for harm. The responsibility for harm production and reduction also includes social, political and economic institutions. Third, the focus on risk as socially situated helps us to understand how risk environments are experienced and embodied as part of everyday practices. Fourth, a risk environment approach implies the incorporation of harm reduction inside broader frameworks that promote human rights approaches to public health.[48]

Within the risk environment framework, it is important to explore the interactions between the micro-, meso- and macro-level environments that shape the development and access to harm reduction in prisons and how these different environments and contexts shift and influence one another. This analysis would examine the micro-risk environment, which is shaped by the interplay of norms, rules and values of particular prison settings; social relationships and networks between drug using prisoners; peer group and social influence; and the immediate context in which drugs are used in prisons. It would also explore those conditions of local prison environments (including the physical space, nature of the regime, drug markets and policy frameworks) that increase and/or decrease the capacity of drug users to reduce harm. Finally, it would consider how macro public health, drug and welfare and economic policies and politics at both national and international levels shape micro social relations of risk and risk resistance and the inequalities in health and access to services both inside and outside prison walls. Rhodes argues that the analysis needs to occur at various levels and explore the influence of social forces beyond the local.[49] Moreover, there is a need to develop multilevel interventions. In analysing prisons, there is a need to look beyond the prison walls and the dynamic interaction between individuals and social structural processes at multiple levels.

A key benefit of employing a risk environment framework is that it allows for the consideration of non-drug and non-health specific factors in harm reduction such as housing, employment, training and community development.[50] This is crucial in relation to prisoners because of the multiple deprivations they experience both before and after custody. It mainstreams drugs and harm reduction as part of wider social movements in public health, and it shifts the locus and politics of change from individual drug use to wider issues of vulnerability and human rights. The aim is to create enabling environments for harm reduction that alleviate situational and structural constraints of risk and vulnerability. This helps to make it a human rights approach to the alleviation of harm.[51]

Rhodes sees the development of 'enabling environments' as the policy goal of risk environment research. However, Duff argues that the concept of 'enabling environments' has been under-theorised and under-researched within the work on risk environments.[52] Research thus far has focused on identifying environmental factors and processes that facilitate risk reduction rather than on the processes and relationships that promote health and development. There is a need for a more balanced and dynamic analysis that explores the deeper environmental processes that support health, resilience and well-being and identifies enabling resources that buffer risk, inequality and vulnerability and the influence on health.[53] While the distribution of enabling resources may be limited within the extreme environments of prisons, Duff argues that they exist in some form in all settings.[54] The strengths, opportunities and assets within the drug use contexts of prisons need to be identified and harnessed in order to devise innovative harm reduction strategies tailored to the specifics of particular prisons and prison populations (see 'Creating an enabling environment for harm reduction'). Within prisons, opportunities for engagement need to be created that move beyond the individual and explore the communities or networks of drug users in prisons and their shared norms, values and practices. Enabling environments are the result of practice and interaction as much as they are a product of social, political and economic processes.[55]

In focus

Creating an enabling environment for harm reduction

Lessons from Moldova

A promising example of creating an enabling environment and innovative delivery for harm reduction emerges from prisons in Moldova.[a] The starting point was a pragmatic acceptance that drugs could not be eradicated and a commitment to understand how the prison environment was amplifying drug-related harm. Within this project, some of the key barriers to harm reduction in prison, such as prisoners' fears of being stigmatised and punished for drug use and/or HIV status, were dealt with carefully. In order to increase access, prisoners were trained as outreach volunteers to provide harm reduction services to their fellow prisoners. These services (i.e. needle and syringe exchange, information and advice, and provision of condoms and alcohol wipes) were provided confidentially and anonymously on a 24-hour basis. Prisoners were allowed to exchange the injecting equipment of other prisoners who were reluctant to contact the outreach volunteers. The initiative promoted a high degree of trust and interaction between the peer volunteers and the prisoners, enabling prisoners to reduce drug-related harm effectively. Evaluation of the initiative indicated a decline in HIV cases, decreases in discarded injecting equipment, prisoner empowerment around health issues, reduction of sexually transmitted infections, reduced safety risks for prison staff, reduction in

> HIV-related stigma and discrimination, and general benefits to public health. It is important to note that these harm reduction measures were accompanied by key structural reforms, including reductions in the prison population and improvements to prison conditions such as reductions in overcrowding, better work opportunities and improved nutrition, which also help to promote the health and well-being of prisoners.
>
> a Hoover & Jurgens, *Harm Reduction in Prison*.

Conclusion

Since the HIV crisis of the 1980s, there has been some progress in implementing harm reduction services in prisons. However, provision still lags behind that offered to drug users in the community in many countries. In the prison environment, it is necessary to balance the medical models of prevention, care and treatment with the requirements of custody, security and control. Harm reduction benefits individual prisoners, staff working inside the prison walls and the wider community. However, simply ensuring that harm reduction is available to prisoners is not an end in itself. Although there are benefits to extending the neoliberal perspective to drug using prisoners in terms of viewing them as equal citizens, this must be balanced with a more contextualised analysis that explores how their agency is constrained by particular environments and power relations. This needs to be accompanied by policy and practice that tackles the social, political, economic and cultural contexts that contribute to the marginalisation, stigmatisation and discrimination experienced by drug users.[56] Under the risk environment approach, responsibility for harm and harm reduction is redistributed and shared between individuals and social economic structures.[57]

Effective harm reduction requires the involvement of and cooperation between governing bodies, agencies, prison staff and those with personal experience. Many different sectors need to work in partnership including health services, legal frameworks, law enforcement and the cultural, social and economic environment. All levels of government need to be involved, including civil society, non-governmental organisations and community organisations.[58] It is necessary for action to occur at a number of different levels: international, national, regional, local and within individual prisons and prisoner networks. Macro-level guidelines and policies for harm reduction in prisons require translation down to the micro or local level. Harm reduction must be culturally sensitive and respond to local needs, cultures and contexts of prisons. Further research is needed on how the various levels of environmental influence interact and affect the development and experience of harm reduction within prison settings. Although the risk environment approach provides an important corrective to the individualism that has dominated harm reduction in prisons, the exploration of 'enabling resources' and 'enabling places' holds promise in the development of further research and practice on harm reduction in prisons.

Within a context of economic recession, increasing unemployment, and growing poverty and deprivation, drug use is likely to increase. Repressive drug policies exacerbate the harm experienced by drug users, particularly if they are arrested, convicted and imprisoned for their drug use. As Stimson argues, the criminalisation of drug users is a major obstacle to harm reduction.[59] The risk environment framework offers the possibility of conceptualising harm reduction more widely to include interventions that aim to reduce harms from drug use as well as other public policies. This includes policy reform and legal change to ensure that drug users are positioned within enabling environments that seek to reduce drug-related harms.

Notes

1   Rhodes & Hedrich, 'Harm reduction and the mainstream'.
2   Stimson, 'Editorial: Harm reduction', p. 92.
3   Hedrich, Pirona & Wiessing, 'From margins to mainstream'.
4   Smart, 'Social policy and drug addiction'.
5   Duke, *Drugs, Prisons and Policy-making*.
6   Rhodes, 'The "risk environment"'.
7   Rhodes, 'Editorial essay: Risk environments and drug harms', p. 193
8   Rhodes, Singer, Bourgois et al., 'The social structural production of HIV risk among injecting drug users', p. 1028.
9   Kerr, Wood, Betteridge et al., 'Harm reduction in prisons'.
10   Ball, *Multi-Centre Study on Drug Injecting and Risk of HIV Infection*.
11   WHO, *Status Paper on Prisons, Drugs and Harm Reduction*.
12   Thomas, 'HIV/AIDS in prison'.
13   Boys et al., 'Drug use and initiation in prisons'.
14   Sykes, *The Society of Captives*.
15   Cope, 'It's no time or high time'.
16   Dolan, Wodak & Penny, 'AIDS behind bars'.
17   Kerr, Wood, Betteridge et al., 'Harm reduction in prisons'.
18   Wright, Vanichsem, Akarasewi et al., 'Was the 1988 HIV epidemic among Bangkok's injecting drug users a common source outbreak?'; Taylor, Goldberg, Elmslie et al., 'Outbreak of HIV infection in a Scottish prison'.
19   Macalino, Hou, Kumar et al., 'Hepatitis C infection and incarcerated populations'.
20   Kerr, Wood, Betteridge et al., 'Harm reduction in prisons'.
21   Sarang, Rhodes, Platt et al., 'Drug injecting and syringe use in the HIV risk environment of Russian penitentiary institutions'.
22   Crewe, 'Prisoner society in the era of hard drugs'.
23   Sparks, Bottoms & Hay, *Prisons and the Problem of Order*.
24   Duke, *Drugs, Prisons and Policy-making*, pp. 111–12.
25   Singleton, Pendry, Taylor et al., *Drug-related Mortality among Newly Released Offenders*.
26   Stevens, Stover & Brentari, 'Criminal justice approaches to harm reduction in Europe'.
27   Stallwitz & Stover, 'The impact of substitution treatment in prisons'.

28 Duke, *Drugs, Prisons and Policy-making.*
29 Godin, Gagnon, Alary et al., 'Correctional officers' intention of accepting or refusing to make HIV preventive tools accessible to inmates'.
30 Mogg & Levy, 'Moving beyond non-engagement on regulated needle-syringe exchange programs in Australian prisons'.
31 Pratt, 'New punitiveness'.
32 Duke, *Drugs, Prisons and Policy-making.*
33 Melossi, & Pavarini, *The Prison and the Factory.*
34 Berridge, *Opium and the People.*
35 For example ACMD, *AIDS and Drug Misuse.*
36 Rhodes & Hedrich, 'Harm reduction and the mainstream', p. 19.
37 Davoli, Simon & Griffith, 'Current and future perspectives on harm reduction in the EU'.
38 WHO, *Status Paper on Prisons, Drugs and Harm Reduction.*
39 Ezard, 'Public health, human rights and the harm reduction paradigm'.
40 WHO, *Statement from the Consultation on Prevention and Control of AIDS in Prisons*; WHO, *WHO Guidelines on HIV Infection and AIDS in Prisons*; WHO, *Status Paper on Prisons, Drugs and Harm Reduction*; UNHCR, *HIV/AIDS in Prisons*; UNAIDS, *Prison and AIDS.*
41 Kerr, Wood, Betteridge et al., 'Harm reduction in prisons'.
42 Kerr, Wood, Betteridge et al., 'Harm reduction in prisons'.
43 Moore & Fraser, 'Putting at risk what we know'.
44 Fraser, Hopwood, Madden et al., 'Towards a global approach'.
45 Moore & Fraser, 'Putting at risk what we know'.
46 Rhodes, 'Editorial essay: Risk environments and drug harms'.
47 Ibid., p. 193.
48 Ibid.
49 Rhodes, 'The "risk environment"'.
50 Ibid.
51 Ibid.
52 Duff, 'Enabling places and enabling resources'.
53 Duff, 'The drifting city'.
54 Duff, 'Enabling places and enabling resources'.
55 Ibid.
56 Moore & Fraser, 'Putting at risk what we know'.
57 Rhodes, 'Editorial essay: Risk environments and drug harms'.
58 WHO, *Status Paper on Prisons, Drugs and Harm Reduction.*
59 Stimson, 'Editorial: Harm reduction'.

References

Advisory Council on the Misuse of Drugs (ACMD). (1988). *AIDS and Drug Misuse.* Part 1. London: HMSO.
Ball, A. (1995). *Multi-Centre Study on Drug Injecting and Risk of HIV Infection.* Geneva: World Health Organisation.
Berridge, V. (1999). *Opium and the People: Opiate Use and Drug Control in Nineteenth and Early Twentieth Century England.* London: Free Association Books.
Boys, A., Farrell, M., Bebbington, P., et al. (2002). Drug use and initiation in prisons: Results from a national prison survey in England and Wales. *Addiction*, 97(12): 1551–60.

Cope, N. (2003). It's no time or high time: Young offenders' experiences of time and drug use in prison. *Howard Journal of Criminal Justice*, 42: 158–75.

Crewe, B. (2006). Prisoner society in the era of hard drugs. *Punishment and Society*, 7(4): 457–81.

Davoli, M., Simon, R. & Griffith, P. (2010). Current and future perspectives on harm reduction in the EU. In T. Rhodes & D. Hedrich (eds), *Harm Reduction: Evidence, Impacts and Challenges*. EMCDDA Monograph 10. Lisbon: EMCDDA.

Dolan, K., Wodak, A., & Penny, R. (1995). AIDS behind bars: Preventing HIV spread among incarcerated drug injectors. *AIDS*, 9: 825–32.

Duff, C. (2009). The drifting city: The role of affect and repair in the development of 'enabling environments'. *International Journal of Drug Policy*, 20: 202–8.

—— (2010). Enabling places and enabling resources: New directions for harm reduction research and practice. *Drug and Alcohol Review*, 29: 337–44.

Duke, K. (2003). *Drugs, Prisons and Policy-making*. London: Palgrave Macmillan.

Ezard, N. (2001). Public health, human rights and the harm reduction paradigm: From risk reduction to vulnerability reduction. *International Journal of Drug Policy*, 12: 207–19.

Fraser, S., Hopwood, M., Madden, A., et al. (2009). Towards a global approach: An overview of harm reduction 2008: IHRA's nineteenth International Conference. *International Journal of Drug Policy*, 20: 93–7.

Godin, G., Gagnon, H., Alary, M., et al. (2001). Correctional officers' intention of accepting or refusing to make HIV preventive tools accessible to inmates. *AIDS Education and Prevention*, 13: 462–73.

Hagan, H. & Thiede, H. (2003). Does bleach disinfection of syringes help prevent hepatitis C virus transmission? *Epidemiology*, 14: 628–9.

Hedrich, D., Pirona, A., & Wiessing, L. (2008). From margins to mainstream: The evolution of harm reduction responses to problem drug use in Europe. *Drugs: Education, Prevention and Policy*, 15: 503–17.

Hoover, J., & Jurgens, R. (2009). *Harm Reduction in Prison: The Moldova Model*. New York: Open Society Institute Public Health Program.

Kerr, T., Wood, E., Betteridge, G., et al. (2004). Harm reduction in prisons: A 'rights based' analysis. *Critical Public Health*, 14(4): 345–60.

Lines, R., Jurgens, R., Betteridge, G., et al. (2006). *Prison Needle Exchange: Lessons from a Comprehensive Review of the International Evidence and Experience* (2nd edn). Toronto: Canadian HIV/AIDS Legal Network.

Macalino, G.E., Hou, J.C., Kumar, M.S., et al. (2004). Hepatitis C infection and incarcerated populations. *International Journal of Drug Policy*, 15: 103–14.

Melossi, D., & Pavarini, M. (1981). *The Prison and the Factory: The Origins of the Penitentiary System*. London: Macmillan.

Mogg, D., & Levy, M. (2009). Moving beyond non-engagement on regulated needle-syringe exchange programs in Australian prisons. *Harm Reduction Journal*, 6(7): 1–9.

Moore, D. & Fraser, S. (2006). Putting at risk what we know: Reflecting on the drug-using subject in harm reduction and its political implications. *Social Science and Medicine*, 62: 3035–47.

Pratt, J. (2008). New punitiveness. In Y. Jewkes & J. Bennett (eds), *Dictionary of Prisons and Punishment* (pp. 181–3). Cullompton, Devon: Willan Publishing.

Rhodes, T. (2002). The 'risk environment': A framework for understanding and reducing drug-related harm. *International Journal of Drug Policy*, 13: 85–94.

—— (2009). Editorial essay: Risk environments and drug harms: A social science for harm reduction approach. *International Journal of Drug Policy*, 20: 193–201.

Rhodes, T., & Hedrich, D. (2010). Harm reduction and the mainstream. In T. Rhodes & D. Hedrich (eds), *Harm Reduction: Evidence, Impacts and Challenges*. EMCDDA Monograph 10. Lisbon: EMCDDA.

Rhodes, T., Singer, M., Bourgois, P., et al. (2005). The social structural production of HIV risk among injecting drug users. *Social Science and Medicine*, 1026–44.

Sarang, A., Rhodes, T., Platt, L., et al. (2006). Drug injecting and syringe use in the HIV risk environment of Russian penitentiary institutions: Qualitative study. *Addiction*, 101: 1787–96.

Singleton, N., Pendry, E., Taylor, C., et al. (2003). *Drug-related Mortality among Newly Released Offenders*. London: Home Office.

Smart, C. (1984). Social policy and drug addiction: A critical study of policy development. *British Journal of Addiction*, 79: 31–9.

Sparks, R., Bottoms, A.E., & Hay, W. (1996). *Prisons and the Problem of Order*. Oxford: Clarendon Press.

Stallwitz, A., & Stover, H. (2007). The impact of substitution treatment in prisons: A literature review. *International Journal of Drug Policy*, 18: 464–74.

Stevens, A., Stover, H., & Brentari, C. (2010). Criminal justice approaches to harm reduction in Europe. In T. Rhodes & D. Hedrich (eds), *Harm Reduction: Evidence, Impacts and Challenges*. EMCDDA Monograph 10. Lisbon: EMCDDA.

Stimson, G. (2010). Editorial: Harm reduction: Moving through the third decade. *International Journal of Drug Policy*, 21: 91–3.

Stover, H., Hennebel, L., & Casselmann, J. (2004). *Substitution Treatment in European Prisons: A Study of Policies and Practices of Substitution Treatment in Prisons in 18 European Countries*. London: Cranstoun Drug Services.

Sykes, G. (1958). *The Society of Captives*. Princeton, NJ: Princeton University Press.

Taylor, A., Goldberg, D., Elmslie, J. et al. (1995). Outbreak of HIV infection in a Scottish prison. *British Medical Journal*, 310: 289–92.

Thomas, P.A. (1990). HIV/AIDS in prison. *Howard Journal*, 29(1): 1–13.

UNAIDS. (1997). *Prison and AIDS: UNAIDS Point of View*. Geneva: Joint United Nations Programme on HIV/AIDS.

United Nations Commission on Human Rights (UNHCR) (1996). *HIV/AIDS in Prisons: Statement by the Joint United Nations Programme on HIV/AIDS (UNAIDS)*. Geneva: UNCHR.

World Health Organization (1987). *Statement from the Consultation on Prevention and Control of AIDS in Prisons*. Geneva: WHO Global Programme on AIDS.

—— (1993). *WHO Guidelines on HIV Infection and AIDS in Prisons*. Geneva: WHO.

—— (2005). *Status Paper on Prisons, Drugs and Harm Reduction*. Copenhagen: WHO Europe.

Wright, N., Vanichsem, S., Akarasewi, P., et al. (1994). Was the 1988 HIV epidemic among Bangkok's injecting drug users a common source outbreak? *AIDS*, 8: 529–32.

Possessed

The unconscious law of drugs

Desmond Manderson

Although the balance of power waxes and wanes in line with social and political circumstances, the rhetorical battle between 'zero tolerance' and 'harm minimisation' has endured for a generation. Politicians in the English-speaking world continue to have consistent recourse to the language of 'zero tolerance', despite the manifest success of what is sometimes called 'harm minimisation' in reducing deaths from drug overdose, levels of HIV infection among the population of injecting drug users and so on.[1] In fact, one might reasonably surmise that the calls for a return to zero tolerance have grown in intensity precisely *as a result of* the practical success of such measures.

These two approaches are profoundly different. Harm minimisation measures seek to improve the health and longevity of drug users *even if* those measures lead to an overall increase in use. Zero tolerance measures seek to decrease drug use *even if* those measures worsen the health and longevity of those who use drugs. The former asks of drug users: are they well? Are they stable? Do they resort to crime? Do they have a job? The latter asks of drug users: are they still using? The former are relativists in every meaningful sense, including believing that illegal drugs can be more or less bad depending on the circumstances. The latter are absolutists in every meaningful sense, including believing that illegal drugs are absolutely bad under all circumstances. From the point of view of public policy or effective legal regulation, such absolutism is puzzling. It is not, of course, that the consumption of drugs such as heroin is harmless, by any means, but at the same time it is surely almost beyond dispute that the current legal regime of prohibition makes matters worse from the point of view of every conceivable indicator of health and social efficacy.[2] Yet the position seems ultimately resistant to all argument.

When our friends and family behave irrationally, indulging in fears and behaviours that even they concede are dysfunctional, perhaps we suggest that they see an analyst. It is their *irrational* impulses that need to be understood if they are to change. After 50 years of drug prohibition, we know that the current regulatory structure is a catastrophic failure. Yet the language and policies of zero tolerance, which constituted and defend this structure, remain an enduring feature in the developed world. This is certainly the case in the United States and through the regime established by the international drug control treaty system, over which it has exerted a crushing influence.[3] The question is why. The puzzle I wish to explore concerns what law is 'for' and why the categorical opposition to harm minimisation has remained so impervious to evidence. It is time to psychoanalyse our drug policies, searching for what lies beneath.

Recent psychoanalytic work in law and literature[4] and in legal theory[5] has drawn increasingly on the work of Freud and Lacan. This framework has been most explicitly elaborated in the writing of Peter Goodrich and Pierre Legendre,[6] Slavoj Zizek[7] and, above all, Shoshana Felman,[8] who has used psychoanalytic theory to connect legal and cultural analysis in new and powerful ways. The trajectory of this scholarship is extremely varied and not always well articulated. But in this chapter I want to make a very specific intervention. Much of the field of psychoanalytic jurisprudence, particularly in its earlier manifestations,[9] drew on psychoanalytic theories to explain individual and social motivation. I offer a psychoanalytic account of institutional action. Contrary to how we tend to think of it, in the drug reform literature in particular, law is not a purely instrumental or regulatory structure. That is the *conscious* of law. But law also has an unconscious.[10] I mean that it does more than directly permit and prohibit action. Like other cultural productions such as politics and art, law serves as the medium for the symbolisation and social transmission of ideals, desires and anxieties. Now the privileged form in which the individual unconscious expresses these deep and structuring drives is through their metaphorical representation and transformation in dreams. Institutions similarly express themselves through metaphors – symbols that stand in for *something else*, something implicit and deeply felt but poorly understood. Laws have a daily meaning, but they also have a night-time meaning, the unconscious and metaphorical representation of a drive.

There are many consequences of this argument, which I hope to explore in this chapter. First, the fact that drug laws appear to many eyes unreasonable and unworkable should no longer arouse consternation, because their functions are not related to reason. Second, since these laws are metaphorical *representations*, or *symptoms*, their goal is to perform something rather than to eliminate it. The flourishing of drugs in societies with harsh and dogmatic drug laws is again not at all surprising, for the laws are a dream whose purpose is to use the metaphor of a drug to structure and symbolise elements of the social imaginary.

In teasing out this argument, I wish to draw a parallel between two legal frameworks that endured not despite their apparent irrationality but because of it: the witchcraft laws of early modern Europe and the drug laws of today. This parallel illuminates the ways in which 'zero tolerance' as an ideology, and the laws that continue to instantiate it, serve not instrumental purposes but psychological ones: like the symbols in a dream, the objects they refer to – witch-demons and drug-demons – are not to be eliminated but rather brought forth and given form. The continuance of the 'drug problem' in the face of laws whose stated aim is to destroy it is evidence not of the legal structure's conscious or rational failure but of its unconscious and irrational *success*.

A quick historical excursus will help set the scene, for I wish to remind readers that modern drug laws were always the manifestation of social anxieties. Around the world, the first 20 or 30 years of the twentieth century involved a radical shift in the taxonomy of 'drugs'. What had previously been a question of science or habit[11] or of desire or shame[12] became reconceived as criminal. But it was not just the valency of a pre-existing category that changed. On the contrary, the definition of certain drugs *as* criminal reorganised the field in quite a new way, establishing new connections and weakening established ones. As I have argued at greater length elsewhere,[13] the animating logic behind these new distinctions was initially racial. In Australia, in a way that was emblematic of the histories of countries all over the world, notably the US, Canada and, somewhat later, Great Britain, the first laws against drug possession were enacted around the turn of the century[14] and focused on opium smoking precisely because of its association with Chinese immigrant labourers.[15] This Orientalist legislation was the expression of a very specific social anxiety. The stories that circulated in the mainstream media at the end of the nineteenth century consistently treated opium as an agent of seduction.[16] Time and again, the Chinese dealer was depicted as a trafficker in young white women. Opium was the device by which the sexual inhibition or revulsion of young (white) girls towards the (alien) Chinese could be overcome.[17] Miscegenation was the fear, and the 'Chinaman's' opium was presented as playing a causal role in bringing about sexual relationships across the racial divide. Opium was a *scapegoat* for a social anxiety about race and sexuality that the laws addressed but did not name. As such, it was not a social evil to be eliminated by law but rather a social function to be given formal recognition by law.

Witchcraft, drug law and anxiety

We have seen such legal logic before – a law that professes to destroy what in fact it preserves. The parallel with witchcraft is uncanny, as Thomas Szasz once remarked.[18] Entwining the two stories together, this chapter argues that our drug laws are *not* intended to get rid of drugs, any more than the Inquisition wanted to ban the devil or the earliest 'drug laws' wanted to eliminate opium. Certainly, we no longer believe in witches, but we cannot comprehend the hysteria that led to such an extreme response without reframing what it is the laws are trying to accomplish. Drug laws present another example from our own time.

Neither the legislative prohibition of witches, then, nor of drugs, now, was of ancient lineage. Drug laws emerge in their modern form only around 1900. In England, Witchcraft Acts lasted from 1542 to 1736.[19] In both cases, we are confronted not by an explosion in the incidence of witches, or drugs, but an explosion in *fear* of them.[20] In both cases, what we are facing is an intense fear of change, articulated through a metaphor that serves as a scapegoat to control and alleviate the anxiety.

Let us begin with witches. The idea of devils taking over the bodies of women was a metaphysically near-perfect method of social control. It defined abnormality as evil and invisible: evil and hence insupportable, invisible and hence indisputable. To be in the thrall of the Devil and his minions was to forfeit all responsibility in the sense of any moral agency over one's behaviour and at the same time to be deprived of the protection of any responsibility that society owed you. *You* no longer existed at all since you had been suborned by this thing. On the one hand, you were not 'really' doing these things at all while, on the other, society was not 'really' doing these things to you. The attribution of all activity to the Devil and his minions rendered passive any challenge to the authority of the Church and the male order at a time of profound crisis brought on by the Reformation.

Within this ideology, the notion of possession was important. Sexual possession by the Devil was the almost universal initiation of women into witchcraft.[21] The result is not as horrible as one might imagine. On the contrary, the 'demon lover' is sexually irresistible.[22] The women, having been tricked (to begin with) by the Devil's adoption of a human disguise, quickly find themselves 'addicted'.[23] 'Women', says the *Malleus Maleficarum*,[24] 'willingly subject themselves to this stinking, miserable servitude for sheer pleasure.'[25]

It will be apparent how closely the idea of drug-taking conforms to this structure, right down to the magical sexual potency with which it is endowed. The Devil, like the drug or, indeed, like the opium pusher, seduces and suborns the will. The role of possession, in all its senses, is remarkably similar.

First, it provides a causal explanation for unacceptable social behaviour. Second, it provides tangible corporeal proof of the intangible degradation of the spirit. The legal possession of a drug, like the witches' sexual possession, offers *physical evidence* of an evil that is otherwise entirely metaphysical. The legal category of *crimen exceptum* recognises the need to abandon normal criteria of proof in cases 'composed of secret crimes unlikely to produce the usual kinds of evidence or witnesses'.[26] Its prime example, before modern drug laws replete with their deeming provisions and reverse onuses, were the laws of witchcraft.

In focus

Witchcraft and the dramatisation of religious belief

In *Demon Lovers: Witchcraft, Sex, and the Crisis of Belief*, Walter Stephens argues that the origins of the witch craze lie, ironically, in the growing influence of empiricism and scientific rationality on the Western mind. The Reformation challenged the very structure of belief and authority in the Christian world: the immediate divinity of the Book replaced the mediated divinity of priests, overturning the hierarchy of the church, rejecting the doctrine of transubstantiation and undermining the centrality of the sacraments. The Inquisition, in turn, attempted to justify the incorporeal reality of the Catholic faith not just by rejecting empirical evidence (as in the case of Galileo) but also by making its own case for the existence of spirits.

The witchcraft trials that swept through Europe were not a product of a strong belief but a shaky one. Witchcraft theorists were 'doubting Thomases' – the very model of Christian empiricism. They demanded physical proof of the Devil and, in turn, of the invisible power of God and the sacraments. They did not fear witches: they *needed* them. As for torture, 'what is universally recognised or firmly believed', Stephens remarks, 'does not need constant reaffirmation through violent coercion'.[a] The Inquisitors needed to touch and feel the wounds in Christ's side – even if that meant putting them there themselves. Witchcraft provided empirical evidence of the invisible, and at the same time offered a much-needed argument for the continuing weakness and impurity of the world. The spirit world exists, as the Devil's marks proved; if evil still exists, the fault lies with the Devil and not with God or humanity.

a Stephens, *Demon Lovers*, pp. 185, 37, 6–7.

Drugs and the dramatisation of philosophical belief

We live in a time in which our structures of belief are again under severe stress. This time it is not Christianity that is in crisis (except tangentially) but modernism. At least since the trauma of World War I, deep philosophical challenges have emerged 'with regard to the twin ideologies of political liberalism and the "objective" scientific quest for truth'. The 'snags and inconsistencies' beneath the surface of liberal individualism have been relentlessly unpicked by 'the entire "French" or even "German" orientation',[27] radically unsettling the relationship of agency to structure. Yet the idea of human autonomy and identity continues to form the basis of our law, economy, rights and ethics.[28] This intellectual tension goes to the heart of what counts as a valid or relevant explanation of behaviour. The very distinction between 'right' and 'left' in politics is an aspect of this disagreement, as is that between prosecution and defence in law, or between punishment and rehabilitation. Such questions speak to the distinction between persons and things – between possessors and possessed – that established a model for agency founded on the subjectivity of the one and the objectivity of the other.[29] Bioethical debates over cloning, genetic engineering and the ownership of genetic information provide recent examples of the dimensions of the problem.[30]

In the Reformation, the presence of an all-powerful God was in question; now, according to Foucault, it is the presence of an all-powerful human subjectivity that is in danger of being erased.[31] So too the critique of 'the metaphysics of presence' may be described as an argument against the possibility of finding any still point, any foundation, whether intellectual or moral, from which the truth about what we know or who we are may firmly be built.[32] The end result 'would be the destruction of the very idea of a field, a specialised professional discourse that arrives at a true account of a limited domain by progressive and rational means. It would mean the end of life as we know it.'[33] This is the long shadow cast not only over modern philosophy but also modern politics.

Just as we saw in relation to witches, this crisis of belief – not in the efficacy and reality of God, but in the efficacy and identity of human beings, not a crisis of faith but of progress – may be allayed by being represented and dramatised. For if drugs show us what it is like to be 'possessed', and therefore to lose one's identity and one's capacity for individual agency, we rest assured, by way of contrast, in our own autonomy. The standard portrayal of the drug addict, dulled and immured in incapacity, reassures us of their absolute *otherness*. The solidity, the certainty, of our identity is shored up by vivid contrast with theirs. The possessed addict depicts a world where night and day are clearly marked, where we are awake and they are asleep, relieving us of our fears of twilight and insomnia.[34] The possessed witch performed much the same service at a parallel moment of crisis. And of course both must be punished for this failure; both are to be held to a standard of agency and responsibility that they *ipso facto* cannot attain, and are then destroyed for their failure. The drug user, like the witch, is held up as a – perhaps *the* – threat to the modern ideology of autonomy and freedom: held up, set apart and scapegoated. And just as witchcraft reconciled God's infinite capacity with the continuing injustice of the world by making tangible the demons working against Him, so too the symbolic role of illegal drugs reconciles humanity's infinite capacity with the continuing injustice of the world by making tangible the objects working against our autonomous rationality.

Law as drama

Drug laws, like witchcraft laws, bring to life a metaphorical representation of deep-seated anxieties and give them formal recognition. The witchcraft laws were symbolically satisfying and powerful, although no doubt impotent to actually achieve their stated goals. They represented the last roll of the dice in the face of the encroaching scepticism of early modern identity. And drug laws are no less symbolically satisfying and powerful. They represent the last roll of the dice in the face of the encroaching scepticism of late modern identity. Witchcraft laws and drug laws are indeed mirror images: the former sought to shore up supernatural agency in a world becoming gradually disenchanted *by* human rationality. The latter seeks to shore up human agency in a world becoming gradually disenchanted *with* human rationality.

The parallel I have explored cautions us against understanding law in purely functional, instrumental or intentional terms. Instead it asks us to read law's subtext, to reimagine legal structures not as an attempt to solve a problem but instead as a means of staging a drama. The drug laws we have been considering are no more designed to outlaw drugs than the Inquisition wanted to outlaw the Devil. On the contrary, they need them. The purpose of the laws in each case is not to destroy those symbols but to frame and use them. Viewed in this way, much that seems opaque about the current regime of prohibition becomes explicable – particularly its counter-productive over-reaction and its unremitting failure. Every drugs seizure, every boatload or shoot-out, is clearly of only the most trivial significance. But it is presented, by police, lawyers, government and the media, as an elaborate morality play staged for the public benefit. The farcical display of the captured drugs is in some ways the sole and certainly the most tangible achievement of law enforcement. The law provides a stage on which this drama can take place. This is not simply a sideshow made possible by law, or a consequence of the failure of the legal principles to achieve their promised goal. On the contrary, this drama is precisely what drug laws have always been 'for'.

The function of illegality is not to stamp out a phenomenon, but to make it *more public*, more dramatic, more theatrical. We are being asked to witness the captured drugs as we were once asked to witness the stories of witches in all their fleshy, gruesome detail. The point is that the hysterical register of the discourse of drugs has the paradoxical effect of defending the notion of individual autonomy and agency and of identifying and cauterising its enemies. More than this, the drugs themselves function as the substance through which this psychological and philosophical crisis of belief can be objectified, materialised, explained and expiated. All the same, one must surely wonder about the merits of keeping open what amounts to a long-running theatre of the absurd. Like a dream, law's power as metaphor lies in its ability to symbolise and control anxieties and desires. But with this difference: the lives of those in our dreams are not thereby destroyed. And like the *Sorcerer's Apprentice*,[35] our fantasies are starting to run riot, ruining whole societies and economies in their wake.

Case study

One would not expect the witch-hunters of the sixteenth century to have countenanced any tolerance of witches. From their point of view, it would not have made sense to acknowledge a continuum between witchcraft and other practices, because it was precisely the *distinction* that needed to be preserved. The same is true in respect of the continuing rhetorical dispute between harm minimisation and zero tolerance in relation to drug policy. Zero tolerance expresses not a social policy but, on the contrary, an ontological principle. Its absolutism and its belief in the existence of a categorical distinction between normal and abnormal, between good and bad drugs and so on, is precisely the point. Its resilience in the face of its failure is to be understood symbolically and psychologically, and on that level no compromise is possible.

To illustrate this, I propose to look at a small and forgotten battle in an ongoing social struggle. In 1997 the government of the Australian Capital Territory (ACT), Australia's smallest and most liberal jurisdiction, proposed a trial that would have involved the legal distribution of managed quantities of heroin to some 40 long-term addicts, in order to study the effect of such a policy on social and health outcomes. The proposal drew on policies that had already shown some success in Switzerland and elsewhere, leading to a decrease in deaths from overdose, as well as considerable other benefits to some drug users.

The trial was developed over several years by a multidisciplinary team based at the National Centre for Epidemiology and Public Health at the Australian National University. The development process had been exceptionally carefully handled in order to respond to input from health, academic, government, community and police groups at every stage. It had garnered bipartisan support in the local parliament. Research had been conducted that consistently showed strong public support for the trial in the ACT. At a meeting of the Ministerial Council on Drugs Strategy, consisting of health and law enforcement ministers from around Australia, the trial received warm approval, leading ACT Chief Minister Kate Carnell to describe it as 'the most dramatic breakthrough in drug treatment in 25 years'.[36]

Within three weeks, however, the trial had been scuppered. A relentless campaign waged on talk-back radio and in the pages of the *Daily Telegraph*, Australia's largest circulation morning paper, coupled with the Prime Minister's own implacable opposition, doomed the project. Carnell, who was described in the media as the 'drug pedlar' for a 'profoundly evil' plan, said that the *Telegraph*'s decision not to provide balanced coverage 'marks a watershed in Australian journalism'. Its editor, Col Allen, conceded as much: 'I think that in the last week particularly, as we fought to have this thing canned, that we were pretty single-minded about it.'[37]

The discourse against the proposed trial exposes exactly the kind of anxieties that drug laws serve to articulate and govern. Foremost was the theme that a society committed to principles of identity and responsibility, agency and choice, could not tolerate *any* level of heroin use, regardless of the social and personal costs of such a policy. Drug users 'must be told they have a choice and if they take the anti-social option society will punish them', said one of the *Telegraph*'s many editorials.[38] It was precisely the importance of the twin themes of identity and autonomy that led the Prime Minister's own adviser on drugs to remark that 'there are worse things than death when it comes to heroin addiction'.[39] With some regularity, this theme of free choice and personal responsibility was tied to broader anxieties about the breakdown of standards.[40] Most users, says one typical correspondent, 'took up this illegal habit of their own volition'.[41] Here we see in its starkest form the striking paradox of possession. Although drug dependence is feared precisely *because* of the loss of agency it connotes, the institutional principle of personal autonomy and responsibility must be maintained and enforced at all costs. It is the anxiety that this idea of responsibility is being steadily undermined that explains both the focus on drug use as the cause of the contagion and an insistence that it must be stamped out in the name of that autonomy.

The other recurring element of the discourse was the notion of surrender. Anything other than absolute prohibition was taken to imply that Australia would have 'run the white flag up the pole, we've surrendered. We've surrendered to the drug dealers.'[42] Prime Minister Howard himself elaborated on the theme during his 2001 general election policy speech, referring contemptuously to those 'who want to run up the white flag and throw up [*sic*] in surrender'.[43]

But what exactly is being 'surrendered' here? The language of war, of 'retreat' and 'weakness' and 'going soft',[44] implied that the defeat which the ACT heroin trial would inflict if it went ahead would not be suffered by those with drug addiction problems but rather by the rest of us. *We* would be 'giving up' our faith in the perfectibility of society and the idea that law could solve our social problems in some absolute fashion. If the so-called evils of drug use were to be understood as falling on a *continuum* with our own behaviour and as a consequence of currently existing social policies, then we would be no longer be able to blame the drugs and the 'drug pedlars' for the undeniable failure of those laws and hopes.

Accordingly, it was not what we ought to do about the 'drug problem' that was under threat in August 1997, but rather whose fault it was. If heroin is to blame, then the established order is not. Witchcraft theory insisted on the reality of the Devil in order to exculpate God from the daily tragedies of the world. Compromise was impossible. So, too, zero tolerance theory insists on the reality of Evil in order to exculpate both humanity and law from the daily tragedies of the world. Compromise is likewise impossible. On that basis, harm minimisation policies represent a very significant white flag indeed: they adopt a posture of humility in the face of human and legal hubris.

As a direct response to Prime Minister John Howard's narrow escape over the ACT heroin trial, his conservative government (1996–2007) replaced or forced mass resignations in his peak advisory body on drugs and appointed as his senior adviser on illegal drugs, Brian Watters, a Major in the Salvation Army, of holding dogmatic prohibitionist views.[45] Nothing could have signalled more clearly the triumph of symbolism over substance.

> *John Howard:* And I feel in very safe hands, with the police on the one side and the Salvation Army on the other.
> *Major Brian Watters:* It's the law and the prophets.
> *John Howard:* It's the law and the prophets. That's right.[46]

The policy overhaul launched by Howard's government was pointedly called 'Tough On Drugs' – 'a national *illicit* drug strategy' designed to overturn the consensus of the previous 15 years, which had focused on harm minimisation and whose centrepiece was a 'national drug strategy' specifically dedicated to breaking down the distinctions between licit and illicit drug problems.[47] The government's policy therefore was about the necessity of separating good from evil, right from wrong, and normal from abnormal behaviour. It was about maintaining the nature of personal identity and autonomy, and the power and promise of law. Agnosticism in respect of what Alex Wodak frequently calls 'utopia' was thus Howard's principal enemy;[48] it was more important to symbolise the fight than to obtain the victory.

Conclusion

The debate between 'zero tolerance' and 'harm minimisation' continues to frame drug policy debates the world over. In this chapter, I have sought to explore not the conscious intentions of law but its subconscious drives. Law is not just instrumental but also symbolic, a vehicle for the representation and organisation of our underlying anxieties, fears and desires. Its targets are metaphors that perform a central role in how we articulate and manage those underlying forces. Alas, our lives are full of things that we profess to hate but which nevertheless structure our lives and with which we cannot do without. So, too, the law. The list of law's perversity, the underlying tension between its rational ends and its irrational desires, which only an unconscious reading can explain, is long. Drugs and witchcraft laws are but two instances, and we could easily think of more – for example, international sanctions (those against Serbia in the 1990s, Gaza today and so on) that claim to be directed against governments but perversely serve only to expand the power of those same interests.[49]

Like a symptom – like drug use itself, even – law acts obsessively, repetitively, predictably and destructively.[50] The legal structure of drugs is not an attempt to solve a problem but to dramatise an ideology and to *entrench* an anxiety by the obsessive, repetitive, predictable and destructive performance of a symptom. Zero tolerance is not a policy but a faith, at the heart of which lies the importance of social rules, obedience and respect for the distinctions between right and wrong, and which sees the legal system as an all-powerful arbiter and enforcer of social norms. Behind that faith lies fear: fear of the consequences of a loss of certainty, fear of a weakened legal capacity and fear of a 'permissive' world in which such distinctions can no longer be drawn. Such a world is not being brought into existence by drug users themselves. They are merely symptoms or metaphors in the dream that law enacts in order to stave off a rupture in the categorical fabric of social belief. It is a dream with which the authors of *Malleus Maleficarum* ('The Hammer of Witches', 1486) would have sympathised. Like these men, former Prime Minister John Howard did not fear witches: he *needed* them. In pursuing and insisting upon this need, against all the evidence and with ever more shrill and inflexible determination, those who continue to advocate such policies behave as though possessed.

Acknowledgement

This chapter is based on Manderson, D. (2005). Possessed: Drug policy, witchcraft and belief. *Cultural Studies*, 19(1): 35–62. Reprinted by permission of Taylor & Francis Ltd, www.informaworld.com.

Notes

1 See Wodak & Owens, *Drug Prohibition*; Wodak & Moore, *Modernising Australia's Drug Policy*; Hamilton, King & Ritter, *Drug Use in Australia*; Erickson, Riley, Cheung et al., *Harm Reduction*.
2 The literature is vast. For synopses of the debates and arguments, see Stokes, Chalk & Gillen, *Drugs and Democracy*; Wodak & Moore, *Modernising Australia's Drug Policy*; Wodak &

Owens, *Drug Prohibition*; Heather, Wodak, Nadelmann et al., *Psychoactive Drugs and Harm Reduction*.

3   UN, *Single Convention on Narcotic Drugs*.
4   Aristodemou, *Law and Literature*; MacNeil, *Lex Populi*.
5   Caudill, 'In the wake, or *at* the wake, of psychoanalytic jurisprudence?'; Schroeder, 'The end of the market'; Douzinas & Gearey, *Critical Jurisprudence*.
6   Legendre, 'Oedipus Lex' and 'Law and the Unconscious', in Legendre, *Law and the Unconscious* (ed. Goodrich).
7   For example Zizek, *Enjoy Your Symptom!*
8   Felman, *Jacques Lacan and the Adventure of Insight*; *Testimony*; and *The Juridical Unconscious*.
9   Ehrenzweig, *Psychoanalytic Jurisprudence*; Goldstein, 'Psychoanalysis and jurisprudence'.
10 Felman, *The Juridical Unconscious*; Goodrich (ed.), *Law and the Unconscious*.
11 Freud, *The Cocaine Papers*, or Conan Doyle, *The Annotated Sherlock Holmes*; and see especially Musto, 'A study in cocaine'.
12 De Quincey, *Confessions of an English Opium-Eater*.
13 Manderson, *From Mr Sin to Mr Big*.
14 For example Victoria, *Opium Smoking Prohibition Act*.
15 Manderson, *From Mr Sin to Mr Big*, pp. 17–58.
16 Ibid., pp. 20–7.
17 For example *Bulletin*, 'The Chinese in Australia', 21 August 1886, p. 11.
18 Szasz, 'Drug prohibition and the fear of autonomy'.
19 See Trevor-Roper, *The European Witch-Craze*; Levack, 'Possession witchcraft and the law in Jacobean England'; Durston, *Witchcraft and Witch Trials*.
20 Stephens, *Demon Lovers*, p. 44.
21 Ibid., pp. 13–31, 87–124.
22 Ibid., pp. 23, 42–54.
23 Ibid., pp. 23, 39.
24 Sprenger & Krämer, *Malleus Maleficarum* ('The Hammer of Witches').
25 Stephens, *Demon Lovers*, p. 46.
26 Levack, 'Possession witchcraft and the law in Jacobean England', note 25.
27 Zizek, 'Critical response I: A symptom of what?', p. 3.
28 Giddens, *The Consequences of Identity*, and *Modernity and Self Identity*.
29 Pottage & Mundy, *Making Persons and Things*.
30 For example Pottage, 'The inscription of life in law'; Fukuyama, *Our Posthuman Future*.
31 Foucault, *The Order of Things*, p. 387.
32 Derrida, *Writing and Difference*, p. 281.
33 Harpham, 'Doing the impossible', pp. 467–8. See for example Jurist, *Beyond Hegel and Nietzsche*.
34 Blanchot, *The Space of Literature*.
35 Goethe, *Der Zauberlehrling*; Dukas, *L'apprenti sorcier*.
36 *Sydney Morning Herald*, 1 August 1997, p. 1.
37 *Sydney Morning Herald*, 22 August 1997, p. 35.
38 *Daily Telegraph*, 5 August 1997, p. 10.
39 *Daily Telegraph*, 14 August 1997, p. 17.
40 For example William Bush in *Daily Telegraph*, 5 August 1997, p. 12.
41 A. Ellery in *Daily Telegraph*, 19 August 1997, p. 12.
42 Allen, ABC, *Media Report*, 4 March 1999; see also *Sydney Morning Herald*, 15 August 1997, p. 9.
43 Howard, Policy speech. See *Daily Telegraph*, 20 August 1997, p. 1, and 14 August 1997, p. 17; *Sydney Morning Herald*, 19 August 1997, p. 1, and 3 February 2004, p. 1.
44 John Howard in *Sydney Morning Herald*, 3 February 2004, p. 1.
45 *Daily Telegraph*, 14 August 1997, p. 17.

46 ABC, *Four Corners*, 1 April 2002.
47 *Sydney Morning Herald*, 3 November 1997, p. 6, and 4 November 1997, p. 15; *Daily Telegraph*, 3 November 1997, p. 1.
48 Wodak & Moore, *Modernising Australia's Drug Policy*.
49 For an extraordinary and compelling example of this perversity, David Samuels, 'The Pink Panthers', *New Yorker,* 12 April 2010, p. 42.
50 Zizek, *Enjoy Your Symptom!*

References

Allen, C. (1999). ABC, *Media Report*. Retrieved 31 March 2011. www.abc.net.au/rn/talks/8.30/mediarpt/mstories/mr990304.htm.

Aristodemou, M. (2000). *Law and Literature: Journeys from Her to Eternity*. Oxford: Oxford University Press.

Australia (1901a). *Customs Act 1901*.

—— (1901b). *Immigration Act 1901*.

Australian Broadcasting Corporation (1 April 2002). *Four Corners*. Retrieved 20 April 2011. www.abc.net.au/4corners/stories/s517990.htm.

Barry, J., Hester, M., & Roberts, G. (eds) (1996). *Witchcraft in Early Modern Europe*. Cambridge: Cambridge University Press.

Blanchot, M. (1955/1989). *The Space of Literature*. Trans. A. Smock. Lincoln: University of Nebraska Press.

Bulletin (1886). 'The Chinese in Australia', 21 August: 11–14. Sydney: Fairfax Press, 1886.

Carlson, D., & Goodrich, P. (eds). (1998). *Law and the Postmodern Mind*. Ann Arbor: University of Michigan Press.

Clark, S. (1997). *Thinking with Demons*. Oxford: Oxford University Press.

Caudill, D. (1996). *In* the wake, or *at* the wake, of psychoanalytic jurisprudence? *Legal Studies Forum*, 20: 187–95.

Daily Telegraph. (1997–2001). Sydney: News Corp.

De Quincey, T. (1822/1961). *Confessions of an English Opium-Eater*. Garden City, NY: Doubleday.

Derrida, J. (1978). *Writing and Difference*. Trans. A. Bass. Chicago: University of Chicago Press.

—— (1982). *Margins of Philosophy*. Trans. A. Bass. Chicago: University of Chicago Press.

Douzinas, C., & Gearey, A. (2005). *Critical Jurisprudence*. Oxford: Hart Publishing.

Doyle, A.C. (1887–1905/1987). *The Annotated Sherlock Holmes*. New York: CN Potter.

Durston, G. (2000). *Witchcraft and Witch Trials*. Chicester, UK: Barry Rose.

Dvorak, R. (2000). Cracking the code. *Michigan Journal of Race and Law*, 5: 611–65.

England (1542). *Witchcraft Act 1542*.

—— (1604). *An Act Against Conjuration, Witchcraft, and Dealing with Evil and Wicked Spirits, 1 James ch. 12*.

Ehrenzweig, A.A. (1972). *Psychoanalytic Jurisprudence*. Amsterdam: Sijthoff.

Erickson, P., Riley, D., Cheung, Y., et al. (eds) (1997). *Harm Reduction: A New Direction for Drug Policies and Programs*. Toronto: University of Toronto Press.

Felman, S. (1989). *Jacques Lacan and the Adventure of Insight: Psychoanalysis in Contemporary Culture*. Boston: Harvard University Press.

—— (1991). *Testimony: Crises of Witnessing in Literature, Psychoanalysis and Literature*. New York: Routledge.

—— (2002). *The Juridical Unconscious: Trials and Tribulations in the Twentieth Century*. Boston: Harvard University Press.

Foucault, M. (1973). *The Order of Things*. Trans. A. Sheridan. New York: Vintage Books.

Freud, S. (1900/2004). *The Interpretation of Dreams*. New York: Macmillan.

—— (1929/1989). *Civilization and Its Discontents*. New York: W.W. Norton.

—— (1953/1963). *The Cocaine Papers*. Vienna: Dunquin Press.

Fukuyama, F. (2002). *Our Posthuman Future: Consequences of the Biotechnology Revolution*. New York: Farrar, Straus & Giroux.

Giddens, A. (1990). *The Consequences of Identity*. Stanford, CA: Stanford University Press.

—— (1991). *Modernity and Self Identity*. Stanford, CA: Stanford University Press.

Goethe, J. (1797). *Der Zauberlehrling*.

Goldstein, J. (1968). Psychoanalysis and jurisprudence. *Yale Law Journal*, 77: 1053–78.

Goodrich, P. (1995). *Oedipus Lex: Psychoanalysis, History, Law*. Berkeley: University of California Press.

Hamilton, M., King, T., & Ritter, A. (eds) (1998). *Drug Use in Australia: A Harm Minimization Approach*. Melbourne: Oxford University Press.

Harpham, G. (2003). Doing the impossible: Slavoj Zizek and the end of knowledge. *Critical Inquiry*, 29: 453–85.

Heather, N., Wodak, A., Nadelmann, E., et al. (eds) (1993). *Psychoactive Drugs and Harm Reduction: From Faith to Science*. London: Whurr Publishing.

Howard, J. (2001). Policy speech. Retrieved 20 April 2011. www.australianpolitics.com/news/2001/01-10-28.shtml.

Jurist, E. (2002). *Beyond Hegel and Nietzsche: Philosophy, Culture and Agency*. Cambridge, MA: MIT Press.

Larner, C. (1981). *Enemies of God: The Witch-Hunt in Scotland*. Baltimore: Johns Hopkins University Press.

Legendre, P. (1997). *Law and the Unconscious: A Legendre Reader*. Ed. Peter Goodrich. Trans. P. Goodrich, A. Schutz & A. Pottage. London: St Martin's Press.

Levack, B. (1996). Possession witchcraft and the law in Jacobean England. *Washington and Lee Law Review*, 52: 1613–40.

Llewellyn Barstow, A. (1994). *Witch-Craze: A New History of the European Witch-hunts*. London: Pandora.

Macdonald, M. (1991). *Witchcraft and Hysteria in Elizabethan London*. London: Tavistock.

MacNeil, W. (2007). *Lex Populi: The Jurisprudence of Popular Culture*. Stanford, CA: Stanford University Press.

Manderson, D. (1993). *From Mr Sin to Mr Big: A History of Australian Drug Laws*. Melbourne: Oxford University Press.

Musto, D. (1986). A study in cocaine: Sherlock Holmes and Sigmund Freud. *Journal of the American Medical Association*, 204: 125–30.

New South Wales (1881). *Influx of Chinese Restriction Act, 45 Vic. No. 11,1881*.

—— (1888). *Chinese Restriction and Regulation Act, 52 Vict. No. 4, 1888*.

—— (1893). *Royal Commission on Alleged Chinese Gambling and Immorality*.

—— (1985). *Drug Misuse and Trafficking Act, 1985.*

Peele, S. (1985). *The Meaning of Addiction: Compulsive Experience and Its Interpretation.* Lexington, MA: Lexington Books.

Pinker, S. (2002). *The Blank Slate: The Modern Denial of Human Nature.* New York: Penguin.

Pottage, A. (1998). The inscription of life in law: Genes, patents and bio-politics. *Modern Law Review*, 61: 740–65.

Pottage, A., & Mundy, M. (eds) (2003). *Making Persons and Things: Law, Anthropology, and the Constitution of the Social.* Cambridge: Cambridge University Press.

Purkiss, D. (1996). *The Witch in History: Early Modern and Twentieth-Century Representations.* London: Routledge.

Roper, L. (1994). *Oedipus and the Devil: Witchcraft, Sexuality and Religion in Early Modern Europe.* London: Routledge.

Samuels, D. (2010). 'The Pink Panthers', *New Yorker*, 12 April: 42.

Schroeder, J. (1998). The end of the market: A psychoanalysis of law and economics. *Harvard Law Review*, 112: 483–558.

Sprenger, J., & Krämer, H. (1486/1996). *Malleus Maleficarum.* Trans. M. Summers. London: Bracken Books.

Stephens, W. (2002). *Demon Lovers: Witchcraft, Sex and the Crisis of Belief.* Chicago & London: University of Chicago Press.

Stokes, G., Chalk, P., & Gillen, K. (eds) (2000). *Drugs and Democracy.* Melbourne: Melbourne University Press.

Sydney Morning Herald. (1997–2004). Sydney: Fairfax.

Szasz, T. (1992). Drug prohibition and the fear of autonomy. *Daedalus*, 121: 161–4.

Trevor-Roper, H. (1990). *The European Witch-Craze of the Sixteenth and Seventeenth Centuries.* Harmondsworth: Penguin.

United Kingdom (1736). *An Act to Repeal the Statute Made in the First Year of the Reign of King James the First, Intituled, An Act Against Conjuration, Witchcraft, and Dealing with Evil and Wicked Spirits, 9 Geo. II ch. 5.*

United Nations (1961). *Single Convention on Narcotic Drugs.*

Victoria (1905). *Opium Smoking Prohibition Act, 5 Edw. VII No. 2003.*

Wodak, A., & Moore, T. (2002). *Modernising Australia's Drug Policy.* Sydney: UNSW Press.

Wodak, A. & Owens, R. (1996). *Drug Prohibition: A Call for Change.* Sydney: UNSW Press.

Zizek, S. (2001). *Enjoy Your Symptom!* London: Routledge.

—— (2003). Critical response I: A symptom of what? *Critical Inquiry*, 29: 486–504.

Index